Quicken 5

SELF-TEACHING GUIDE

Quicken 5

SELF-TEACHING GUIDE

Peter G. Aitken

John Wiley & Sons, Inc.
New York ▲ Chichester ▲ Brisbane ▲ Toronto ▲ Singapore

Quicken® is a registered trademark of Intuit

Recognizing the importance of preserving what has been written, it is a policy of John Wiley & Sons, Inc. to have books of enduring value published in the United States printed on acid-free paper, and we exert our best efforts to that end.

Library of Congress Cataloging-in-Publication Data

Aitken, Peter G.
Quicken 5: self-teaching guide / Peter G. Aitken.
p. cm. -- (Wiley self-teaching guides)
Includes index.
ISBN 0-471-54889-8 (pbk. : alk. paper)
1. Quicken (Computer program) 2. Finance, Personal--Computer programs. 3. Investments--Computer programs. I. Title.
II. Series.
HG179.A38 1992
332.024'00285'5369--dc20 92-782
CIP

Printed in the United States of America

92 93 10 9 8 7 6 5 4 3 2 1

Contents Overview

Appendixes

Contents

5 Checking Accounts (3), 93

6 Using Quicken for a Home Budget, 117

7 Savings Accounts, Transfers, and Tax-related Categories, 135

Preface

Welcome to the *Self-Teaching Guide* for Quicken, version 5. Quicken is the world's most popular financial management program, and is used by millions of individuals and small businesses to keep track of their bank accounts, investments, loans, and other financial matters. It's a great program, but being so powerful it is unavoidably somewhat complicated. That's where this book comes in. It is designed for the many people who are looking for a quick and easy way to learn Quicken. Once you start reading this book, you'll be using Quicken for your own finances in no time at all!

About This Book

This book is carefully organized to make the learning process as efficient as possible. Topics are covered in the order that most people will need them. You'll find a number of helpful features in this book:

▲ At the beginning of each chapter, you'll find a list of the chapter's major topics.

▲ In each chapter, *Check Yourself* exercises encourage you to practice what you've learned so far. Each exercise includes a brief description of the steps you should follow to complete the exercise.

▲ Brief *Tips* call your attention to important points, shortcuts, and cautions.

▲ At the end of each chapter, a *Quick Command Summary* lists and reviews the important procedures you learned in the chapter.

▲ Also at the end of each chapter, *Practice What You've Learned* exercises suggest additional steps you may wish to complete. Answers are not provided for these exercises. If you have trouble completing them, you should refer back to the chapter for help.

▲ The book is illustrated throughout with *screen shots* that show you what the Quicken screen looks like as you perform various tasks.

This book is a tutorial. I strongly suggest that you make use of the *Check Yourself* and *Practice What You've Learned* exercises. They are an important component of Wiley's *Self-Teaching Guide* series, and have proven to be a valuable learning aid.

How to Use This Book

This book is aimed at users who have no previous experience with Quicken. My intent is for you to read the book chapters in order, from start to finish. Later chapters often build on information that is presented in earlier chapters, so if you skip ahead you may run into difficulties. I have attempted to present information in the order that most readers are likely to need it. For example, the most common use for Quicken is to maintain a checking account, and that's what I cover first.

As with other books in the Wiley *Self-Teaching Guide* series, this book is organized into a series of relatively brief lessons. Each lesson helps you master a particular aspect of Quicken. You should work through the lessons in order, but you can pause between lessons at any time. In fact, it's a good idea to avoid doing too much in a single session. By digesting the lessons in small chunks, perhaps two or three lessons at a time, you'll retain the information better and avoid the frustration that may result from trying to work too quickly.

The Quicken program is well designed and relatively easy to use, but because it is so powerful, it is unavoidably somewhat complicated. You may wish to take things a step at a time, particularly if you are new to computers. For example, you could work through the lessons on checking account basics in Chapters 2 and 3, then start using Quicken for your own checking account. If you run into problems, refer back to the lessons or to the Quicken documentation for assistance. After a few weeks you'll have gained some familiarity with Quicken, and will be ready to move on to the next topic—printing checks and reconciling your accounts, covered in Chapters 4 and 5.

I also suggest that you take the time to work through the *Check Yourself* exercises located throughout each chapter. These exercises are not meant to be exhaustive, but rather to check you on a few important items that were covered in the lesson. Answers are provided for the *Check Yourself* exercises. These answers do not provide nearly as much detail as the body of the chapter, but are intended to be brief descriptions of the steps you must follow to complete the exercise. If you have trouble completing an exercise, you might want to review the lesson before going on.

I have invented a ficticious family, the Smiths, whose financial information is used in the book's lessons. As you work through the lessons, I suggest you use the information that I provide for this typical family. You will be setting up a separate group of accounts for the Smiths, so their data will be kept separate from the real data that you will soon be entering for your own accounts.

I have used certain typographic conventions to help make the material in this book easier to understand. New terms are printed in *italics* when they are first introduced. Information that you enter from the keyboard is printed in **boldface**. Special key combinations are separated by a plus (+) sign. For example, **Ctrl+F1** means to press and hold the Ctrl key, then tap the F1 key.

You're now ready to get started on the way to becoming a Quicken expert. I hope that you find this book to be helpful in learning Quicken. Once you start using Quicken, I think you'll find it to be a terrific program. You may soon wonder how you ever got along without it!

Peter G. Aitken
Durham, NC

1

Introducing Quicken

Before you begin to use this book, you must have installed Quicken on your computer system. If you've already done this, you can continue with the chapter. If not, please turn to Appendix A for installation instructions.

This chapter starts you on your way to becoming a proficient Quicken user. You'll learn

- **What Quicken can do for you**
- **How to start Quicken**
- **How to select commands from Quicken menus**
- **How to create a Quicken file**
- **How to start a checking account**
- **How to exit Quicken**

What Can Quicken Do for You?

You probably already know that Quicken helps you organize your home and small business finances, but you may not be aware of some of the specific things that Quicken can do. Here's a brief description of some of Quicken's more important capabilities:

- **Checking accounts:** With Quicken, you can maintain your checking accounts, keeping track of deposits, checks written, and service fees. You can also print checks using a dot matrix or laser printer, or pay bills electronically using the CheckFree payment service. Quicken makes it easy to reconcile your account records with your bank statement, keeping your balance accurate to the penny and ensuring that you'll never bounce another check.
- **Savings accounts:** You can keep track of all savings account activity, including interest payments and transfers to other accounts.
- **Credit card accounts:** You can set up a Quicken account for each of your credit cards, keeping track of charges, payments, and interest fees.
- **Investment accounts:** Quicken can keep track of your investments, such as stocks and mutual funds, and makes it easy to see how each investment is doing in terms of profit or loss.
- **Other assets and liabilities:** Assets include things you own, such as your home, a coin collection, or business equipment. Liabilities are things you owe, such as your mortgage or an educational loan. Quicken can keep track of these, too.

Much of Quicken's power comes from its categories and reports. Whenever you enter a transaction into Quicken, you assign it to a category. Examples of expense categories include Groceries, Child Care, and Mortgage, and examples of income categories include Salary and Investment Income. With its reports, Quicken lets you view your financial data in just about any format you might need. A report could be a simple list of all charitable contributions you made during the tax year, or could be a complete cash flow statement for your consulting business.

Starting Quicken, Using Menus, and Exiting

Once you've installed Quicken onto your computer system (as explained in Appendix A), you are ready to start the program.

Here are the steps to follow:

1. If you're running Quicken from a hard disk, change to the directory where the Quicken program is installed. If you followed the default installation procedure, this will be C:\QUICKEN5. At the C:> prompt, enter

   cd c:\quicken5

   If you're running Quicken from diskettes, insert the Quicken Program diskette (that you created during installation) in disk drive A.

2. At the C:> (hard disk users) or A:> (diskette users) prompt, press **q**.

   The program will take a few seconds to load, and then the Quicken opening screen will be displayed. If you're starting Quicken for the first time, a special introductory screen is displayed (as shown in Figure 1.1). This screen offers you the option of viewing one of Quicken's two tutorials, and of setting up your own Quicken data. For now, you don't want to do any of these things; you'll be able to do all of them later from the Quicken Main Menu.

3. To get rid of the special opening screen and to display Quicken's Main Menu, press **Esc**, then press **Enter**.

▼ *Figure 1.1. This Display Appears the First Time You Start Quicken*

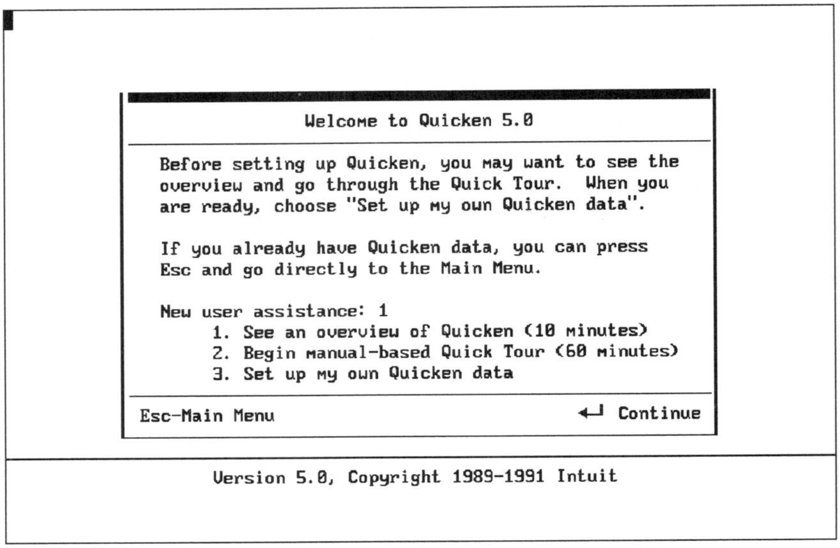

The Quicken Main Menu is shown in Figure 1.2. If you've started and exited Quicken before, this will be the first screen to appear the next time you start Quicken.

▼ *Figure 1.2. The Quicken Main Menu*

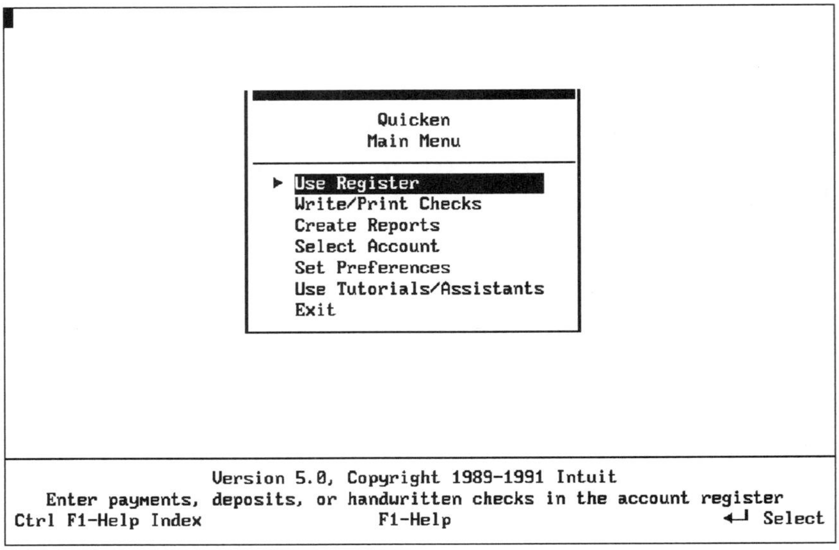

Starting Quicken, Using Menus, and Exiting

Quicken Menu Styles

Using Quicken menus is somewhat complicated by the fact that Quicken offers two styles of menus and selecting menu commands. One style is shown in Figure 1.2. If your Quicken Main Menu does not match Figure 1.2, but instead looks like Figure 1.2a, then the alternative menu style is in effect.

This alternative menu style is provided primarily for compatibility with earlier versions of Quicken. The new style, shown in Figure 1.2, is preferred, and will be used throughout this book. If your screen is displaying the old menu style, as in Figure 1.2a, you can switch to the new style by following the procedure below.

To switch from old- to new-style menus:

1. Select the Set Preferences command by pressing **5**.
2. Another menu is displayed. From this menu select the Screen Settings command by pressing **3**.
3. Yet another menu is displayed. From this menu select the Menu Access command by pressing **4**.

▼ ***Figure 1.2a. Quicken's Alternative Menu Style***

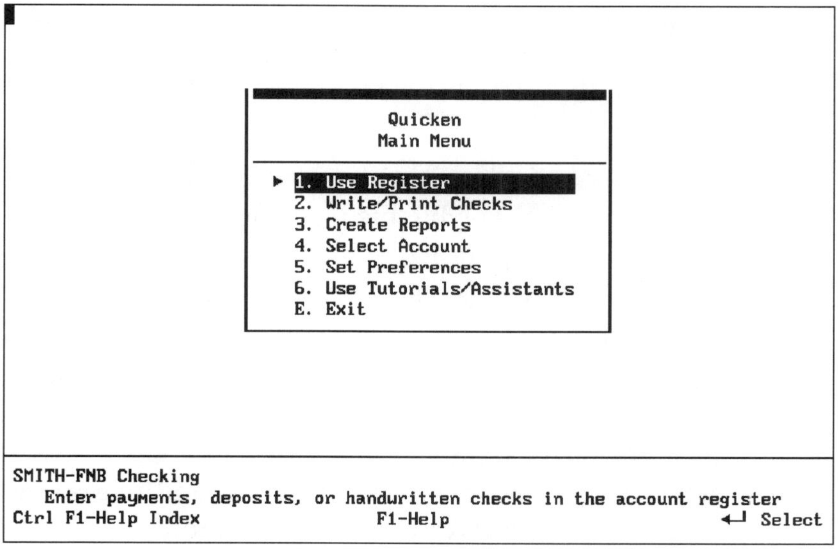

4. A small window is displayed offering you two choices of menu access methods. Press **2** to select the Alt-keys method, then press **Enter**.
5. A message is displayed telling you that the new menu access method will be in effect the next time you start Quicken.
6. Press **Enter** to continue, then press **Esc** twice to return to Quicken's Main Menu.
7. Press **E** to exit Quicken, then restart the program as described earlier in this chapter.
8. Quicken starts and displays its Main Menu. Now, the menu should appear as shown in Figure 1.2.

Using Quicken Menus

When you use Quicken, you are often required to make choices from menus to tell Quicken what you want to do.

There are three ways to select a menu command:

▲ From the keyboard, use the up arrow and down arrow keys to move the highlight bar to the desired menu command, then press **Enter**. Try it now, moving the highlight up and down among the choices on the Quicken Main Menu. Don't press Enter, however, because you're not yet ready to make a choice! As you move the highlight bar, the next-to-last line on the screen displays a brief description of the highlighted command.

▲ From the keyboard, you can also press the single letter key that corresponds to the highlighted letter in the desired menu command. Look at Figure 1.2; you could, for example, press **C** to select the Create Reports menu command.

▲ If your computer has a mouse installed, you can use it to select menu commands. Move the mouse on your desk until the pointer is positioned over the desired command. (The pointer is the small rectangle that moves on the screen as you move the mouse.) Then, rapidly press and release the left mouse button. This is called *clicking* the mouse.

The Esc Key

The Esc (for *Escape*) key, located at the upper left of most keyboards, can be though of as the "Oops!" key. The Esc key lets you recover from some mistakes that you make while using Quicken, such as selecting the wrong menu command.

When you press **Esc**, Quicken stops what it is doing and returns to the previous activity or menu. Give it a try. You should already have the Quicken Main Menu displayed on your screen from the earlier portions of this lesson.

1. Select the Set Preferences command using one of the techniques you learned above (for instance, press the **P** key). The Set Preferences Menu is displayed. However, this is a "mistake" and you want to cancel it.
2. Press **Esc**. The Set Preferences menu disappears and the Quicken Main Menu is displayed again.

TIP

Mouse users: pressing the right mouse button has the same effect as pressing the Esc key.

Exiting Quicken

You're now ready to conclude this lesson by exiting Quicken and returning to the DOS prompt. Each time you finish using Quicken, you must exit before you can run other programs. More important, you must exit Quicken before turning your system off. All data you have entered into Quicken is automatically saved when you exit. To exit, simply select Exit from the main Quicken menu.

CHECK YOURSELF

1. How do you start Quicken? (Go ahead and do it!)

2. What's the quickest way to select a menu command using the keyboard? Use this method to select the Set Preferences command from the Main Menu.

3. If you enter the wrong command, how can you recover? For example, if selecting Set Preferences (in Step 1) was a mistake, how do you redisplay the Main Menu?

ANSWERS

1. From the DOS prompt, type **cd \quicken** and press **Enter**. Then type **q** and press **Enter**.

2. Press the key that corresponds to the single highlighted letter in the menu command. To select Set Preferences, press **P**.

3. Press **Esc**.

Setting Up a Quicken File

Quicken organizes its data at two levels: by account and by file. A single *account* can be a bank account, a mutual fund investment, your petty cash, and so on. A *file* contains as many as 255 separate accounts. You can have more than one Quicken file, but you can work with only one file at a time.

TIP

In previous versions of Quicken, a file was called an account group.

A single file should be sufficient for most people. If you have complicated finances, you may eventually want to set up multiple files for groups of related accounts. For example, if you manage rental properties, you could set up one Quicken file for your household accounts, and another for your rental business accounts. Keep in mind, however, that keeping accounts in a single file has certain advantages:

▲ You can easily transfer money between accounts in the same file.

▲ You can create reports that consolidate data from all accounts in a file.

▲ Report definitions, categories, classes, and memorized transactions can be used in all accounts in a file.

Setting Up a Quicken File

For now, you're going to set up a single file for our fictitious family, the Smiths.

Here are the steps to follow:

1. Start Quicken, and from the Main Menu select Set Preferences. A new menu is displayed.
2. From the new menu, select File Activities.
3. Yet another menu is displayed. From this new menu, select Select/Setup File. The screen shown in Figure 1.3 is displayed. The choice <Set Up File> is already highlighted. If you had already set up one or more Quicken files, their names would be displayed here also. You could select which file to use by

▼ ***Figure 1.3. The Select/Setup File Screen***

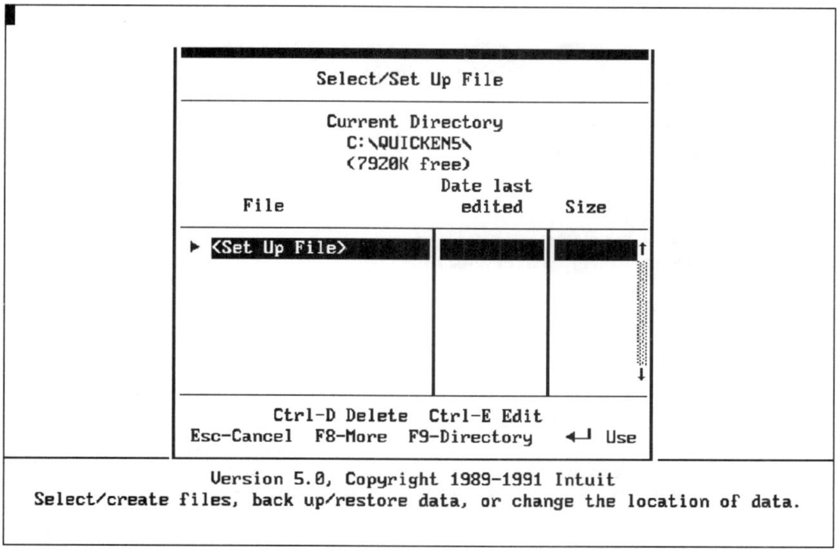

pressing the arrow keys to move the highlight bar to the desired choice, and then pressing **Enter**. Since you have not yet set up any files, only the <Set Up File> choice is available. Press **Enter** to select it.

4. The screen in Figure 1.4 is displayed, with the cursor positioned after the "Enter name for file:" screen prompt. Type the name **SMITH** for our demonstration file, then press **Enter**. If you were setting up your own file, you would type in a descriptive filename up to eight characters long.
5. The cursor moves down to the "Location for file:" prompt. The default entry here is the name of the directory where you installed Quicken, which should be QUICKEN5. You don't need to change this, so accept the default by pressing **Enter**.
6. On the next screen, you specify which categories the new file will use. Quicken offers two predefined sets of categories—one for home use and one for business use. You'll learn more about Quicken categories, including how to define your own custom categories, in future lessons. For now, select Both Home and Business by pressing **3**.

▼ ***Figure 1.4. Screen Used to Specify the Name and Location of a File***

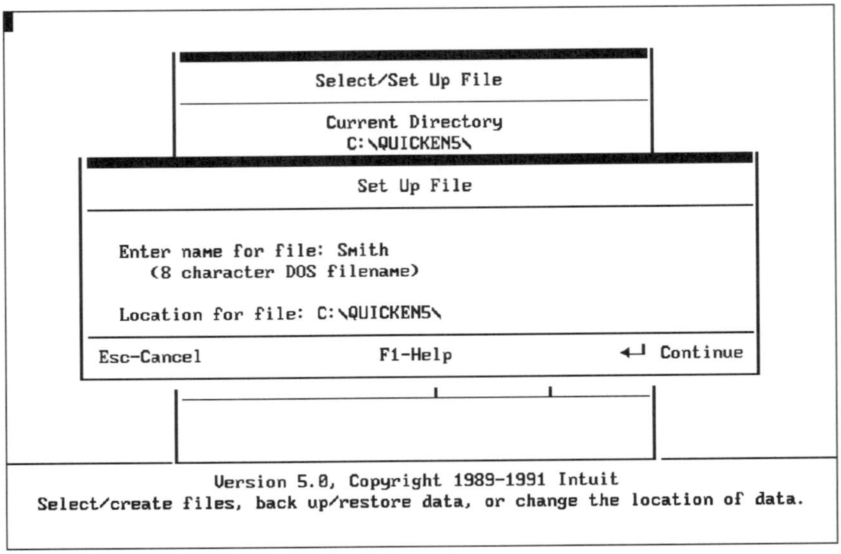

7. You are returned to the Select/Set Up File screen. You'll see that your new Quicken file, SMITH, is now listed under the <Set Up File> choice. You could select SMITH for use at this point, but since you're done with this lesson, press **Esc** three times to return to the Quicken Main Menu. You can now exit Quicken if you want to take a break, or you can go on with the next lesson.

Deleting a File

There may be times when you want to delete a Quicken file and all of the accounts it contains. Use caution when deleting a file. You must be sure you will not need its data again, because once a file has been deleted it is gone forever (unless you made backup copies).

Here's how to delete a file:

1. Display the Select/Set Up File screen. As you probably remember, this is done by selecting Set Preferences from the Main Menu, then selecting File Activities followed by Select/Setup File.
2. Use the arrow keys to highlight the name of the file to be deleted.
3. Press **Ctrl+D**. Quicken prompts you to enter **YES** to delete the file. If you enter anything else, the file will not be deleted. (This is a safety measure to ensure against accidents.) Since you don't want to delete a file at this time, press **Esc** until you return to the Main Menu.

You now know how to create and delete Quicken files. Before you can use a file, you must create one or more accounts in it. That's the topic of the next lesson.

CHECK YOURSELF

Create a new Quicken file named JUNK, then delete it.

ANSWERS

1. Select Set Preferences, then select File Activities.
2. Select Select/Set Up File.
3. Highlight <Set Up File> and press **Enter**.
4. Enter the file name **JUNK** for the new file and press **Enter** twice.
5. Specify the categories to be used for the file.
6. Press **Esc** three times to return to the Main Menu.

To delete the file:

1. Select Set Preferences, then select File Activities.
2. Select Select/Set Up File.
3. Highlight the file name JUNK.
4. Press **Ctrl+D**.
5. Enter **YES** then press **Enter**.
6. Press **Esc** three times to return to the Main Menu.

Note: If you did not create a file named SMITH earlier, do so now (but don't delete it). You'll need it later.

Setting Up a Checking Account

The new Quicken file that you set up in the previous lesson is empty—it doesn't contain any data or accounts. Before you can use Quicken for your financial data, you must set up at least one account. When you set up an account, you tell Quicken the type of account and the account name, and you enter the initial financial information for that account. This lesson shows you how to set up a checking account.

Setting Up a Checking Account

What Information Do You Need?

Whenever you set up an account, you must decide how much, if any, historical data you want to enter in the account. *Historical data* refers to information about financial transactions that occurred in the past. For example, if you're setting up a checking account, you might want to include all checks written since January 1 so that Quicken can produce reports that reflect activity for the entire year. You may not care about historical data, in which case you'll enter only the checks written since your last bank statement.

In either case, you'll need one of your bank statements. If you will not be entering historical data, you need your most recent statement. If you will be entering historical data, you need the last statement before the period of interest. For example, if you plan to enter all checks since January 1, you need the statement for December.

Setting Up the Smiths' Checking Account

Once you have gathered the information you need, you can set up the demonstration checking account for the ficticious Smiths.

Here are the steps to follow:

1. From the Quicken Main Menu, choose the Select Account command. Quicken automatically uses the SMITH file, since it's the only Quicken file you have set up. The screen shown in Figure 1.5 is displayed. Since this file contains no accounts, the only choice available is <New Account>. Select this by pressing **Enter**. The screen shown in Figure 1.6 is displayed.
2. You use the Set Up New Account screen to enter certain information about the new account. The screen contains several blanks, or *fields*, where you enter information. You will

▼ *Figure 1.5. The Select Account to Use Screen*

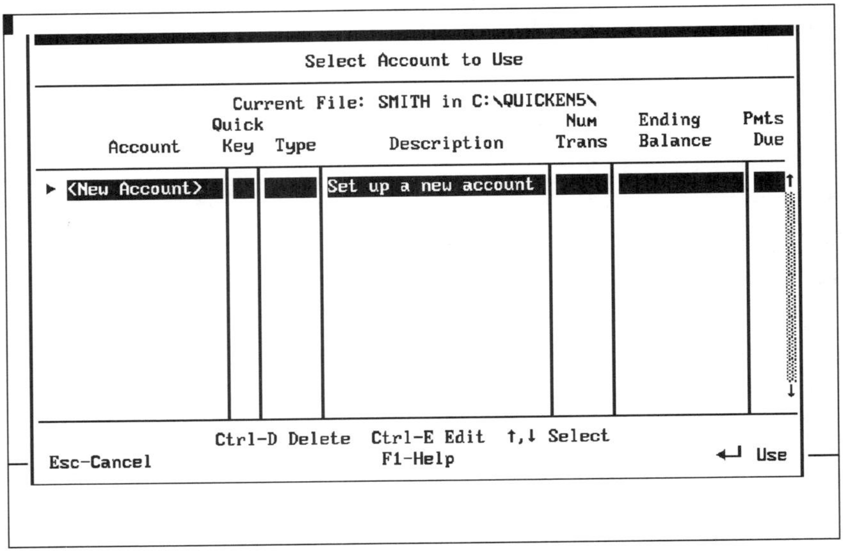

encounter this type of information entry screen frequently in Quicken, so you need to know how to use these screens:

- ▲ Some fields offer you a list of numbered choices, such as the "Account Type:" field in Figure 1.6. Simply enter the number of your choice, then press **Enter** or **Tab**.
- ▲ Other fields require that you type information, such as the "Name for this account:" field in Figure 1.6. Type the information from the keyboard; if you make a mistake, press **Backspace** to erase each character, then retype. When you've finished, press **Enter** or **Tab**.
- ▲ Press **Tab** to move the cursor to the next field. Press **Shift+Tab** to move the cursor to the previous field. You can use the mouse to move directly to any field by pointing to the field and then clicking the mouse.
- ▲ When the cursor is on the last field, pressing **Enter** confirms the information and moves to the next screen. Before doing this, you should carefully check the information you've entered and edit it, if necessary.

3. You're now ready to enter account information for the Smiths' checking account. Under "Account Type:" you can see that

Setting Up a Checking Account

▼ *Figure 1.6. The Set Up New Account Screen*

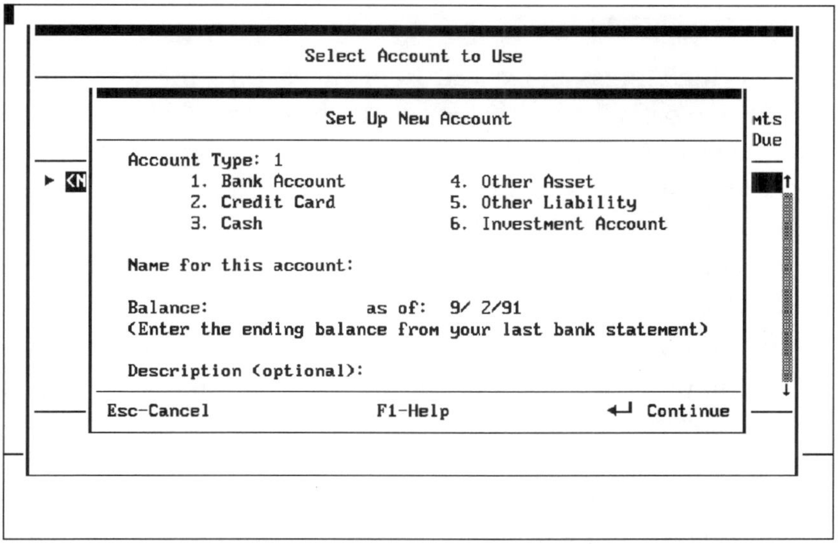

"Bank Account" is already selected, so all you need to do is press **Enter**.

4. In the "Name for this account:" field, you enter a name that will identify the account. The Smiths' account is at First National Bank, so type

   FNB Checking

   then press **Enter**.

5. For the "Balance:" amount you must look at the most recent account statement for the account. For the Smiths, this statement covers the period from December 1, 1991 through December 31, 1991, and shows a closing balance of $1255.46. With the cursor in the "Balance:" field, type

   1255.46

   then press **Enter** or **Tab**. The cursor will move to the "as of:" field, where you enter

   12/31/91

   and again press **Enter** or **Tab**.

6. The final field on this screen is the "Description:" field. As you can see from the screen, this entry is optional. If you

want to, you can enter a label or description that will help you identify the account. For the Smiths' account, type

Household checking

but don't press Enter yet! Remember, pressing Enter with the cursor in the last field will accept your entries and move to the next screen. At this point, check the information you entered and, if you find any mistakes, go back and correct them. When you're sure that everything is okay, move the cursor to the last field (if it's not already there), and press **Enter**.

7. The screen that was shown in Figure 1.5 is displayed again, but now it includes a listing for the checking account that you just created. This listing shows the name, type, description, and balance for the account. There are also columns for other information about the account. The Num Trans column lists the total number of transactions (deposits, withdrawals, and so on) for the account. At present, this is 1, representing the "deposit" of the account's initial balance. You'll learn about the Quick Key and Pmts Due (payments due) columns later.
8. You're finished setting up this account, so you can press **Esc** to return to the Main Menu. Note that, in the lower-left corner of the screen, the names of the current file and account are listed: SMITH-FNB Checking.

Deleting an Account

You can delete an account from a file, perhaps because you've closed the account and no longer need the information it contains. Be careful when thinking about deleting an account: even when the account is closed, you may need to refer to information in that account at some future date.

If you decide that it's okay to delete an account, here's how to do it:

1. From the Main Menu, choose Select Account.

2. On the Select Account screen, use the arrow keys to highlight the name of the account that you want to delete.
3. Press **Ctrl+D**. Quicken prompts you to enter **YES** to delete the account. Since you're just practicing at this point, press **Esc** twice to return to the Main Menu without deleting anything.

Selecting a File and an Account to Use

Each time you start Quicken, it automatically selects the file and account that were in use most recently. The current file and account name are displayed in the lower-left corner of the Main Menu screen.

When you have more than one file and account, you need to be able to switch between them. Here's how:

1. To use a different account in the current file, choose the Select Account command from the Main Menu. Quicken displays a list of all accounts in the file. Use the arrow keys to highlight the desired account, then press **Enter**. Quicken will display the register for the selected account. (You'll learn about the register in the next chapter.)
2. To use a different file, choose the Set Preferences command from the Main Menu, then select File Activities followed by Select/Set Up File. A list of all your Quicken files is displayed. Use the arrow keys to highlight the desired file, then press **Enter**. Quicken then displays the Select Account screen, which lists the accounts in the file you just selected. Choose the account to use, as described above.

TIP

If you get lost or confused, you can always press *Esc* one or more times to return to the Main Menu.

CHECK YOURSELF

Make sure the SMITH file is current, then create a new checking account named TEST. After verifying that the account has been created, delete it. If you did not create the account FNB Checking earlier in the chapter, create it now in the Smiths' file.

ANSWERS

To create the account:

1. Choose Select Account.
2. Highlight <New Account> and press **Enter**.
3. Select the account type **1**, then enter the name and other information for the new account, then press **F10**.
4. Press **Esc** to return to the Main Menu.

To delete an account:

1. Choose Select Account.
2. Highlight the name of the account to delete, then press **Ctrl+D**.
3. Enter **YES** and press **Enter**.
4. Press **Esc** to return to the Main Menu.

Setting Up Your Own Account

After working through the above lessons, you are ready to start your own Quicken checking account.

Here's what you need to do:

1. Find your latest bank statement. If you want to include some historical data in your account, find the last statement before the period of interest.
2. Follow the procedures described in the Setting Up a Quicken File lesson earlier in this chapter. For the file name, choose

Setting Up a Checking Account

something that will reflect the types of accounts you plan to keep in the file.

3. At the end of the procedure, do not press Esc to return to the Main Menu, but leave the Select/Set Up File screen displayed. If you mistakenly return to the Main Menu, you can redisplay this screen by selecting Set Preferences from the Main Menu, then selecting File Activities followed by Select/Set Up File.
4. This screen should display two files: the SMITH file you set up earlier, and your own file. Since you want your checking account to be in your own file, you must select it. To do this, use the arrow keys to move the highlight bar to the file name and press **Enter**.
5. From the next screen, select <New Account>. Then, follow the procedures for Setting Up a Checking Account as described earlier, this time entering the closing balance and date from your bank statement.
6. Return to the Main Menu and exit Quicken by pressing **x**. All of the data that you have entered is automatically saved.

When you're finished, you'll have two Quicken files—the Smiths' file and your own. You'll use the Smiths' file and accounts for practice as you work through the lessons in the book. As you learn how to do different things with Quicken, you can then apply these skills, as needed, to your own accounts.

QUICK COMMAND SUMMARY

This section summarizes the most important Quicken commands that you learned in this chapter. In each case, it is assumed you are starting from the Main Menu.

To create a new Quicken file:

1. Select Set Preferences.
2. Select File Activities.
3. Select Select/Set Up File.
4. Highlight <Set Up File>, then press **Enter**.

5. Enter a name for the file, then press **Enter** twice.
6. Choose a category list to be used by the file.
7. Press **Esc** three times to return to the Main Menu.

To select a file and account for use:

1. Select Set Preferences.
2. Select File Activities.
3. Choose Select/Set Up File.
4. Highlight the name of the file to use, then press **Enter**.
5. Quicken displays a list of accounts in the selected file. Highlight the desired account name, then press **Enter**.

To select an account from the current file:

1. Choose Select Account.
2. Highlight the name of the desired account, and press **Enter**.

PRACTICE WHAT YOU'VE LEARNED

Learning is always improved by practice, and that's the rationale behind these end-of-chapter practices. To help you remember what you've learned in this chapter, try the following:

1. Start Quicken.
2. Create a "dummy" Quicken file to be used for practice. By using a dummy file rather than one containing your real financial information, you'll be free to experiment and won't have to worry about making a mistake.
3. Create several different checking accounts in the file. Practice making each account current in turn.
4. Delete one or more of the accounts. You can also delete the file, but it would be a good idea to keep it—you'll be able to use it for future practices.
5. Exit Quicken.

2

Checking Accounts (1)

This chapter is the first in a series of four chapters that explain how to use Quicken checking accounts. In these chapters you'll learn how to enter checks you've written, edit the check register, print checks, balance your account, and more. This first chapter starts with the basics of checking account use. You'll learn how to

- **Use the register**
- **Enter checks you've written**
- **Record deposits**
- **Work with Quicken categories**

Writing Checks

When you are using Quicken to keep track of your checking account, you have three check-writing options:

- Write the checks manually, in the usual fashion. You keep track of checks in your handwritten checkbook register, and from time to time transfer the information to Quicken.
- Enter the payment information directly into Quicken, then have Quicken print checks using your dot-matrix or laser printer.
- Enter the payment information directly into Quicken, then use your modem to transmit the information to the CheckFree service. CheckFree prints and mails a check to the payee, or makes an electronic transfer to the payee's account.

To use the second method, you must purchase checks and envelopes designed for use with Quicken. To use the third method, you must subscribe to the CheckFree service. Both of these payment methods are described later in the book.

While check printing and the CheckFree service can be very convenient, many Quicken users do just fine without them. The first method—handwriting checks and then transferring the information to Quicken—is the one payment method that just about everyone has to use. After all, you can't use electronic payment or a laser-printed check when you're buying groceries at the corner store!

When you're writing checks manually, you must be sure to transfer information for all checks to Quicken; otherwise, your Quicken account will not be accurate. If you just started an account using the balance from a recent bank statement, you must enter the information for all checks that had not cleared as of that statement. You enter checks using the Quicken register.

The Register

The Quicken register is designed to look a lot like a regular, paper checkbook register. You should now display the register for the Smiths' checking account.

Here's what to do:

1. Start Quicken, then look in the lower-left corner of the Main Menu screen to see if the SMITH file is current. If it is, choose Select Account, then highlight FNB Checking and press **Enter**.
2. If the lower-left corner of the screen indicates that the desired file and account are current, select Use Register.
3. If the SMITH file is not current, select it by using the techniques you learned in the previous chapter.

Any of the above actions will display the register for FNB Checking, as shown in Figure 2.1. Take a good look at the Register screen, because you need to become familiar with it.

▼ *Figure 2.1. The Register Screen*

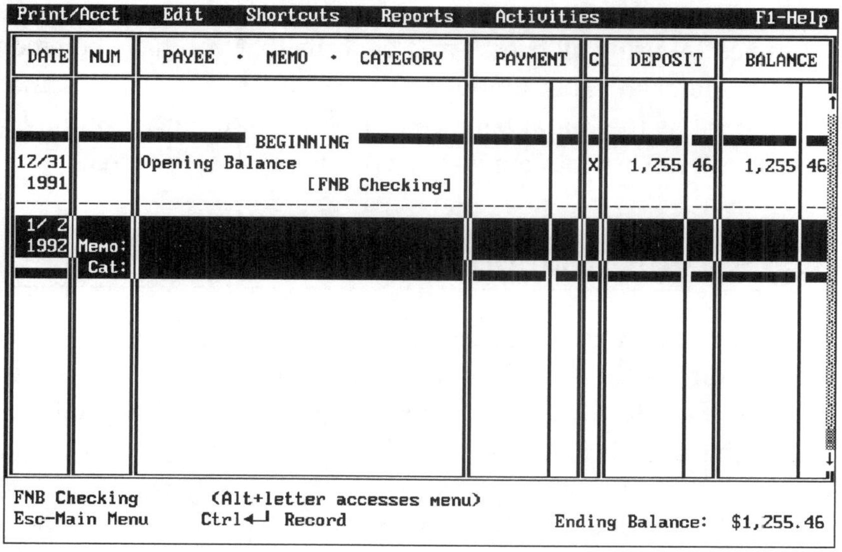

The main part of the screen is designed to look like an actual checkbook register, with columns for check number, date, amount, payee, and other information. Each row holds a single transaction: a payment or a deposit. The first row holds the opening balance transaction that you specified when you set up the account. The second row is highlighted, and is ready to accept information from you. Before you begin entering check information, take a look at the other parts of the register screen:

- ▲ The top row displays a menu. Each item on this menu leads to a submenu that contains additional commands. The submenu commands are used to perform a variety of tasks for you as you work in the register. To display a submenu, press **Alt** plus the first letter of the desired item. For example, to display the Edit submenu, press **Alt+E**. Go ahead and try it—you'll see the Edit submenu pop up over part of the register screen. Then press **Esc** to hide the submenu. You'll learn more about the menu commands as they are introduced in later chapters.
- ▲ The account name is displayed at the lower-left corner of the register screen.
- ▲ The Ending Balance is displayed at the lower-right corner of the screen. This amount is the account balance, and is determined by using all checks and deposits that you have entered into Quicken. This amount should be $1,255.46, the same amount as the initial balance in the account. Since you have not entered any payments or deposits yet, this is correct.

Register Information

You can see that the Quicken register has places, or *fields*, for several different kinds of information. Some of these items are probably familiar to you, while some may not be. We'll take a look at these fields in order:

- ▲ The DATE field holds the date of each transaction. When you first display the register, the DATE field contains today's date (obtained from your computer's clock). You can change the date, which you will learn later on in this lesson.

- ▲ The NUM field holds check numbers. For deposits and other transactions that are unnumbered, this field is left blank. Note that the "Memo:" and "Cat:" labels in the NUM column are not actually part of the NUM field, but refer to fields in the next column to the right.
- ▲ The large column in the middle of the screen holds three fields. The top line is the PAYEE field—the name of the person or company the check is made out to.
- ▲ The MEMO field is the second line in the column. You can enter a memo here to identify the transaction: "Sarah's bike," "Dan's golf clubs," "New tires," and so on. For many transactions, this field will be left blank.
- ▲ The CATEGORY field is used to define a category. Each transaction must be assigned to a category. For example, the electric bill is assigned to Utilities, daycare tuition is assigned to Childcare, and airline tickets are assigned to Travel. Categories are an extremely important part of Quicken, so you'll be reading and learning quite a bit more about them.
- ▲ In the PAYMENT field, you enter the amount for a transaction that takes money out of the account: checks you write, automatic teller withdrawals, and so on.
- ▲ An "X" in the C field indicates that a transaction has cleared (appeared on a bank statement). If the C field is blank, the transaction has not cleared. Don't worry about this field for now. You'll learn more about clearing transactions in the section on reconciling your account in Chapter 5.
- ▲ In the DEPOSIT account, you enter the amount for a transaction that puts money into the account: deposits, interest payments, and so on.
- ▲ The BALANCE field indicates the account balance immediately following the transaction. Quicken calculates this amount for you, and you cannot make an entry in this field.

Moving between Fields

When you're working in the register, you must move the cursor between fields. The *cursor* is the small blinking underline that marks where information you type will appear. When you first display the register, the cursor is in the DATE field. Here's how you move the cursor between fields in a transaction:

- ▲ To move to the next field, press **Tab** or **Enter**.
- ▲ To move back one field, press **Shift+Tab**.
- ▲ To move to any field, click on the field with the mouse. (Of course, you must have a mouse to use this approach.)

There's a lot more to learn about using the register, but you now know enough to make your first entries. The Smiths have written several checks and have made one deposit since they received the bank statement used to start the account. The relevant information is as follows:

1/3/92, check 104 to Miller's Food Market, $56.65
1/4/92, deposit of $3500, Andrea's salary
1/5/92, check 105 to Edison Electric, $45.00
1/5/92, check 106 to Cancer Research Foundation, $25.00

The remainder of this chapter shows you how to enter these transactions into the Smiths' Quicken checking account.

Entering a Check

The most common type of entry you will make in a Quicken checking account is, of course, for checks you have written.

These are the steps to follow (using the Smiths' check 104 as an example):

Entering a Check

1. You should have the register for the FNB Checking account displayed, with the cursor in the DATE field of the first blank transaction (as shown in Figure 2.1).
2. Enter the date. The DATE field initially displays today's date or, if you've already entered one or more transactions, the date entered for the previous transaction. If this is correct, accept it by pressing **Enter** or **Tab**. To change the date, you can type the correct date information using the Quicken format "month/day/year." You can also change the date using the special keys shown in Table 2.1.

   You do not need to press **Shift** when using these keys. For example, you can press either **t** or **T** for today's date. The **+** and **-** keys can be either the ones at the far right of your keyboard (on the numeric keypad) or the ones just to the left of the Backspace key.

TIP

You'll remember the month and year keys better if you note that "M" and "H" are the first and last letters of "month," and "Y" and "R" are the first and last letters of "year."

3. After entering the date, press **Tab** or **Enter** to move to the NUM field. Enter the first check number, **104**. Instead of entering the check number, you can press **+** to get the next number in sequence. If no checks have been entered in the

▼ Table 2.1. Keys Used to Change the Date

To Make This Date Change:	*Press:*
Advance one day	+
Move back one day	–
Today	T
First of the current or previous month	M
Last of the previous month	H
First of the current or previous year	Y
Last of the previous year	R

account, the sequence starts at number 101. After a check number has been entered in the NUM field, you can press + or – to increment or decrement the number by 1.

4. Press **Tab** or **Enter** to move to the PAYEE field. Enter the payee, **Miller's Food Market**, then press **Tab** or **Enter** to move to the PAYMENT field. Enter the amount **56.65**. Note that Quicken automatically formats the entry for you, placing the dollar and cents amounts in the proper locations.
5. Press **Tab** or **Enter** four times to move to the CATEGORY field. (You're leaving the MEMO field blank for this transaction.) In the CATEGORY field, type **Groceries**, but don't press Tab or Enter yet.

Your screen should now look like Figure 2.2. When the cursor is in the CATEGORY field, the Tab and Enter keys work differently than they do in other fields:

- ▲ Press **Tab** to move to the DATE field.
- ▲ Press **Enter** to record the transaction. Quicken prompts you to verify the transaction information. Select Record Transac-

▼ ***Figure 2.2. The Transaction Has Been Entered***

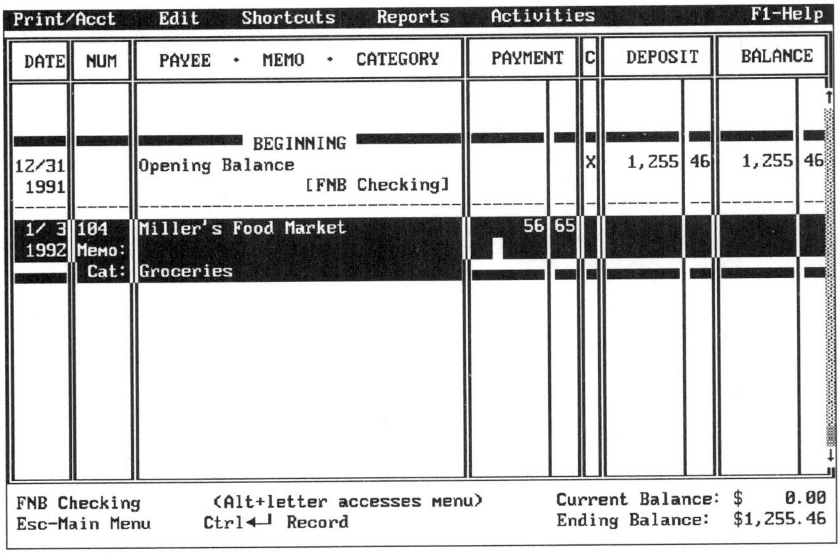

tion to record the transaction and move to the next register entry. Select Don't Record if you notice one or more errors and want to return to editing the transaction.

Entering a Check

At any time when entering a transaction, you can press **Ctrl+Enter** to record the transaction. Quicken will not prompt you to verify, so use this recording method with care. You don't want to record this transaction yet, so please read on.

What If You Made a Mistake?

After you've entered all the transaction information, and the cursor is in the CATEGORY field, you should check your entry for errors. If you find one, use **Tab**, **Shift+Tab**, or the mouse to move to the field with the error, then make the necessary correction. When editing a Quicken field, you can use the following editing keys:

- ▲ The **Left** or **Right** arrow keys move the cursor left or right one character.
- ▲ The **Home** or **End** keys move the cursor to the beginning or end of the field.
- ▲ **Ctrl+Left** arrow or **Ctrl+Right** arrow moves the cursor left or right one word.
- ▲ **Delete** erases the character under the cursor.
- ▲ **Backspace** deletes the character to the left of the cursor.
- ▲ **Ctrl+Backspace** deletes the entire field.

The above editing keys work whenever you're entering or editing information in a Quicken field. New characters are, of course, typed at the keyboard and appear at the cursor location. Quicken has two typing modes:

- ▲ In overstrike mode (the default), new characters you type replace any existing characters at the cursor position. In overstrike mode, the cursor is a blinking underline.

▲ In insert mode, new characters do not replace existing characters. Rather, characters at and to the right of the cursor position "move over" to make room for new characters. In insert mode the cursor is a blinking rectangle.

To toggle between insert and overstrike modes, press the **Ins** key.

Recording the Transaction

At this point, you should have made any needed corrections to the transaction information. You're now ready to record the transaction. Recording saves the transaction in the register and stores it to the disk file. Even after recording a transaction, you can go back and make changes. Of course, it's always better to catch errors at this stage before the transaction is recorded! There are two ways to record a transaction:

▲ With the cursor located in any field in the transaction, press **Ctrl+Enter**.

▲ With the cursor in the CATEGORY field, press **Enter**. Quicken asks if you want to record the transaction. If you've noticed an error that you missed before, select "Do not record" or press **Esc** to return to the transaction for further editing. Otherwise, select Record Transaction.

When the transaction is recorded, Quicken automatically calculates and displays the new account balance, and the highlight moves down to the next blank transaction. Your screen should now look like the one shown in Figure 2.3.

Entering a Deposit

If you're going to write checks on your checking account, you also need to make deposits—at least once in a while! The proce-

▼ Figure 2.3. The New Balance Is Displayed

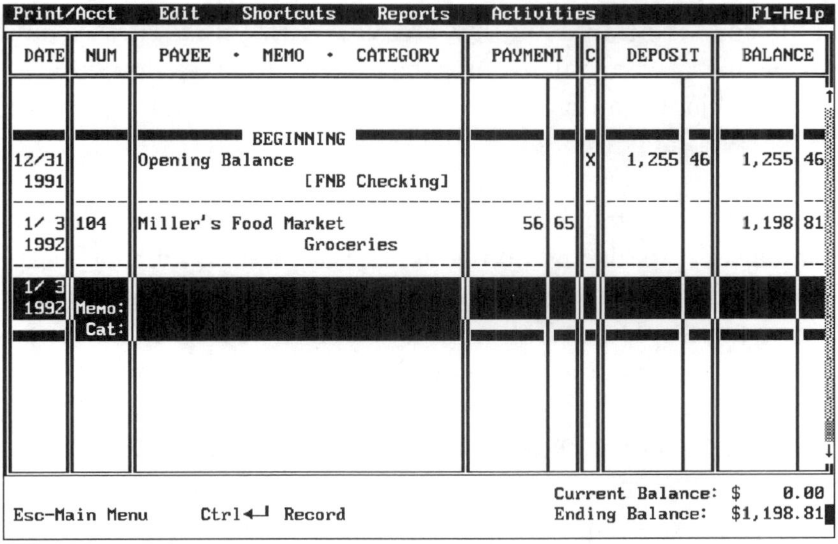

Entering a Deposit

dure for entering a deposit into a Quicken checking account is similar to the procedure for entering a check.

To enter a deposit:

1. Display the account register and be sure the cursor is in the DATE field.
2. Enter the date of the deposit. Remember, you can change the date by typing the correct date or by using the special keys shown earlier in Table 2.1.
3. Press **Tab** twice to move to the PAYEE field. Since deposits are unnumbered, you are leaving the NUM field blank.
4. Enter **Deposit** as the payee, then press **Tab** three times to move to the DEPOSIT field.
5. Enter the deposit amount—in this case **$3500.00** (you do not have to type the cents part of the amount if it is zero).
6. Press **Tab** once to move to the MEMO field, then enter **Andrea's paycheck**.
7. Press **Tab** once to move to the CATEGORY field, then enter **Salary**. Check the information you entered for errors, and if

necessary go back and make corrections (using the editing techniques you learned earlier in this chapter).

8. Record the transaction by pressing **Ctrl+Enter**. The account balance is recalculated and the highlight moves down to the next blank transaction. Your screen should look like the one shown in Figure 2.4.

Note that, after a transaction has been recorded, Quicken condenses it to display on two rows, with the MEMO and CATEGORY fields sharing a row. Only the first 15 characters of a memo are displayed. If the memo is longer than 15 characters, a small, right-pointing arrow is displayed at the end to indicate that more information is stored but not displayed. You can see this in the deposit transaction you just made, as shown in Figure 2.4.

Memos or Categories?

You might be a bit unsure about the distinction between the MEMO and CATEGORY fields in the register. (I know that I was when I first started using Quicken.)

▼ *Figure 2.4. The Register after Entry of a Deposit*

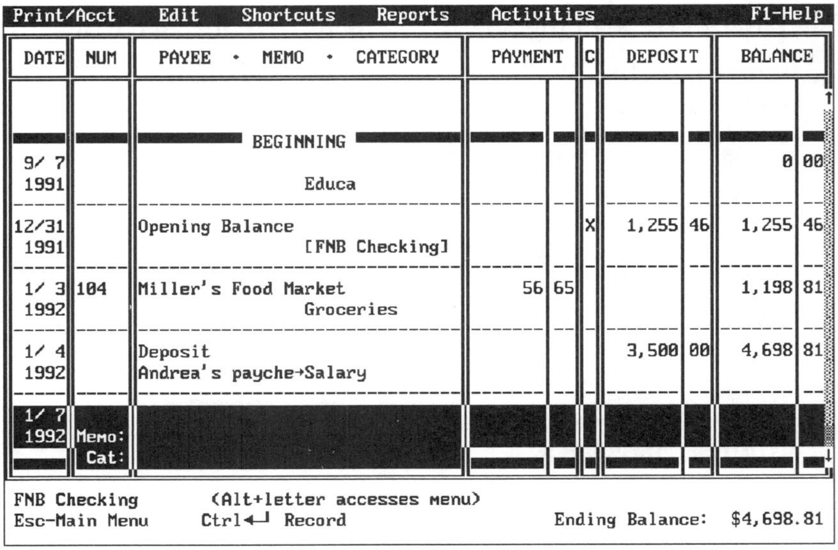

▲ A memo is nothing more than additional information about a transaction for your own records. Quicken records memos for you, but does nothing else with them.

▲ A category specifies the type of expense or income that a transaction represents: Groceries, Clothing, Entertainment, and so on.

Entering a Deposit

Quicken can use categories in reports that provide detailed information about your finances. If you're careful to assign transactions to the proper categories, these reports will give you a detailed and accurate picture of your finances. You'll learn how to create reports later in the book. For now, here's an example of the use of memos and categories.

If you write a $120 check to pay for your son's sneakers (which he absolutely must have to be "cool"), you would assign the transaction to the category "Clothing." When you later create a report of expenses, Quicken will include that amount in the total for "Clothing." You could also enter the memo "Junior's sneakers" in the transaction to remind yourself about the reason for the expense. However, this memo will not appear on reports.

I mentioned earlier that you must make an entry in the CATEGORY field for each transaction. Strictly speaking, this is not accurate. Quicken will not prevent you from leaving the CATEGORY field blank. It's a bad idea, however, and I strongly suggest that you always enter a category for each transaction—even if you have to use a general, catch-all category, such as Misc.

CHECK YOURSELF

You should now enter the remaining two checks (listed earlier) in the Smiths' account. Use the Utilities category for check 105, and the Charity category for check 106.

ANSWERS

1. If necessary, display the register for the Smiths' FNB Checking account.

2. Press the **PgDn** key to move the highlight to the bottom of the register, to the first empty transaction. Be sure the cursor is in the NUM field.
3. Enter the check number (105). Remember that pressing **+** with the cursor in the NUM field automatically enters the next sequential check number.
4. Enter the remaining information for the check. After you enter the category, press **Ctrl+Enter**.
5. Repeat Steps 3 and 4 for the second check. When you have entered both checks, the account balance should be $4,628.73.

More About Categories

Quicken offers predefined categories that cover most home and business needs. Quicken provides one set of categories for home use, and another for business use. When you set up a Quicken file, you select which set of categories to use: home, business, both, or neither. You learned how to do this in an earlier lesson.

Table 2.2 lists Quicken's predefined home categories, and Table 2.3 lists the business categories.

Many people find Quicken's predefined categories sufficient for their needs. If they're not, you can add new categories. You can also delete categories that you don't need.

Subcategories

In the table of home categories, note that certain categories have several subcategories indented under them. For example, the Fuel, Loan, and Service subcategories are listed under the Auto category. Using subcategories gives you additional control over the way Quicken can summarize your financial information when creating reports.

▼ *Table 2.2. Quicken Home Categories*

INCOME

Category Name	Description
Bonus	Bonus Income
Canada Pen	Canadian Pension
Div Income	Dividend Income
Gift Received	Gift Received
Int Inc	Interest Income
Invest Inc	Investment Income
Old Age Pension	Old Age Pension
Other Inc	Other Income
Salary	Salary Income

EXPENSE

Category Name	Description
Auto	Automobile Expenses
Fuel	Auto Fuel
Loan	Auto Loan Payment
Service	Auto Service
Bank Chrg	Bank Charge
Charity	Charitable Donations
Childcare	Childcare Expenses
Christmas	Christmas Expenses
Clothing	Clothing
Dining	Dining Out
Dues	Dues
Education	Education
Entertain	Entertainment
Gifts	Gift Expenses
Groceries	Groceries
Home Rpair	Home Repair and Maintenance
Household	Household Miscellaneous Expenses
Housing	Housing
Insurance	Insurance
Int Exp	Interest Expense

continued

More About Categories

▼ *Table 2.2. Quicken Home Categories (continued)*

Expense Category Name	***Description***
Invest Exp	Investment Expense
Medical	Medical & Dental
Misc	Miscellaneous
Mort Int	Mortgage Interest Expenses
Other Exp	Other Expenses
Recreation	Recreation Expenses
RRSP	Regular Retirement Savings Plan
Subscriptions	Subscriptions
Supplies	Supplies
Tax	Taxes
Fed	Federal Tax
FICA	Social Security Tax
Other	Miscellaneous Taxes
Prop	Property Tax
State	State Tax
Telephone	Telephone Expense
UIC	Unemployment Insurance Commission
Utilities	Water, Gas, Electric
Gas & Electric	Gas and Electricity
Water	Water

For example, if you use the Auto subcategories, Quicken can provide a total of all your auto expenses, plus a breakdown of expenses for Fuel, Loan, and Service subcategories. Subcategories are entered in the CATEGORY field, following the category name and separated by a colon, as shown below:

Category:subcategory

For example, to assign a check to the Fuel subcategory under the Auto category, you would enter **Auto:Fuel** in the CATEGORY field.

More About Categories

▼ *Table 2.3. Quicken Business Categories*

INCOME

Category Name	*Description*
Gr Sales	Gross Sales
Other Inc	Other Income
Rent Income	Rent Income

EXPENSE

Category Name	*Description*
Ads	Advertising
Car	Car and Truck
Commission	Commissions
Freight	Freight
Int Paid	Interest Paid
L&P Fees	Legal and Professional Fees
Late Fees	Late Payment Fees
Office	Office Expenses
Rent Paid	Rent Paid
Repairs	Repairs
Returns	Returns and Allowances
Tax	Taxes
Travel	Travel Expenses
Wages	Wages and Job Credits

Viewing the Category List

You can view a file's category list any time you are in the register. You should do this now, as follows:

1. Display the register for the Smiths' FNB Checking account. If this register is not already displayed, make sure that SMITH is the current file, then select Use Register from the Main Menu.
2. Press **Ctrl+C**. A window opens, displaying the category list. This list is shown in Figure 2.5.

▼ Figure 2.5. The Category and Transfer List

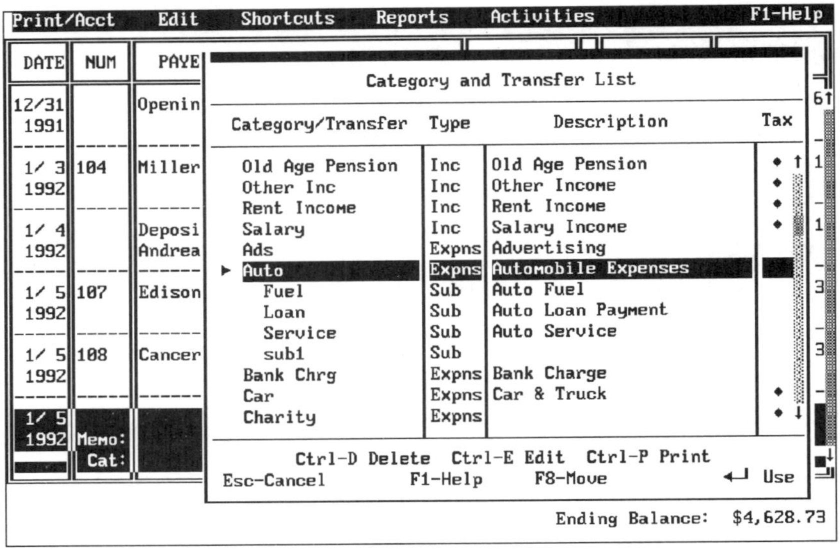

3. The list is too long to display entirely in one window. To scroll up and down through the list, press **PgUp** and **PgDn**. When you're finished viewing the list, press **Esc** to return to the register. Before you do, however, you should note that the category list has four columns:

   ▲ The Category/Transfer column lists the category name. The first entry in this column is <New Category>, which you select when creating a new category. The "Transfer" part of this column heading reflects the fact that each of your Quicken accounts is itself considered a "category" for the purpose of transferring funds between accounts.

   ▲ The Type column lists the category type: "Expns" for expense, "Inc" for income, or "Sub" for subcategory.

   ▲ The Description column lists the category description.

   ▲ The Tax column contains a bullet if the category is tax related. You'll learn about this in Chapter 7.

Once you've finished viewing the category list, press **Esc** to return to the register.

Entering Categories and Subcategories

More About Categories

When you're adding transactions to the register, you have several methods available for entering the category (and, if used, subcategory) in the CATEGORY field. You can, of course, simply type the entire category name, as you did earlier in this chapter when you entered the Smiths' checks. There are two other ways that save time and reduce mistakes.

The first method lets you select from the category list:

1. When you enter a transaction, move the cursor to the CATEGORY field. Do not enter anything, but instead press **Ctrl+C**.
2. Quicken displays a window containing the file's category list. Presss the **PgUp**, **PgDn**, **Up** arrow, and **Down** arrow keys to move the highlight bar to the desired category or subcategory, then press **Enter**.
3. Quicken returns to the register and automatically enters the selected category name in the CATEGORY field. If you selected a subcategory, both the category and subcategory names are entered.
4. You then continue with the transaction just as if you had typed the category name yourself.

The other method of entering category names requires you to type in part of the name, then lets Quicken fill in the rest:

1. With the cursor in the CATEGORY field, type the first few letters of the desired category name. For example, for "Groceries" you could enter **Gro**.
2. Press **Enter** or **Tab**. Quicken looks through the file's category list. If it finds a single category or subcategory name that matches the letters you typed, it enters that category into the CATEGORY field. You then continue entering the transaction.
3. Sometimes, however, there will be more than one match. For example, if you enter **Hou**, Quicken matches two categories in the list: Household and Housing. When this happen, Quicken displays a small window offering you two choices:

Add to Category List or Select from Category List. Choose the latter command.

4. Quicken displays the category list with the highlight on the first matching category. Since the category list is alphabetical, the other matching category or categories will be shown immediately below. Press the **Up** arrow and **Down** arrow keys to select the correct category, then press **Enter**. Quicken enters the selected category in the register.

CHECK YOURSELF

Try practicing the new methods you've just learned for entering categories into the register. Here is the information for three more checks that the Smiths have written:

1/6/92, check 107, Coastal Seafood, $16.35
1/6/92, check 108, Sears, $38.10
1/7/92, check 109, Mobil Oil, $25.00

1. If necessary, display the register for the Smiths' FNB Checking account.
2. Press the **PgDn** key to move the highlight to the bottom of the register, to the first empty transaction. Be sure the cursor is in the NUM field.
3. Enter the information for check 107, up to but not including the CATEGORY.
4. For check 107, the category is Groceries. Enter **Gro** in the CATEGORY field and press **Enter**. You'll see how Quicken automatically finds and enters the matching category.
5. Repeat Step 3 for check 108.
6. For check 108, the category is Household. Enter **Hou** in the CATEGORY field and press **Enter**. Since there are two categories that match, you'll have to select the correct one from the category list.
7. Repeat Step 3 for check 109.
8. For check 109, you want to use the category Auto and the subcategory Fuel. Enter **Fuel** in the CATEGORY field and press

Enter. Quicken finds Fuel as a subcategory under Auto, and enters both the category and subcategory in the transaction.

More About Categories

Adding Categories

As you work with Quicken, you may find that the predefined categories are not sufficient for your needs.

You can add new categories and subcategories to a file's category list by following these steps:

1. There are two ways to add a new category or subcategory:

   ▲ Display the file's category list, then select <New Category>. (Remember, this is the first entry in the list.) You must use this method if you are adding a subcategory.

   ▲ When entering a transaction, type the new category in the CATEGORY field, then press **Enter**. Since it's a new category, Quicken will not find the entry in the existing category list. You are offered the choice of Add to Category List or Select from Category List. Choose the first command.

   In either case, Quicken displays the Set Up Category window, as shown in Figure 2.6.

2. If you used the first method above, the cursor is in the "Name:" field. Type a name for the category. The name can be up to 15 characters long and can contain spaces, but cannot contain the characters [,], /, or :.

3. Next, press **Tab** or **Enter** to move the cursor to the "Income, Expense or Subcategory" field. If you used the second method, the category name you entered in the register's CATEGORY field is already inserted in the "Name:" field, and the cursor is in the "Income, Expense or Subcategory" field.

4. Enter **E**, **I**, or **S** to specify the type. Remember, you can add a subcategory only if you started from the category list. Then press **Tab** or **Enter** to move to the "Description:" field. This entry is optional. Enter a description if the category name

▼ *Figure 2.6. The Set Up Category Window*

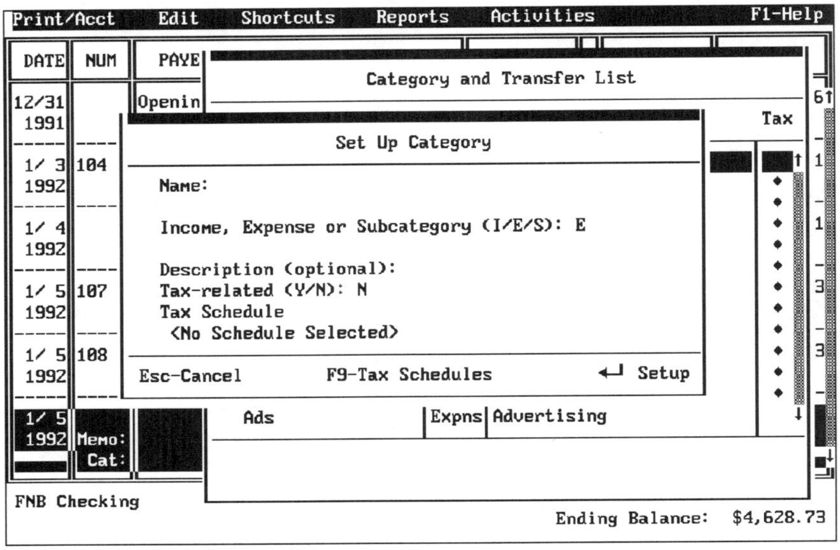

alone is not enough to make its purpose clear. A category description can be up to 25 characters long. Press **Tab** or **Enter** to move to the "Tax-related:" field.

5. This is a Yes/No field, and is used to specify whether the new category is tax related. You'll learn later in the book (Chapter 7) about using Quicken categories to help with your tax preparation. For now, press **Tab** or **Enter** to accept the default answer of **N** (for "No").

6. If the new addition is an Income or Expense category, it is added to the category list and Quicken returns you to either the category list or the register, depending on where you started.

7. If the new addition is a subcategory, you must tell Quicken the category under which the new subcategory is to be placed. Quicken displays a list of all existing categories and subcategories. The name of the new subcategory is highlighted at the top of the list. Press the **Up** arrow, **Down** arrow, **PgUp**, and **PgDn** keys to move the highlight to the desired category, then press **Enter**. The subcategory is added under that

More About Categories

category. The new subcategory is given the same expense or income classification as the category it has been placed under.

8. Finally, press **Esc** to return to the register.

At this point, you should have a clear understanding of how to insert a category in a transaction, and how to add new categories and subcategories to the category list.

CHECK YOURSELF

The Smiths are avid tennis players and are also active in off-road bicycling. They need a "Sports" category to use for all sports-related expenses. Under "Sports" they need "Tennis" and "Biking" subcategories so that expenses for the two activities can be kept separate. Add these categories to the category list for the SMITH file.

ANSWERS

1. Make the SMITH file current, and display the register for FNB Checking (or any account).
2. Press **Ctrl+C** to display the category list.
3. Press **PgUp** one or more times to scroll to the top of the list, and highlight the <New Category> entry.
4. In the Set Up Category window, enter **Sports** as the Category name and **E** to indicate that it is an expense.
5. Press **F10**. Quicken redisplays the category list, with <New Category> highlighted. Press **Enter**.
6. The Set Up Category window is displayed. Enter **Tennis** as the name and enter **S** to specify this as a subcategory.
7. Press **F10**. Quicken displays the category list. Press the **PgDn** and arrow keys to scroll the list until the Sports category is highlighted, then press **Enter**. Tennis will be added as a subcategory under the Sports category.
8. Scroll to the top of the list to highlight <New Category>, and press **Enter**.

9. Repeat Steps 6 and 7 for the Biking subcategory.
10. Press **Esc** to return to the Main Menu.

Deleting a Category

If your category list contains categories that you don't use, you may wish to delete them. Deleting unused categories makes the list shorter and therefore easier to work with.

To delete a category:

1. Display the category list. Remember, this is done by first displaying the register, and then pressing **Ctrl+C**.
2. Move the highlight bar to the category you want to delete, then press **Ctrl+D**.
3. Quicken displays a message box asking you to confirm the category deletion. Press **Enter** to delete the category or **Esc** to cancel.

TIP

You cannot delete a category that has subcategories. Although Quicken will allow you to delete a category or subcategory that has transactions assigned to it, you should avoid doing so. When you delete a subcategory, all transactions assigned to that subcategory are merged with its parent category. When you delete a category, transactions assigned to it become unclassified—that is, the CATEGORY field is blank.

Editing a Category

You can edit an existing category by changing its name, description, and other information. To edit a category, the procedure is similar to the procedure you used to initially define a category. You can edit Quicken's predefined categories as well as categories you have created yourself.

To edit a category:

More About Categories

1. Display the category list. Remember, this is done by first displaying the register, then pressing **Ctrl+C**.
2. Move the highlight bar to the category you want to edit, then press **Ctrl+E**.
3. Quicken displays the Edit Category window, as shown in Figure 2.7. This window contains the same fields as the Set Up Category window. Initially, the fields display the current information about the selected category.
4. Move the cursor to the field(s) you want to edit, and make the desired changes.
5. To save your changes, press **Enter** one or more times until the Edit Category window is hidden and the category list is again displayed. To cancel your changes, press **Esc**.

If you change the category name (for instance, the entry in the Category/Transfer column), and then save the change, Quicken will automatically make the change in the CATEGORY field of all transactions assigned to that category.

▼ ***Figure 2.7. The Edit Category Window***

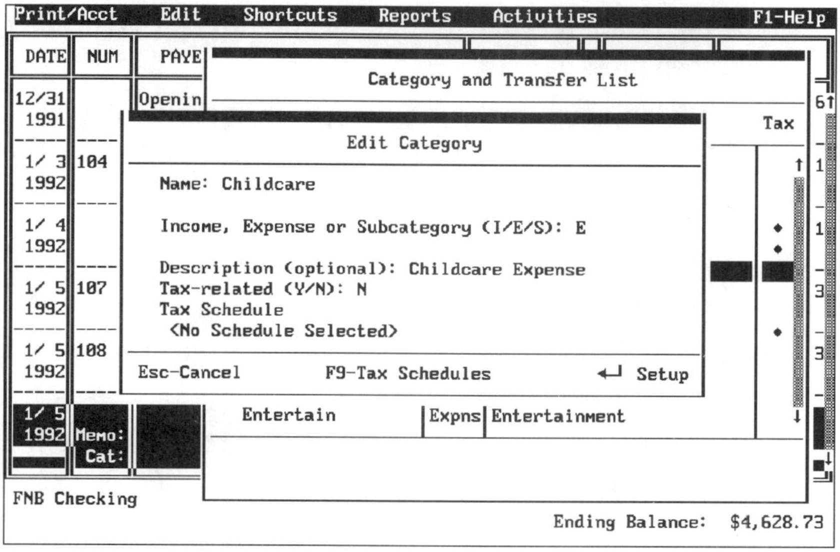

QUICK COMMAND SUMMARY

To enter handwritten checks in the Quicken register:

1. Display the register.
2. With the cursor in the DATE field, enter the check date. Remember the special keys (**+**, **-**, **T**, **M**, **H**, **Y**, **R**) that you can use to change the date.
3. Press **Tab** to move to the NUM field and enter the check number. Press **+** to automatically enter the next sequential number.
4. Use **Tab** and **Shift+Tab** to move between fields. Make entries in the PAYEE and PAYMENT fields and, optionally, the MEMO field.
5. Enter an expense category in the CATEGORY field, then press **Ctrl+Enter** to record the transaction.

To have Quicken help you enter a category:

1. With the cursor in the CATEGORY field, press **Ctrl+C** to display the category list.
2. Highlight the desired category, then press **Enter**.

or:

1. Type the first few letters of the category in the CATEGORY field, then press **Tab**.
2. If there's only one matching category, Quicken enters it in the field. If there is more than one matching category, Quicken displays all matching categories. Choose one; Quicken then enters the category in the field.

To add a category to the category list:

1. Display the register, then press **Ctrl+C** to display the category list.
2. Press **PgUp** one or more times to scroll to the top of the list, highlight <New Category>, and press **Enter**.

3. In the Set Up Category window, enter the name and other information about the category.
4. Press **Enter** to record the new category.

PRACTICE WHAT YOU'VE LEARNED

To get a better feel for working with checking accounts, you can make use of the dummy Quicken file that you set up earlier. Make that file current, and display the register for a checking account. Enter some checks and deposits, and try your hand at the various methods for entering a category in each transaction. You should also add some new categories and subcategories to the file's category list.

If you've started a Quicken account for your own checking account, now would be a good time to enter your own checks into that account. Remember to first switch to your own file. While you should be careful, don't worry about making a mistake. You can always make corrections.

3

Checking Accounts (2)

This is the second chapter on Quicken checking accounts. It covers some additional important checking account activities that you need to know in order to use Quicken efficiently. It also covers the built-in calculator and the on-line help system. You'll learn how to

- **Use the Quicken calculator**
- **View the register and make corrections**
- **Split transaction between two or more categories**
- **Find information in your register**
- **Use the help system**
- **Print the register**

Using the Quicken Calculator

Quicken includes a *pop-up* calculator that can be very handy for doing quick calculations. The term "pop-up" means that the calculator can be displayed (popped up) on the screen at any time by pressing a set of keys. After you've finished using the calculator, you can hide it by pressing **Esc**. If you like, the result of your calculations can be automatically transferred (pasted) into a file.

To pop up the calculator, press **Ctrl+O** (the letter "O," not a zero). Figure 3.1 shows the calculator popped up over the register screen. When you pop up the calculator, Quicken turns on your keyboard's NUM LOCK so that the keypad can be used to enter numbers into the calculator (although you can also use the number keys along the top of the keyboard). When you exit the calculator, NUM LOCK is turned off (unless it was on initially, in which case it will stay on).

The calculator works much like any typical hand-held calculator. It offers the four basic arithmetic operations: addition (+),

▼ *Figure 3.1. The Quicken Calculator*

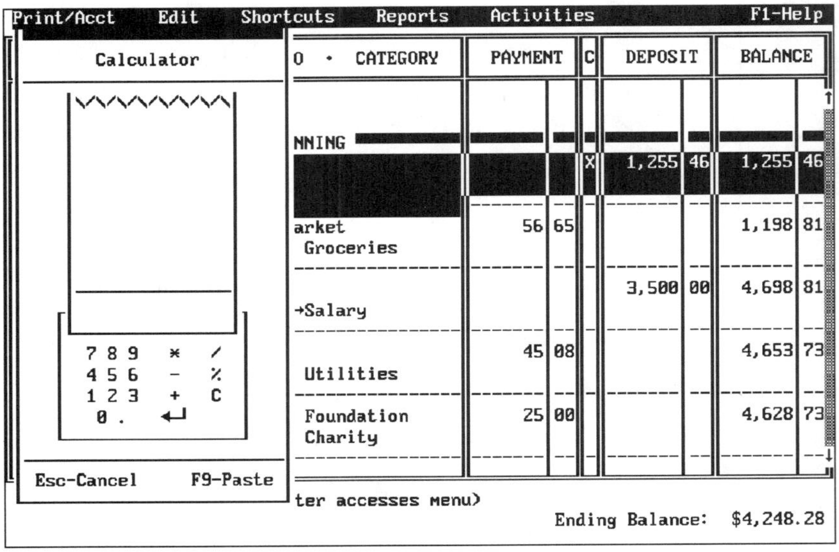

Using the Quicken Calculator

subtraction (-), multiplication (*), and division (/). Percent and Clear functions are also available.

Calculations are performed with eight-digit accuracy, and a simulated paper tape allows you to view the results of previous calculations. The best way to learn the calculator is to use it, so we'll run though some practice calculations. If necessary, press **Ctrl+O** to pop up the calculator.

To add 105 and 234:

1. Type **105**.
2. Press +.
3. Type **234**.
4. Press = or **Enter**. The answer, 439, is displayed in the calculator entry window.

To calculate 12 percent of 1500:

1. Type **1500**.
2. Press *.
3. Type **12**.
4. Press %.
5. Press = or **Enter**. The answer, 180, is displayed.

To perform a chain calculation, where the result of one calculation is used as input to the next, do not press Enter or = until the final calculation is entered.

For example, to add 46 and 190, and then multiple the sum by 50:

1. Type **46**.
2. Press +.
3. Type **190**.
4. Press *. The sum, 236, is displayed in the entry window.
5. Type **50**.
6. Press = or **Enter**. The answer, 11,800, is displayed in the entry window.

The calculator can paste its answer into any Quicken field where a number is needed. This can be very useful, saving you time and reducing errors. For example, suppose you have received two bills from your dentist—one for your checkup and one for your daughter's filling. You want to pay the total amount with a single check.

Here's how to calculate and paste the total:

1. Display the check register, and enter the check information up to, but not including, the amount. The cursor should be in the PAYMENT field.
2. Press **Ctrl+O** to display the calculator, then add the amounts for the two bills. The total amount will be displayed in the calculator entry window.
3. Press **F9**. The total is transferred, or pasted, into the PAYMENT field of the register, and the calculator is hidden.
4. Continue entering the transaction information, then transfer the check amount to your handwritten check.

Making Corrections

Information that you have entered in the register can always be changed later. You may discover that you made a mistake entering a check amount, or you may decide to change the category that a transaction is assigned to.

When you first display the register for a given account, the highlight is at the bottom of the register, on the first blank transaction. To edit a previous transaction, you must first move to it, as follows:

- ▲ Press the **Up** or **Down** arrow key to move up or down one transaction.
- ▲ Press **PgUp** or **PgDn** to move up or down one screen.
- ▲ Press **Ctrl+PgDn** or **Ctrl+PgUp** to move to the first transaction in the next or previous month.

Making Corrections

▲ Press **Ctrl+Home** or **Ctrl+End** to move to the first or last transaction in the register.

If you have a mouse, you can use the *scroll bar* to move around between transactions. The scroll bar is displayed along the right edge of your screen, and is shown in Figure 3.2.

The position of the *elevator box* in the scroll bar represents your relative position in the register. If the elevator box is at the bottom of the scroll bar, you are at or near the end of the register. If the elevator box is at the center of the scroll bar, you are at or near the middle of the register. You can use the mouse to perform the following actions with the scroll bar:

▲ To move up or down one transaction, click on the Up or Down *scroll arrows*.

▲ To move up one screen, click on the scroll bar between the elevator box and the Up arrow.

▲ To move down one screen, click on the scroll bar between the elevator box and the Down arrow.

▲ To move a variable distance, position the pointer on the elevator box, press and hold the left mouse button, then move

▼ *Figure 3.2. The Scroll Bar*

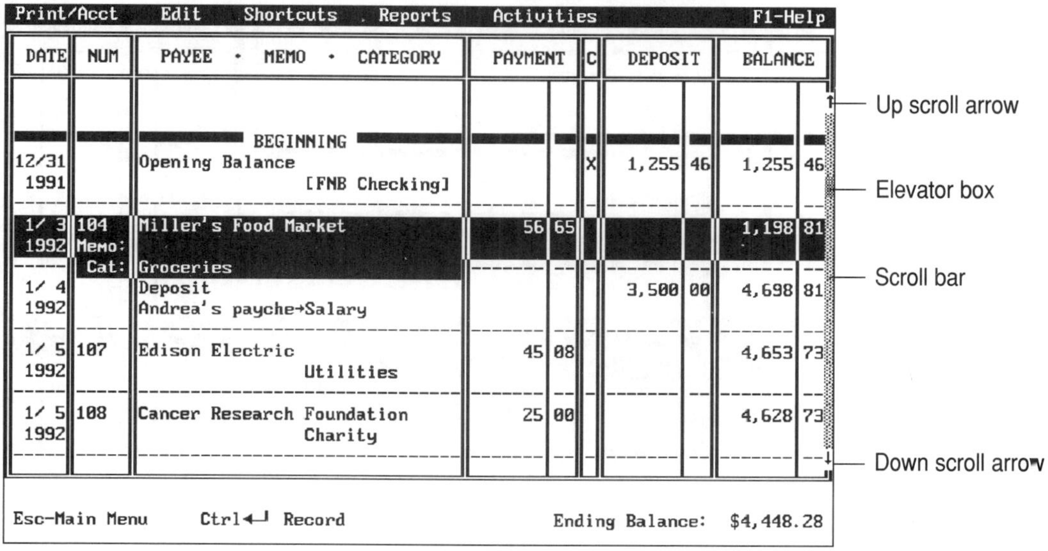

the elevator box to the new position and release the mouse button. (This is called *dragging*.)

After you have moved to the desired transaction, you make changes by first moving the cursor to the proper field. As always, this is done by pressing **Tab** or **Shift+Tab**, or by clicking on the field with the mouse. Then, edit the information in the field by using the editing keys you learned in the previous chapter.

After making the needed changes, you can record them in two ways. If you press **Ctrl+Enter**, the changes are recorded and the highlight moves to the next transaction. If you try to move the highlight off the changed transaction, Quicken prompts you to either record or cancel the changes, by displaying the message window shown in Figure 3.3. Select either Record changes and leave or Cancel changes and leave.

Deleting a Transaction

There may be times when you want to delete an entire transaction from the register. Perhaps you mistakenly entered the trans-

▼ *Figure 3.3. Quicken Prompts You to Record or Cancel Changes*

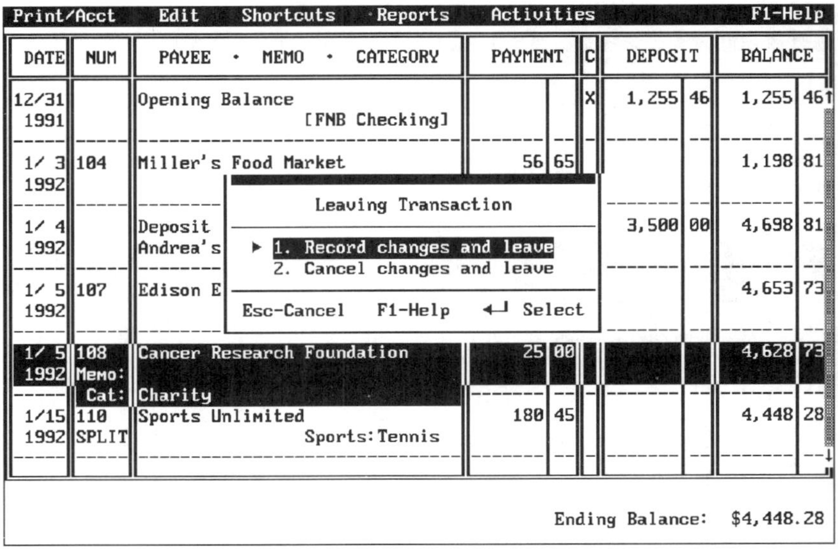

action twice, and you must delete the duplicate. Or, a check you wrote to a mail-order company has been returned because the item you ordered was not available.

Making Corrections

Here's how to delete a transaction:

1. Display the register, then move the highlight to the transaction you want to delete.
2. Press **Ctrl+D**. Quicken asks you whether the transaction should be deleted. Select Delete Transaction to delete it. Select "Do not delete" or press **Esc** to cancel and retain the transaction.

When you delete a transaction, the deletion is permanent. There is no way to recover the transaction. You can, of course, reenter it from scratch.

Finding Specific Transactions

If your register contains only a few dozen transactions, it's not too difficult to find a specific transaction by simply browsing through the register. However, this approach is not practical when a register grows to several hundred transactions.

Quicken lets you search your register for specific information in the NUM, PAYEE, MEMO, PAYMENT, CLEARED, DEPOSIT, or CATEGORY fields. By using Quicken's Find command, you can easily locate any transaction.

To perform a search, you must first display the register. Then, select the Find command by pressing **Ctrl+F**. You can also select Find by pressing **Alt+E** to display the Edit menu, then selecting Find from the submenu. When you select Find, Quicken displays the Transaction to Find window, which is shown in Figure 3.4.

You'll note that this window is a replica of a register entry, with fields for the same information (except for DATE). To perform a search, you enter the information you're looking for—the *template*—in the corresponding field in the Transaction to Find window.

▼ *Figure 3.4. The Transaction to Find Window*

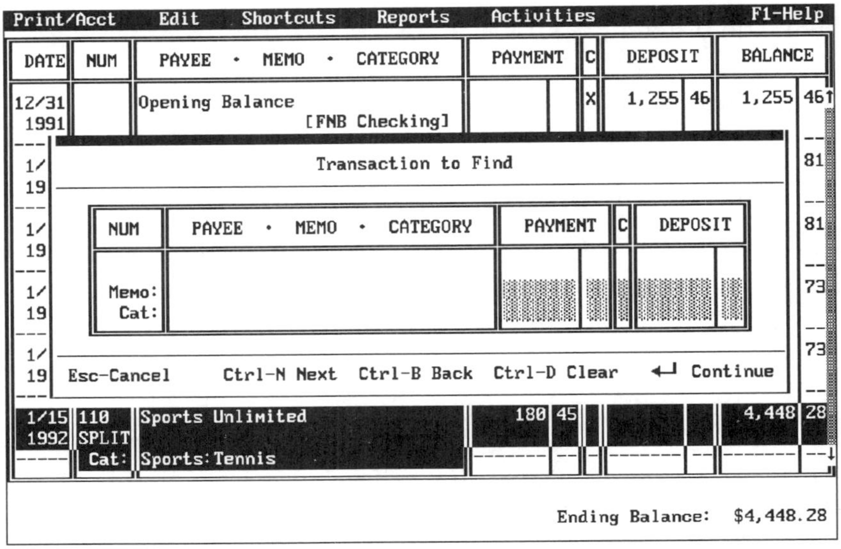

Here are some examples:

▲ To find checks with "Herb's Auto Shop" in the PAYEE field, enter **Herb's Auto Shop** in the PAYEE field of the Transaction to Find window.

▲ To find a deposit in the amount of $1000, enter **1000** in the DEPOSIT field of the Transaction to Find window.

▲ To find checks assigned to the Charity category, enter **Charity** in the CATEGORY field of the Transaction to Find window.

In the Transaction to Find window, you move the cursor and edit fields just as you do in the register. If the window already contains template information, you can clear all fields by pressing **Ctrl+D**. To find a transaction that matches two or more templates, enter search information in two or more fields. For example, to find a check that you wrote to K Mart for $75.00, enter **K Mart** in the PAYEE field and **75.00** in the PAYMENT field of the Transaction to Find window.

Once you have entered the template information in the Transaction to Find window, press either **Ctrl+N** or **Ctrl+B** to begin the search. **Ctrl+N** searches forward for the next matching transaction; **Ctrl+B** searches backward toward the start of the register. (**N** stands for Next, **B** stands for Back.)

Quicken searches through the register in the specified direction. If it finds a transaction that matches all the templates, it highlights the transaction. You can edit the transaction, delete it, or perform any other register actions that you wish. There's no need to exit the search routine. However, the template(s) that you entered in the Transaction to Find window remain active until you change or delete them. You can continue the search at any time by pressing **Ctrl+N** or **Ctrl+B** again.

If Quicken reaches the end (forward searches) or beginning (backward searches) of the register without finding a match, it displays a message to that effect. You can then terminate the search by pressing **Esc**. You can also press **Enter** to continue the search from the beginning of the register (if you're conducting a forward search) or from the end of the register (if you're conducting a backward search). These latter options make sense, of course, only if you started the search from somewhere in the middle of the register.

Finding Specific Transactions

Search Strategies

Quicken will, of course, find any exact matches to your template. It will also find transactions that contain the template (partial matches). For example, if you enter **Smith** in the PAYEE field of the Transaction to Find window, Quicken will consider it to be a match with transactions that have any of the following in their PAYEE field:

Smiths' Market
George Smith Auto Service
William's Blacksmith Shop

The last example shows you that Quicken does not care whether characters are uppercase or lowercase. An uppercase template matches a lowercase target, and vice versa.

You can tell Quicken to find only exact matches, if that's what you prefer. There are actually two ways to do this. To limit a specific search to exact matches, precede the template with a = sign. For example, if you enter

=tax

Quicken will match

tax
TAX
Tax

but will not match

tax deduction
withholding tax
taxable income

You can include a few other characters in your search templates to narrow what Quicken will find. These characters are:

..	Any sequence of zero or more characters
?	Any single character
~	Anything except what follows

The use of these special characters is illustrated by the examples shown in Table 3.1.

CHECK YOURSELF

It's time to try searching the Smiths' register. You want to find the most recent check written to Miller's Food Market. Hint: you'll start at the end of the register and search backwards. This guarantees that you'll find the most recent matching transaction.

ANSWERS

1. Display the register for the Smiths' FNB Checking account.
2. If necessary, press **PgDn** to move the end of the register.

3. Press **Ctrl+F** to display the Transaction to Find window.
4. In the PAYEE field, enter **Miller's Food Market**.
5. Press **Ctrl+B**.

Finding Specific Transactions

Splitting Transactions

Quicken lets you split a single transaction between two or more categories or subcategories. This can be a very useful feature, since it's not uncommon to write a single check to pay for items that fall into multiple expense categories. When you later create reports, Quicken will assign the different portions of a split transaction to their proper categories and subcategories.

Here's an example. The Smiths have written a check for $180.45 to Sports Unlimited. The amount includes $119.67 for new bicycling helmets, and $60.78 for restringing tennis rackets. You'll recall from the previous chapter that the Smiths want to keep tennis and biking expenses in separate subcategories.

▲ *Table 3.1. Using special characters in Quicken searches*

Template	*Matches*	*Does not match*
tax..	tax tax penalty taxes	withholding tax 1990 tax
..tax	tax withholding tax	tax due tax penalty
t?x	tax tox tex	tx taxes tax deduction
~tax	tax deduction payroll tax green eggs	tax TAX tAx
t..x	tx tax trax trhgnvbfgrx	taxable tax deduction payroll tax

The following steps show you how this is done. You probably have already created the category Sports and, under it, the subcategories Tennis and Biking. (This was one of the *Check Yourself* exercises in the previous chapter.) If you have not done so, you can create these categories while you're splitting the transaction.

To split a transaction:

1. Make the Smiths' FNB Checking account current, and display the register.
2. Enter the date, number, payee, and amount of the check in the normal fashion.
3. With the cursor in the CATEGORY field, press **Ctrl+S**. Alternately, you can press **Alt+E** to display the Edit menu, then press **S** to select Split Transaction.
4. The Split Transaction window is displayed, as shown in Figure 3.5. Note that the check amount is entered in the Amount column, but all other fields in the window are empty. The cursor is in the first line in the Category column.

▼ *Figure 3.5. The Split Transaction Window*

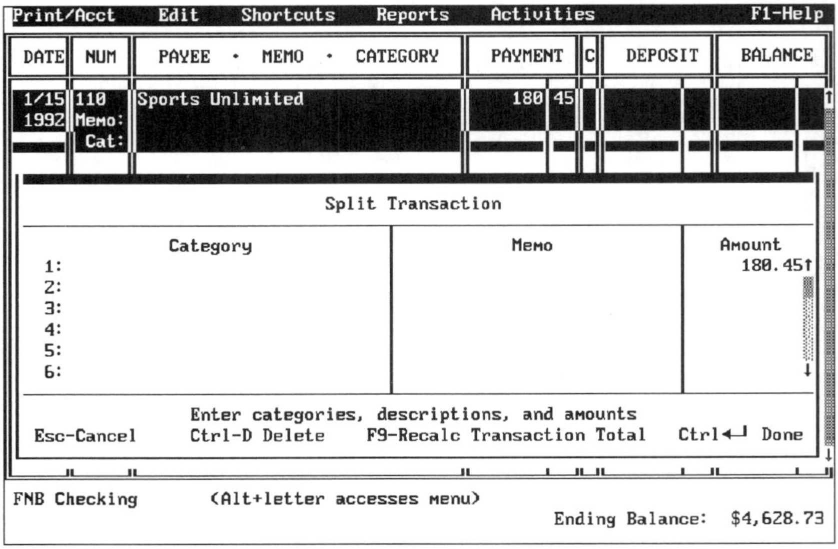

Splitting Transactions

5. In the first column, enter the first category/subcategory that the transaction is to be assigned to. For our example, enter **Sports:Tennis**.
6. Press **Tab**. If the category and/or subcategory already exists, the cursor moves to the Memo column. If the category and/or subcategory does not already exist, you are given the option of selecting from the category list or adding to the category list. If Sports:Tennis has not already been added to the category list for the SMITH file, add it now.
7. With the cursor in the Memo column, you can enter a memo for this split portion of the transaction. Memos entered in the Split Transaction window are just like memos entered in the register's MEMO field—they provide information for your own record keeping. You do not need a memo here, so press **Tab** to move the cursor to the Amount column.
8. The Amount column already contains the total check amount. The next step is to enter the portion of the total that belongs to this part of the split transaction—the $60.78 to be assigned to the Tennis subcategory. Simply type **60.78**. When you press the first key, the total figure is erased and what you type appears in its place.
9. When you've entered the entire figure, 60.78, press **Tab**. The cursor moves to the second line in the Category column. In addition, Quicken automatically subtracts the amount you entered from the total check amount and enters the difference in the next line of the Amount column. In our example, this figure is 119.67, as shown in Figure 3.6.
10. You're now ready to enter the next category for the split transaction. Enter **Sports:Biking** in the second line of the Category column, then press **Tab**.
11. As it did before, the cursor moves to the Memo column or, if the category/subcategory are not found in the file's category list, you are given the option of adding them to the list.
12. In the Memo column, enter a memo if desired. For this example, you don't need to enter a memo.

▼ *Figure 3.6. The First Part of a Split Transaction*

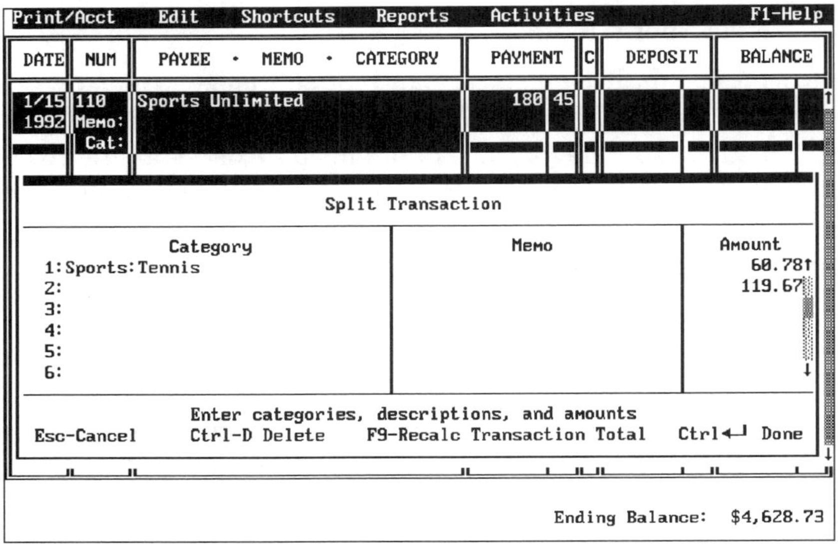

13. Press **Tab** to move the cursor to the Amount field. Quicken has already calculated the correct amount for the Biking expense, so there's no need to enter anything here.

14. Press **Ctrl+Enter**. The Split Transaction window closes and you are returned to the register. The cursor is still in the CATEGORY field, which displays the name of the first category you assigned in the split. In the NUM column, the transaction displays the word SPLIT to indicate that the transaction has been split among two or more categories.

15. Enter remaining information for the transaction, in the normal fashion. After checking the transaction for accuracy and making any changes that are needed, press **Ctrl+Enter** to record the transaction. Your screen should look like the one shown in Figure 3.7. Note that SPLIT is still displayed in the NUM column to indicate a split transaction.

TIP

You can split a transaction into as many as 30 categories and subcategories. To do this, simply repeat Steps 8 through 12 above, for each split. Each

time you enter a new amount in the Amount column, Quicken re-calculates the remaining balance and displays it. Once you have entered all the splits, complete the process by following Steps 13 through 15.

Splitting Transactions

CHECK YOURSELF

To check your ability to split a transaction, enter the following split transaction in the Smiths' register:

Check # 111, dated 1/16/92 to WalMart, total amount $212.65
Assign $98.04 to Auto:Service
Assign $54.12 to Clothing
Assign $16.75 to Household
Assign the balance to Supplies

ANSWERS

1. Display the register for the Smiths' FNB Checking account.
2. If necessary, press **PgDn** to move to the end of the register.

▼ ***Figure 3.7. The Completed Split Transaction***

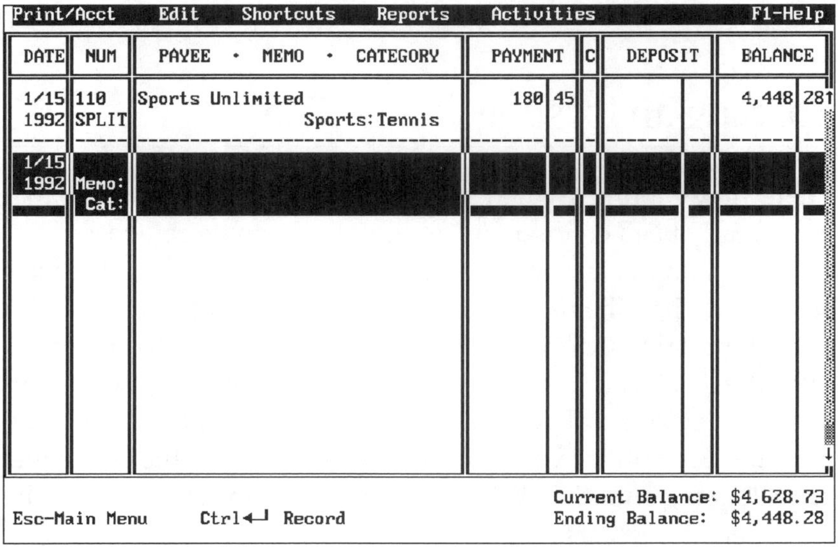

3. Enter the check date, number, payee, and total amount in the proper fields, then press **Tab** to move the cursor to the CATEGORY field.
4. Press **Ctrl+S** to display the Split Transaction window.
5. In row 1, enter **Auto:Service** in the Category column. Press **Tab** twice to move the cursor to the Amount column.
6. Ignoring the numbers already displayed there, enter **98.04**, then press **Enter**. The cursor moves to row 2 of the Category column.
7. Enter **Clothing** in the Category column, then press **Tab** twice to move the cursor to the Amount column.
8. Ignoring the numbers already displayed there, enter **54.12** then press **Enter**. The cursor moves to line 3 of the Category field.
9. In row 3, enter **Household** in the Category column and **16.75** in the Amount column.
10. In row 4, enter **Supplies** in the Category column. The correct amount is already entered in the Amount column.
11. Press **Ctrl+Enter** to return to the register, then press **Enter** to record the transaction.

Splitting an Existing Transaction

There may be times when you want to split a transaction that has already been entered and assigned to a single category.

For example, suppose you took your car to the local service station and had the mechanics tune the car and fill the tank with gas. The total was $75.00. When you initially entered the check into Quicken, you assigned the entire amount to the Auto category. Later you realize that the amount should have been split, with the $20.00 that you paid for gas assigned to the Auto:Fuel subcategory, and the $55.00 for the tune-up assigned to the Auto:Service subcategory.

Splitting Transactions

Here's how to split an existing transaction:

1. Display the register and move to the transaction you want to change. Remember, you can use the Edit Find command to locate the correct transaction.
2. Move the cursor to the CATEGORY field, and press **Ctrl+S**.
3. The Split Transaction window is displayed, with the previously assigned category listed in the top line.
4. Press **Ctrl+D** to delete the category.
5. Enter the split categories, as described above, just as if you were entering the transaction for the first time.

The Help System

The Quicken program includes a detailed, online help system that can save you time when you're working and are not quite sure how to do something. The help system is *context sensitive.* In other words, when you activate the help system, the system "knows" what you are currently doing in Quicken, and displays information related to that topic. For example, if you activate the help system while you're working in the register, Quicken will display a window containing information about the register. This window is shown in Figure 3.8.

To activate help, press **F1** at any time. You can also activate help by selecting the Help command, which is displayed on many Quicken menus. Most Help windows contain more text than can be viewed at one time. You can scroll through a Help window with the **Up** and **Down** arrows, and the **PgUp** and **PgDn** keys; if you have a mouse, you can also use the scroll bar.

The Quicken help system uses cross references that make it easy to move back and forth between related help topics. In the Help window, cross references are displayed in a different color from other text (assuming you have a color monitor). You can move a highlight bar forward and backward among cross references by pressing **Tab** and **Shift+Tab**. When the highlight is on

▼ Figure 3.8. A Help Window

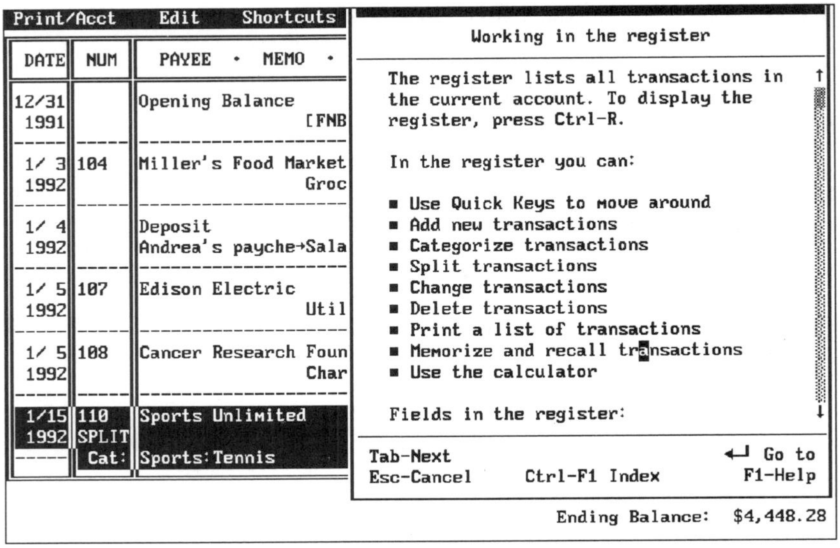

a cross reference, pressing **Enter** takes you to that topic. When you're viewing a cross-reference screen, pressing **Backspace** returns you to the previous screen—that is, the screen from which you selected the cross reference.

TIP

A few additional keys are available for use within a Help window. Any time a Help window is displayed, pressing *F1* will display "Help on Help" information. (In other words, help on using the help system itself.) Pressing *Ctrl+F1* displays the help index, an alphabetical listing of all available help topics. Pressing *Esc* closes the Help window and returns you to whatever you were doing before you activated the help system.

CHECK YOURSELF

Try using the help system. Find help information about setting up subcategories.

ANSWERS

The Help System

1. From the Main Menu, press **F1** to display the Help window.
2. Press **Ctrl+F1** to display the help index.
3. Press **Tab** twice to highlight the "Categories and subcategories" index entry, then press **Enter**.
4. Press the **PgDn** key to scroll through the information displayed. Near the bottom is a list of related topics. Press **Tab** to highlight "Setting up subcategories."
5. Press **Enter**. Information about setting up subcategories is displayed.
6. Press **Esc** to close the Help window and to return to the Main Menu.

Printing the Register

If you have a printer, you can create a printout of a register. The printer must be properly connected to your computer, and you must have specified your printer type when you first installed Quicken. Be sure the printer is turned on and is online. ("Online" means that your printer is ready to accept characters from your computer. Many printers have a separate online button or switch.)

To print a register, first display the register, then press **Ctrl+P**. You can also select the Print/Acct command from the menu, then select Print Register from the submenu. The Print Register window will be displayed, as shown in Figure 3.9.

Information that you enter in this window controls which transactions are printed and how they are formatted. Remember, press **Tab** and **Shift+Tab** to move between fields in the window:

▲ In the "Print transactions from...to:" fields, specify the date range of transactions to be printed. When the cursor is in either of these date fields, you can use Quicken's special

▼ ***Figure 3.9. The Print Register Window***

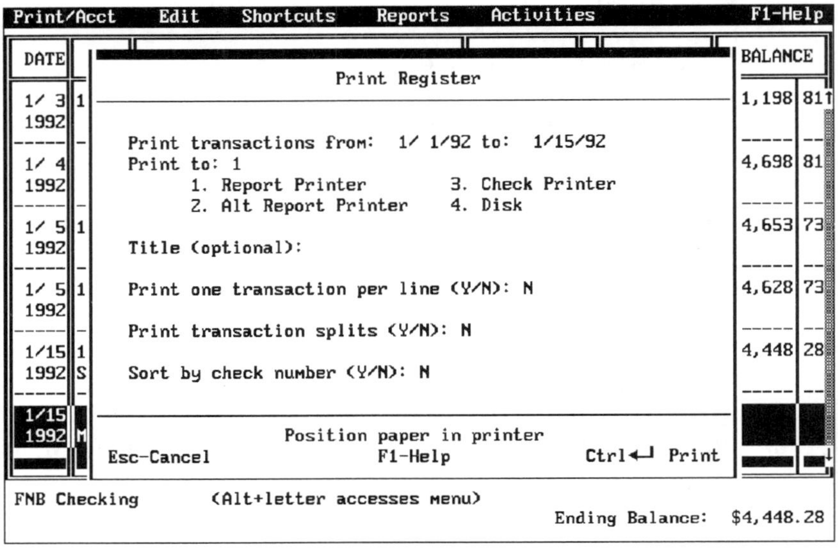

date keys: **T** for today's date, **+** and **–** to increment/decrement by one day, and so on. To print all transactions, enter any From date before the account was started, and enter a To date in the future.

▲ In the "Print to:" field, specify the destination for the report. Selections 1 through 3 refer to one or more printers that you set up when you initially installed Quicken. Most users will have a single printer, the Report Printer. Select Disk to have Quicken save the output to a disk file rather than to create an actual printout. You can later retrieve the information from the file into your word processor or other program. You do not need to have a printer installed to use the Disk option.

▲ In the "Title:" field, enter the report title that will be printed at the start of the report. If you do not specify a title, Quicken uses "Register" as the report title.

▲ In the "Print one transaction per line:" field, specify **Y** to print each transaction on a single line. Quicken will abbreviate transactions slightly to fit each transaction on a single line. Specify **N** to print transactions in full.

▲ In the "Print transaction splits:" field, enter **Y** or **N** to specify whether information about splits will be printed.

▲ In the "Sort by check number:" field, enter **Y** to sort transactions by check number, or enter **N** to sort transactions by date. If you sort by check number, Quicken prints an asterisk in the report to indicate gaps in the check number sequence.

Printing the Register

After you have entered the necessary information in the window, check to be sure your printer is ready. It must be turned on, of course, and the "online" or "ready" indicator should be displayed on the printer's control panel. If you're using a laser printer, be sure there is paper in the paper cassette. For a dot-matrix printer, be sure the printhead is aligned with the top of a page. Then, press **Ctrl+Enter** to start printing. (If the cursor is in the "Sort by check number:" field, you can also press **Enter** to start printing.)

Quicken will print the report, then return to the register screen. If there's some problem with the printer—perhaps you forgot to turn it on, or it's out of paper—Quicken displays the message "Waiting for printer...." If this happens, press **Esc** to cancel the print job. Then, check the printer to determine the cause of the problem. After you've corrected the problem, restart the print job.

Printing to Disk

If you chose selection 4 in the "Print to:" field, Quicken saves the report to a disk file rather than sending it to your printer. When you start "printing" by pressing **Ctrl+Enter**, Quicken displays the Print to Disk window, as shown in Figure 3.10.

Information entered in this window controls the way Quicken saves the report to a disk file:

▲ In the "DOS File:" field, enter the name you want Quicken to use for the file. A file name consists of a one- to eight-character name, followed by an optional period and an optional one- to three-character extension. If you enter a file

▼ Figure 3.10. The Print to Disk Window

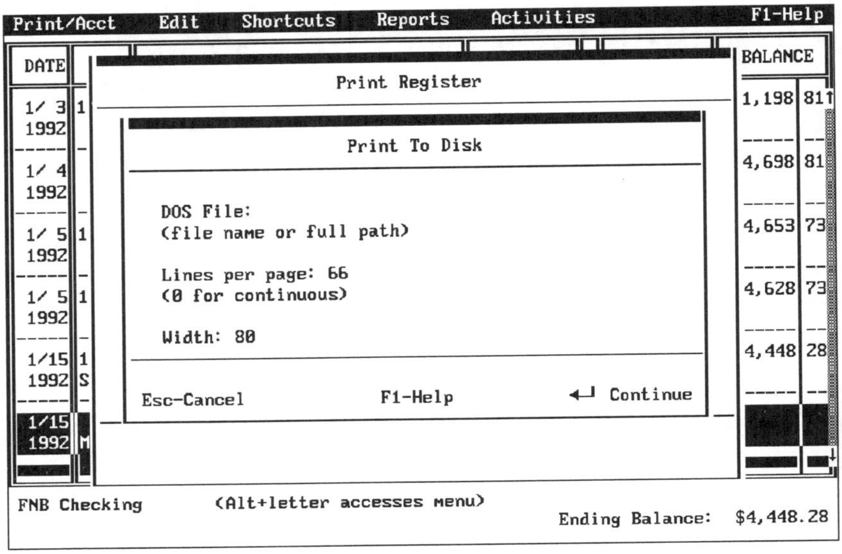

name, Quicken saves the file in the current directory (where the Quicken data files are stored). You can also specify a different disk and/or path before the file name.

▲ In the "Lines per page:" field, specify how many lines to print per page. This setting is not particularly useful, since there are no "pages" in a disk file. You should enter **0** here to tell Quicken to save the report without page breaks.

▲ In the "Width:" field, specify the width of the report—for instance, the number of characters to place in each line of the disk file.

After specifying the Width, press **Enter** to continue. Quicken saves the report in a disk file with the name you specified. If a file with that name already exists, Quicken allows you to either overwrite the existing file with the new one, or to cancel the operation and enter a different file name.

If there's a disk problem, such as leaving a diskette drive door open, Quicken displays a message to that effect. You can correct the problem and try again, or cancel the operation.

CHECK YOURSELF

If your system has a printer installed, you should create a printout of the register for the Smiths' FNB Checking account. Print all the transactions in the register.

ANSWERS

1. Be sure your printer is turned on and is online.
2. Display the register for the Smiths' FNB checking account.
3. Press **Ctrl+P**.
4. In the window, enter the date range of transactions to print, and specify the print destination.
5. Press **Ctrl+Enter**.

QUICK COMMAND SUMMARY

To use the Quicken calculator:

1. Press **Ctrl+O** to display the calculator.
2. Perform the desired calculations.
3. Press **F9** to paste the calculator's answer into Quicken at the current cursor position. Press **Esc** to hide the calculator without pasting.

To delete a transaction:

1. Display the register and move the highlight to the transaction.
2. Press **Ctrl+D**.
3. In response to the prompt, select Delete Transaction to confirm. To cancel, select "Do not delete" or press **Esc**.

To find a specific transaction:

1. Display the register.
2. Press **Ctrl+F** to display the Transaction to Find window.

3. In the correct field, enter the template that you want to search for.
4. Press **Ctrl+B** to search backward through the register. Press **Ctrl+N** to search forward through the register.
5. Repeat Step 4 until you locate the desired transaction.

To split a transaction between two or more categories:

1. Enter the transaction as you normally would, up to but not including the CATEGORY field.
2. With the cursor in the CATEGORY field, press **Ctrl+S**. The Split Transaction window is displayed.
3. In this window, enter the splits, one per line.
4. When all splits are entered, press **Ctrl+Enter** to close the Split Transaction window and return to the register.
5. Continue entering the transaction in the usual manner. The transaction will display SPLIT in the NUM field to indicate it has been split.

To print all or part of a register:

1. Display the register.
2. Press **Ctrl+P** to display the Print Register window.
3. In this window, enter information about the date range of transactions to print, the print destination, and the print format.
4. Press **Ctrl+Enter** to begin printing.

PRACTICE WHAT YOU'VE LEARNED

This chapter has covered many topics, including sections on using the calculator, checking accounts, and the help system. You should become familiar with each topic in order to use Quicken effectively. Here are some suggestions for practice activities. Remember, you can use your "dummy" file for practice if you like.

▲ Display the calculator and perform some calculations. Try using the "paste" feature to enter the calculator total into a register.

▲ Enter some transactions that are split between two or more categories.

▲ Use the Find command to locate specific transactions in the check register.

▲ As you work through the above practices, try using the help system. See how the context-sensitive nature of Quicken's help system works. Try exploring the help system by using the system's cross-references to move from topic to topic.

4

Printing Checks

This third chapter on checking accounts shows you how to print checks with Quicken and your printer. If you will be using only hand-written checks, you can go ahead to the next chapter. You need to read this chapter only if you are going to print checks. You will learn how to

- ▲ **Order Quicken checks**
- ▲ **Enter check information**
- ▲ **Set up your printer**
- ▲ **Print checks**

Ordering Quicken Checks

To print checks using Quicken, you must have special, personalized checks that are available from Intuit. An order form for checks is included in your Quicken package. If you've misplaced this form or need to reorder checks, you can print another order form from within Quicken.

Follow these steps to print the order form:

1. From the Main Menu, select Write/Print Checks.
2. A screen with a blank check appears. You use this screen when writing checks, as you'll learn later in this chapter.
3. Select Activities from the menu, then select Order Supplies. A screen is displayed that lets you print an order form on your printer. This screen also lists a phone number you can call for additional information.
4. Select the printer to use. The order form is printed. Be sure to order the correct checks for your printer.

While waiting for your check order to arrive, you can practice printing by using the sample checks provided with Quicken.

Writing Checks

Before Quicken can print checks, you must *write* the checks by entering information into Quicken. Writing a check in Quicken is much like writing a paper check. When you write a Quicken check, the information is automatically entered in the register. Please note that the following procedure is only for checks that you want Quicken to print. Handwritten checks, deposits, and bank fees must be entered directly into the register, as you learned earlier.

To write checks, select Write/Print Checks from the Main Menu. The screen shown in Figure 4.1 is displayed.

Writing Checks

▼ *Figure 4.1. The Write Checks Screen*

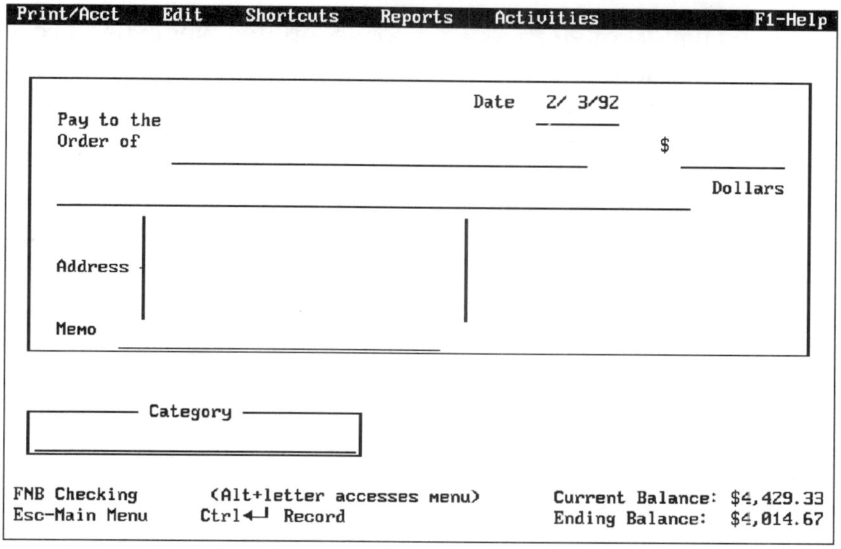

Note that this screen looks a lot like a regular, paper check. This screen has a menu across the top, and several other components. Some of them are fields in which you enter information that will be printed on the check:

- ▲ The Date field initially displays the current date. You can change this if necessary.
- ▲ In the "Pay to the Order of" field, you enter the name of the payee.
- ▲ In the amount field (preceded by a dollar sign), you enter the check amount.
- ▲ In the Address field, you can optionally enter the name and address of the payee. Use this field if you will be mailing the check using a Quicken window envelope.
- ▲ In the Memo field, enter an optional memo to describe the check.

Other items on this screen are for your information and record-keeping purposes—they do not print on the check:

- ▲ In the Category field, you enter the category to which the check is assigned.

- ▲ The name of the current account is displayed in the lower-left corner of the screen.
- ▲ If you have written checks but not yet printed them, the Checks to Print field displays the total amount for these checks. This field is not displayed in Figure 4.1.
- ▲ If you have written post-dated checks (checks with a future date), the "Current Balance:" field is displayed. This field provides the account balance, but disregards the post-dated checks.
- ▲ The "Ending Balance:" field displays the account's ending balance. This balance reflects all checks, including post-dated checks.

The procedure for writing checks is:

1. From the Main Menu, select Write/Print Checks.
2. Be sure the proper account is current. (Look at the account name in the lower-left corner of the screen.) If not, select Print/Acct from the menu, then choose Select/Setup Account. From the list that is displayed, select the desired account.
3. The Date field displays today's date. If you want to change the date, move the cursor to the Date field and type the correct date. You can also use Quicken's special date keys, as explained in Chapter 2, to change the date.
4. In the "Pay to the Order of" field, enter the name of the payee exactly as you want it printed on the check.
5. In the amount field, to the right of the dollar sign, enter the check amount, then press **Tab**. Quicken automatically spells out the amount on the next line.
6. Enter the optional address and memo in their respective fields. The address can contain as many as five lines.
7. In the Category field, enter the check's category and, if appropriate, the subcategory. You have all the same options here as you do when entering a category in the register. For example, press **Ctrl+C** to display a list of categories from which you can choose, or press **Ctrl+S** to split the transaction between two or more categories:subcategories.

Writing Checks

8. Review your entry for accuracy. If you find a mistake, return to that field and make the necessary corrections.
9. To record the check, press **Enter** when the cursor is in the Category field, then verify that the transaction should be recorded. You can also record the transaction by pressing **Ctrl+Enter** while the cursor is in any field.
10. Quicken records the transaction and removes the completed check from the screen. Another blank check is displayed. You can continue writing more checks.

TIP

You don't need to immediately print checks that you've written. In fact, you can exit Quicken and wait as long as you like before printing the checks—Quicken will remember everything you entered, and will keep track of which checks have been printed and which have not. Some people like to write checks on a day-to-day basis as their bills come in, then print them in a group at the end of the month.

CHECK YOURSELF

To make sure you understand how to write checks, you should practice writing some checks for the Smiths' checking account. Here are details you can use to write three checks:

First check:

Date:	Today
Payee:	Ford Motor Credit
Amount:	$378.95
Address:	Ford Motor Credit, P.O. Box 12345, Detroit, MI 43210
Memo:	None
Category:	Auto, subcategory Loan

Second check:

Date:	Last day of the current month. (Tip: press **h** with the cursor in the Date field.
Payee:	Natural Gas Service
Amount:	$35.71

Address: None
Memo: None
Category: Utilities

Third check:

Date: Today
Payee: Citywide Cable TV
Amount: 18.95
Address: None
Memo: None
Category: Entertainment

ANSWER

1. Be sure the Smiths' FNB Checking account is current.
2. From the Main Menu, select Write/Print Checks.
3. Enter the information for the first check. Remember, use **Tab** and **Shift+Tab** to move forward and backward between fields.
4. When the check is complete, press **Ctrl+Enter**.
5. Repeat Steps 3 and 4 for the remaining checks.
6. Press **Esc** to return to the Main Menu.

Reviewing Checks

After writing a number of checks, you can review them and correct any mistakes that you find. This applies only to checks you have written but not yet printed. Checks that have been printed can be reviewed only, using the register.

To review checks:

1. From the Main Menu, select Write/Print Checks to display the Write Checks screen.
2. A blank check is displayed. Checks are stored in date order, with a blank check at the end. To review checks:

- Press **PgUp** to view the previous check.
- Press **PgDn** to view the next check.
- Press **Ctrl+Home** to view the first check.
- Press **Ctrl+End** to view the last check (which is blank).

3. To find a specific check, select Edit Find, then use Quicken's searching capabilities to find checks that match specific information. This is similar to finding information in the register, which you learned about in Chapter 3.
4. If you need to make changes to a check, use **Tab** and **Shift+Tab** to move between fields and edit information in the usual manner. Press **Ctrl+Enter** to record your changes.
5. To delete a check that you have written, display the check and then select Edit Delete Transaction or press **Ctrl+D**. Quicken asks for verification, then deletes the check from the Write Checks screen and from the register.

To close the Write Checks screen and return to the Main Menu, press **Esc**.

What About Check Numbers?

You may be wondering why there is no field for check number on the Write Checks screen. Quicken checks are prenumbered. When you write the check, you won't be able to identify the check number—because the number doesn't exist yet. When you actually print the checks, Quicken will assign the proper check number to each transaction. In the register, unprinted checks are listed with a row of asterisks in the NUM field.

Setting Up Your Printer

When you installed Quicken on your computer system, you specified one or more printers to use. You specified at least two printers: the check printer and the report printer. For many people, these will be the same printer. For checks to print properly, Quicken must have the correct information about the printer being used. Now is a good time to check your printer settings.

To set up your printer or to check printer settings:

1. From the Main Menu, select Set Preferences.
2. Next, select Printer Settings, and then select Settings for Printing Checks.
3. The screen shown in Figure 4.2 is displayed. The information on your screen will probably differ from the contents shown in the figure.
4. If there is no entry for the "Name of Printer:" field, or if the entry is incorrect, press **F9** and select your type of printer from the list that is displayed.
5. Examine the other information on the screen and verify that it is correct for the printer you will be using to print checks. Quicken's default settings will be okay for most situations. Remember, you use **Tab** and **Shift+Tab** to move forward and backward between fields. With the cursor on the last field, press **Enter** to record the information and exit.

▼ *Figure 4.2. The Check Printer Settings Screen*

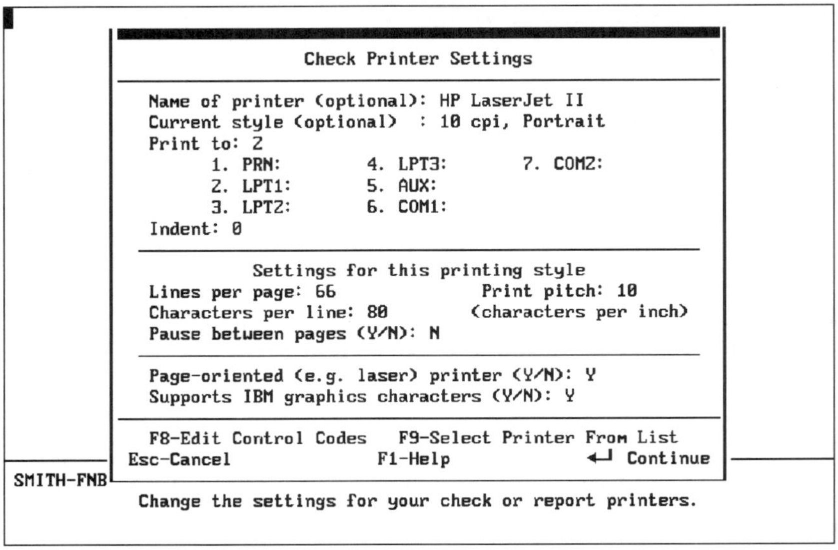

Positioning Checks in the Printer

Positioning Checks in the Printer

Before printing checks, you must make sure that the blank checks are positioned properly in the printer. Quicken can print a sample check to test paper alignment.

Dot-Matrix Printers

If you're using a dot-matrix printer, your Quicken checks are supplied on continuous paper with perforated tractor strips along each edge. You insert the checks into your printer in the same way that you insert regular printer paper. You must, of course, remove any paper from the printer before loading the checks.

Use the following procedure to position the checks properly:

1. Load the checks into the printer, with the first check positioned under the print head.
2. Turn the printer on and be sure it is online.
3. From the Main Menu, select Write/Print Checks.
4. If you have one or more checks to print, you can proceed directly to the next step. If not, you must enter one blank check before proceeding.
5. Select Print/Acct, then select Print Checks. As a shortcut, simply press **Ctrl+P**.
6. The Print Checks window is displayed, as shown in Figure 4.3.
7. In the "Print to:" field, enter **3** to specify the check printer.
8. In the "Type of checks to print on:" field, enter the number corresponding to the type of checks you purchased.
9. Press **F9**. Quicken will print a sample check that looks like the one shown in Figure 4.4. *Do not* move the checks up or down in the printer.

▼ Figure 4.3. The Print Checks Window

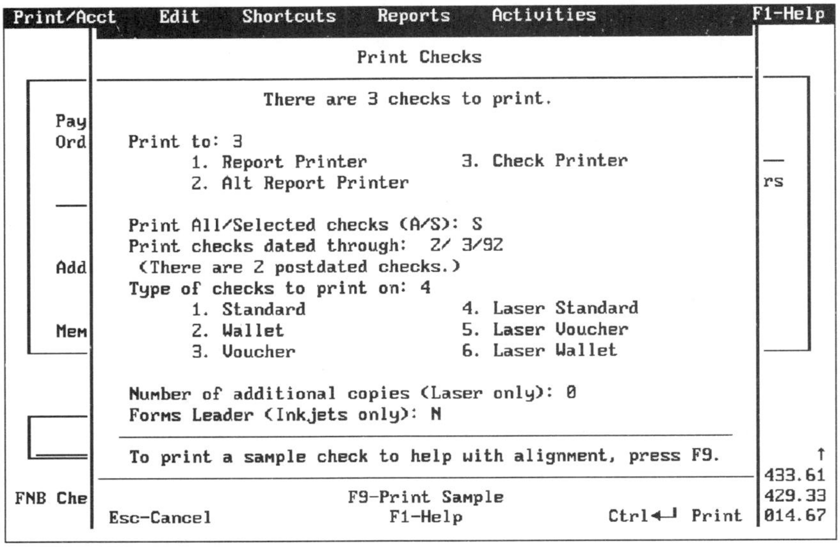

10. Examine the sample check. There are rows of X's printed in the date and amount blanks, and the word "Payee" in the "Pay to the Order of" line. These items should have been printed just above the lines on the check, as shown in Figure 4.4. If the vertical and horizontal positioning is correct, you can press **Enter** and continue to the next section, *Printing Checks.*

▼ Figure 4.4. A Sample Check Correctly Printed by Quicken

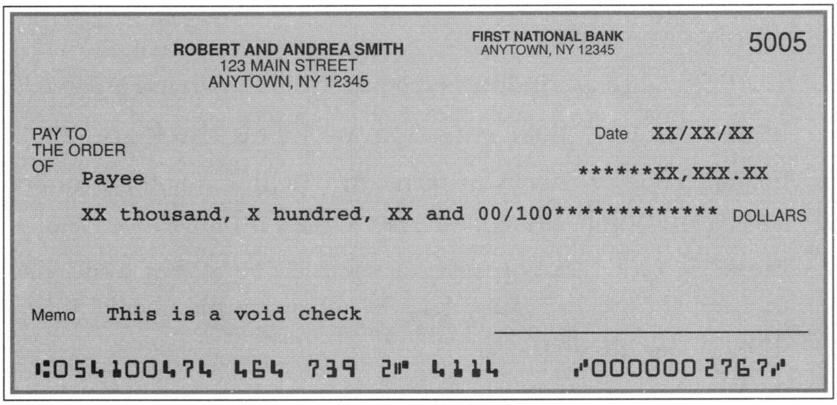

11. If the vertical position is incorrect, look at the pointer line that Quicken printed on the check. The arrows at either end of this line point to a number printed on the tractor strip along the edges of the check. This is the position number. The pointer line is printed only if you're using a dot-matrix printer, and is not shown in Figure 4.4, which was printed on a laser printer.

Positioning Checks in the Printer

12. Enter the position number, and press **Enter**. Quicken advances to the next blank check and prints another sample check. This time, the sample should be correctly aligned. If the paper is still vertically too high or low, by a significant amount, return to Step 11. If the paper is off by a fraction of a line, use the adjustment knob on the side of your printer to align the paper.
13. If the side-to-side position of the print sample is off, loosen the paper clamps on your printer and slide the paper left or right to the proper position.
14. Your checks are now positioned properly. Look at the position relative to the printer and try to remember it for the future. With a little practice, you may be able to position your checks perfectly on the first try.

Laser Printers

Quicken checks for laser printers are grouped three to a page (or one to a page for voucher-style checks). You insert the sheets of checks into your laser printer paper tray. If you're unsure how to do this, refer to your printer's documentation.

Laser printer checks are aligned automatically by the printer. If you have entered your printer settings correctly, you should have no problem with alignment. You can print a sample check as described above for a dot-matrix printer. If the alignment is wrong, you probably entered an incorrect printer setting.

Resolving Printer Problems

The check-printing procedure in Quicken is relatively foolproof. It's likely that you will be successfully printing checks on your first try. If problems arise, however, you should refer to your Quicken manual, which contains a detailed section on the most common printing problems and their solutions.

Printing Checks

Once you have verified that your checks are aligned correctly, you are ready to print real checks. You can print checks as soon as you enter them, or you can "save them up" and print them in a batch at the end of the month (when you get your paycheck!).

Also, you can print post-dated checks before their date, or wait until payment is due. When you print checks, you must provide Quicken with the following information:

- ▲ The printer to use (usually the check printer).
- ▲ Which checks to print. You can print all checks, checks through a certain date, or individually selected checks.
- ▲ The check number of the next check.

The procedure to follow is:

1. Display the Print Checks window (Figure 4.3). To do this, select Write/Print Checks from the Main Menu, then either press **Ctrl+P** or select Print/Acct and then select Print Checks.
2. At the top of this window, Quicken displays the number of checks to be printed.
3. In the "Print to:" field, enter the number of the printer to use (usually the Check Printer, item 3).
4. In the "Print All/Selected checks:" field, enter **A** to print all checks (except post-dated checks), and enter **S** to select checks to print.
5. If you have written post-dated checks, the window will display Print Checks Date Through, followed by today's date. Accept this date by pressing **Enter** if you don't want to print any post-dated checks. Otherwise, enter the date of the latest check to print.

Printing Checks

6. In the "Type of checks to print on:" field, enter the number corresponding to the type of checks you purchased. Quicken will remember the entry you make here, so you won't have to reenter it in future check-printing sessions (unless you change check types, of course).
7. The "Number of additional copies" entry is required only if you are using multi-part voucher checks in a laser printer. Otherwise, leave this set at 0.
8. In the "Forms Leader:" field, enter **Y** only if you are using a forms leader with an inkjet printer.
9. When the information in the Print Checks window is complete, press **Ctrl+Enter**. If you specified printing all checks, the Type Check Number window is displayed. If you specified printing selected checks, the Select Checks to Print window is displayed (Figure 4.5).
10. The Select Checks to Print window lists all the checks you have written. Press the **Up** and **Down** arrow keys to move between checks, then press the **Spacebar** to select and deselect individual checks. A check selected for printing has Print displayed in the right column. Press **F9** if you want to

▼ *Figure 4.5. The Select Checks to Print Window*

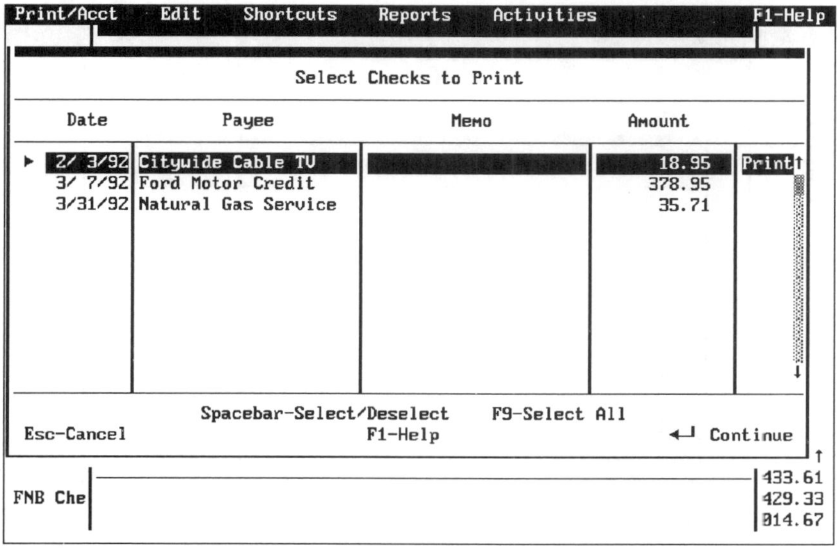

select all checks. When you're done, press **Enter** to display the Enter Check Number window.

11. Look at the check forms in your printer to find the number of the first check—the check that is about to be printed. If necessary, type the correct check number in the window. You can also press the + and – keys to increase/decrease the check number.
12. Press **Enter** to print all checks. Quicken starts printing and, when finished, displays the window shown in Figure 4.6, which asks you to verify whether the checks printed correctly.
13. Remove the printed checks from the printer, and examine them carefully. If they are all okay, press **Enter**. Quicken marks all the checks as having been printed, and returns you to the Write Checks screen.
14. Occasionally, some checks do not print properly. The printer may have jammed, you may have run out of checks, and so on. Determine the number of the first check that did not print properly, and then type the number and press **Enter**. Quicken marks lower-numbered checks as having been printed, and marks other checks as unprinted. You are then returned to the Print Checks window.

▼ ***Figure 4.6. The "Did checks print OK?" Window***

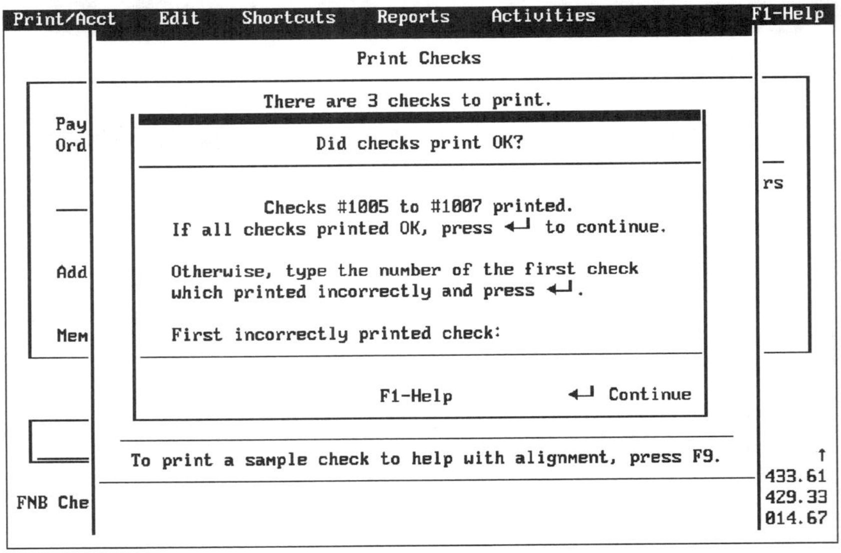

Printing Checks

15. Correct whatever problem caused the checks to print improperly, then reprint the checks. When the Enter Check Number window is displayed, the correct number for the next check should be shown. (Quicken automatically keeps track of check numbers.) Verify this number, and then press **Enter** to reprint the checks.

When Quicken prints a check, it enters the correct check number in the register. Your checks are now ready to be mailed. Separate them and, for continuous checks, remove the tractor perforations. Don't forget to sign the checks!

CHECK YOURSELF

You should practice printing checks by using the three checks you wrote for the Smiths' account earlier in this chapter. Use the sample checks that are provided with the Quicken package. These are the continuous-style checks designed for use in a dot-matrix printer. If you have a laser printer, you can still use these checks by separating them into sheets of three, then removing the tractor-feed strips.

ANSWER

1. Position the checks in your printer.
2. From the Main Menu, select Write/Print Checks.
3. Press **Ctrl+P**.
4. In the window, specify the print destination (Check Printer) and that all checks should be printed.
5. Specify the type of checks being used.
6. Print a sample check to verify alignment by pressing **F9**.
7. Press **Ctrl+Enter**.
8. Enter the number on the first check that will be printed.
9. Press **Enter** to begin printing.

Reprinting Checks

Even after a check has been successfully printed, you may need to reprint it. Perhaps you spilled coffee on the original, or your pen leaked while signing the check. You can reprint any check at any time.

Follow these steps to reprint a check:

1. Display the register for the account.
2. Find the check in question, and move the cursor to the NUM field.
3. Enter * (an asterisk). Quicken replaces the check number with a row of asterisks, which marks the check as unprinted.
4. Press **Ctrl+W** to display the Write Checks screen. If you had entered an address on the original check, you will have to reenter it. (Quicken does not save the address after a check has been printed.) Press **PgUp** and **PgDn** to display the check in the Write Checks window, then reenter the address.
5. Print the check(s) in the usual manner.

QUICK COMMAND SUMMARY

To write checks for later printing:

1. From the Main Menu, select Write/Print Checks to display the Write Checks screen.
2. On the blank check that is displayed, enter the payee and the check amount. Change the date if necessary.
3. In the Address field, enter an address of up to five lines if you will be mailing the check in a window envelope.
4. Enter a memo in the Memo field.
5. Enter a category and, optionally, a subcategory in the Category field. You can display the category list by pressing **Ctrl+C**, and split the transaction by pressing **Ctrl+S**.

6. Record the transaction by pressing **Enter** with the cursor in the Category field, or by pressing **Ctrl+Enter** while the cursor is in any field. Quicken records the check and displays another blank check.
7. Repeat Step 2 to write additional checks. Press **Esc** to return to the Main Menu.

To print checks that you have written:

1. Load your printer with special checks ordered from Intuit.
2. From the Main Menu, select Write/Print Checks, then press **Ctrl+P** to display the Print Checks window.
3. Fill in the necessary information in the window. Press **F9** to print a sample check to test alignment, or press **Ctrl+Enter** to begin printing checks.
4. Make sure your checks are aligned properly in the printer.
5. Enter the first check number, then press **Enter**. The checks are printed.

PRACTICE WHAT YOU'VE LEARNED

If you plan to use Quicken to print real checks, it's a good idea to practice until you have the procedure down pat. Better to make a mistake printing a few practice checks than when printing a large number of real checks! Use your "dummy" file, if you wish, entering checks and printing them until you are confident that you have mastered the process (particularly the alignment of checks in the printer).

TIP

You will probably want to minimize the number of "real" checks used for practice. If you're using a laser printer, you can make photocopies of checks onto standard 8-1/2" x 11" printer paper, and use the copies for practice. With a dot-matrix printer, you can use checks twice: Print on the front the first time, then turn the pages over and print on the back.

5

Checking Accounts (3)

This is the last of 4 chapters dealing with Quicken checking accounts. It covers some additional activities that you need to know in order to fully realize the benefits of using Quicken. You'll learn how to

- **Reconcile your Quicken account with your bank statement**
- **Deal with reconciliation errors**
- **Use Quicken classes**
- **Memorize recurring transactions**
- **Recall memorized transactions**

Reconciling Your Account

The term *reconciling* refers to the process by which you ensure that your Quicken account agrees with the statement you receive from the bank. For most accounts, you will receive a statement once per month and perform reconciliation once per month. If you have accumulated more than one statement, you reconcile one at a time, starting with the earliest statement.

Here's a quick overview of the reconciliation process: you start by entering into Quicken certain information from your bank statement, such as beginning and ending balances, interest earned, bank fees, and so on. Quicken then displays a list of all uncleared transactions. A transaction is *uncleared* if it has not yet appeared on a bank statement. From this list, you mark as cleared those transactions that appear on the current bank statement. When all transactions have been marked, Quicken calculates the account's ending balance and compares it with the ending balance you entered from the bank statement. If the amounts match, your account is properly balanced and reconciliation is complete. If the amounts do not match, you then locate and correct the mistake(s).

Starting the Reconciliation Process

To begin the process of reconciling your account, you will need your latest bank statement and, optionally, a pen or pencil. Start Quicken and make sure the proper account is current.

To reconcile your account:

1. Begin from either the Register screen or the Write Checks screen. With either of these screens displayed, select Activities, then select Reconcile from the pull-down menu. The Reconcile Register with Bank Statement window is displayed, as shown in Figure 5.1.
2. The first field in this window is titled Bank Statement Opening Balance. Here Quicken displays what it thinks your

Reconciling Your Account

▼ *Figure 5.1. The Reconcile Register with Bank Statement Window*

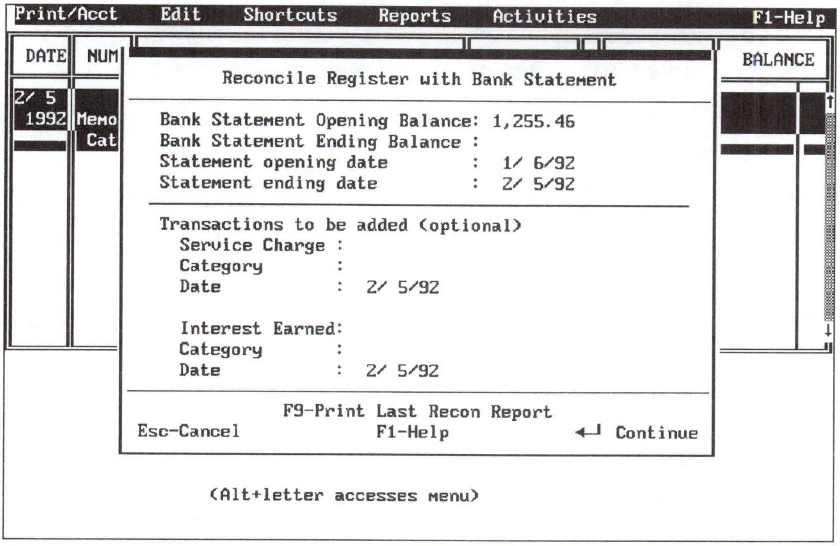

statement's opening balance should be. If you have reconciled the account before, this amount will be the same as the closing balance on the previous statement. If this is a new account and has not yet been reconciled, this amount will be the Initial Balance that you entered when you set up the account. If you regularly reconcile your account, this amount should be correct. At times, and particularly when you're working with a new account, the amount may not agree with your bank statement. If the amount displayed here disagrees with your bank statement, enter the opening balance amount from your bank statement.

3. In the Bank Statement Ending Balance field, enter the ending balance from your bank statement, then press **Enter**.
4. In the "Statement opening date" field, Quicken displays the closing date of the previous reconciliation, or for new accounts, the date the account was set up. You can change this date if it is incorrect.
5. In the "Statement ending date" field, Quicken displays the date one month from the statement opening date. This is

based on the fact that most bank statements cover a one month period. Again, you can change this date if necessary.

6. The "Transactions to be added" section of this window contains fields for entering bank service charges and interest payments. These entries are optional, and need to be used only if applicable to your account.
7. In the Service Charge field, enter the amount of any account service fees that appear on your statement. If you have multiple fees (for instance, a monthly account fee and a check printing charge), you may want to use the Quicken calculator (**Ctrl+O**) to calculate the total.
8. In the Category field, enter the category to be assigned to the service charges. Usually the Quicken category, Bank Chrg (Bank Charge), is used for account fees.
9. In the Date field, Quicken displays the statement ending date. You can change this if you want the service charge listed on another date.
10. If your account pays interest, enter the amount in the Interest Earned field. You can also enter a category for the interest in the Category field; usually interest income is assigned to the Int Inc (Interest Income) category. You can also change the date for the interest income, if desired.
11. When you're done entering information in the Reconcile Register with Bank Statement window, your screen will look like Figure 5.2 (of course, the amounts may differ).
12. Press **Enter** with the cursor in the last field, or press **Ctrl+Enter** from any field. Quicken closes the window and displays the Reconciliation screen, which lists all the uncleared transactions in the account (Figure 5.3). The next step in reconciliation is marking transactions as cleared.

Marking Transactions as Cleared

Figure 5.3 shows the screen in which you mark transactions as cleared.

▼ ***Figure 5.2. Updated Reconcile Bank Statement with Register Window***

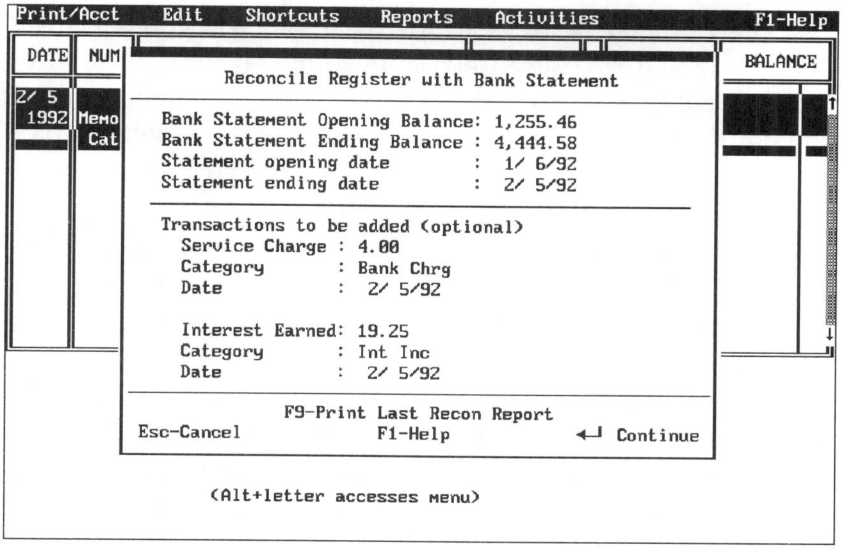

Reconciling Your Account

In this window, all uncleared transactions are listed at the top. Quicken lists deposits first, followed by checks and other payments. At the end of the list, Quicken lists any service charges and/or interest payments. Note field C. In this field, Quicken

▼ ***Figure 5.3. Screen Used to Mark Transactions as Cleared***

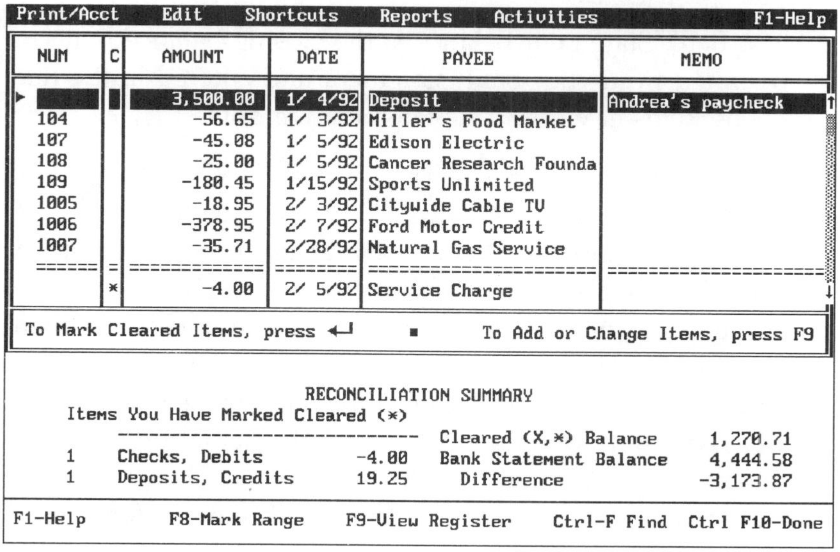

displays an asterisk for transactions that you mark as cleared. Initially, this field is blank for all listed transactions except service charges and/or interest payments that you entered in the previous window. These transactions are "cleared" in that, by entering them, you have indicated to Quicken that they are listed on your bank statement. The service charge and/or interest payment transactions will be automatically entered in the account register when reconciliation is complete.

At the bottom of the Reconciliation screen, Quicken displays the RECONCILIATION SUMMARY. On the left, Quicken summarizes the total for items you have marked as cleared. Two totals are displayed. For Checks, Debits, Quicken totals all cleared payment transactions (any transactions that take money out of the account). For Deposits, Credits Quicken totals all cleared income transactions (any transactions that add money to the account). When this screen is first displayed, the only cleared transactions are those service charges and/or interest payments (if any) that you entered in the Reconcile Register with Bank Statement window.

On the right side of the RECONCILIATION SUMMARY, Quicken displays several calculated items:

- ▲ The Cleared (X,*) Balance is Quicken's calculation of the balance, taking into account only the transactions that have been marked as cleared.
- ▲ The Bank Statement Balance is the closing balance that you obtained from your bank statement and entered in the Reconcile Register with Bank Statement window.
- ▲ The Difference is the difference between the two previous amounts.
- ▲ A field titled Opening Balance Difference (not shown in Figure 5.3) is displayed only if you changed the bank statement opening balance calculated by Quicken to match the opening balance shown on your bank statement. The amount displayed in this field is the difference between Quicken's calculation of opening balance and the actual opening balance that you entered from your statement. Later, you will have to instruct Quicken how to deal with this difference.

Reconciling Your Account

You're now ready to start marking items in the list. Here are the keys you will use:

- ▲ Press **Up** arrow or **Down** arrow to move the highlight to the next or previous transaction.
- ▲ Press **PgUp** or **PgDn** to move up or down in the list by one page.
- ▲ Press **Ctrl+PgUp** or **Ctrl+PgDn** to move to the first or last transaction in the list.
- ▲ Press **Enter** to mark the current transaction as cleared and move down one transaction.
- ▲ Press **Spacebar** to toggle the current transaction between cleared and uncleared.

Look at your bank statement and mark as cleared each transaction that appears in the statement. It's useful to place a check mark next to each transaction on the bank statement as you clear it. (That's what the pen or pencil is for!) In the C field of the screen, each transaction that you clear is marked with an asterisk. As you clear transactions, the amounts displayed in the RECONCILIATION SUMMARY at the bottom of the screen are immediately updated.

Most of the time, reconciliation proceeds smoothly and your account balances perfectly. After you mark as cleared all the transactions that appear on your bank statement, the Cleared (X,*) Balance displayed in the RECONCILIATION SUMMARY will agree to the penny with the Bank Statement Balance, and the Difference field will display 0. Congratulations! Your account is balanced and you know exactly how much money it contains. Your screen will appear like the one shown in Figure 5.4. (Amounts and transaction details will differ, of course.) You can now go on to the *Completing Reconciliation* section, found later in this chapter.

Sometimes, however, the account does not balance after all statement transactions have been marked as cleared. The Difference field in the RECONCILIATION SUMMARY will then display an amount other than 0. This amount is the difference between what Quicken thinks the account balance is, and what the bank thinks it is. If this happens to you, don't worry. It

▼ ***Figure 5.4. Balanced Account with the Difference Field Displaying 0***

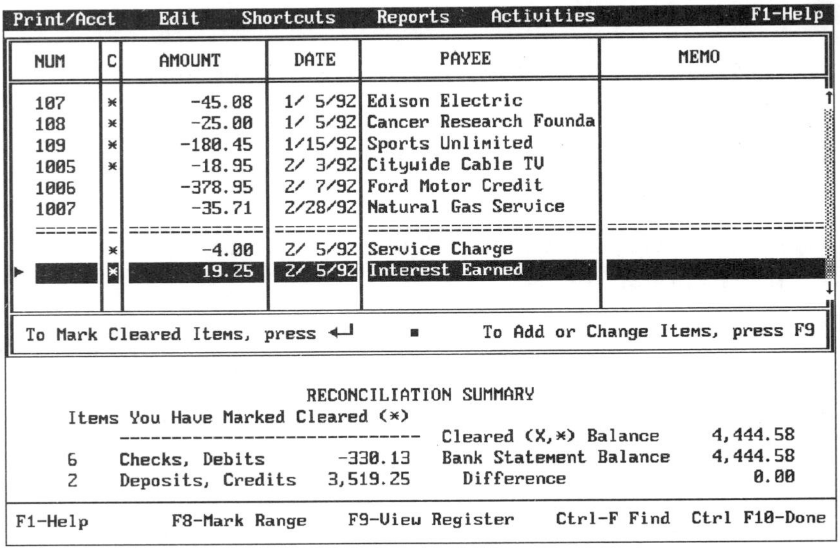

happens to everyone at least once, and it's usually quite simple to find the error or errors that are causing the imbalance, as you will see in the next section.

Dealing with Reconciliation Errors

If you've marked as cleared all of the transaction on your bank statement, but your account still doesn't balance, there must be a mistake somewhere. And, to be honest, it's probably *your* mistake. It's true that banks occasionally make errors on the statement, but it's pretty rare. Your error is probably one of the following:

- ▲ You forgot to enter one or more transactions into Quicken.
- ▲ You made a mistake entering the dollar amount of one or more transactions.
- ▲ You marked as "cleared" one or more transactions that have not cleared.
- ▲ You did not mark as "cleared" one or more transactions that have cleared.

Reconciling Your Account

The first type of error, forgetting to enter one or more transactions, is the easiest to find because the transactions will appear on your bank statement but not in the Quicken transaction list.

Here's how to enter forgotten transactions during reconciliation:

1. From the Reconciliation screen (Figure 5.3), press **F9** to view the register.
2. Press **Ctrl+End** to move to the blank transaction at the end of the register.
3. Enter one or more transactions in the usual manner.
4. When you have entered all the forgotten transactions, press **F9** to return to the Reconciliation screen. The newly entered transactions are now included in the list of uncleared transactions.
5. Assuming these transactions appear on your bank statement, mark them as cleared.

If you have forgotten any transactions, entering them will usually bring your account into balance. If not, you will have to consider the other possible errors.

Next, see whether you've marked too many or too few transactions as cleared. It's a simple matter of going over your bank statement again and comparing it with the transactions listed by Quicken on the Reconciliation screen. Double check that you have marked as cleared only those transactions that appear on the bank statement and all of the transactions that appear on the bank statement.

If your account imbalance is not corrected by either of the previous procedures, the remaining possibility is that you entered an incorrect dollar amount for one or more items. While it is sometimes a bother to do so, I strongly suggest that you make the effort to find and correct the error. If you do not, your Quicken account will not accurately reflect the actual account balance. And, after all, one of the major reasons for using Quicken is accuracy!

To find the erroneous amount:

1. Scroll to the top of the transaction list in the Reconciliation screen.
2. Starting with the first transaction, compare it to the corresponding entry on your bank statement.
3. If the amounts match, press the **Down** arrow to move to the next transaction.
4. If they do not match, press **F9** to display the register. The highlight will be on the same transaction. Move the cursor to the AMOUNT field, and make the necessary correction.
5. Press **Ctrl+Enter** to record the changes, then press **F9** to return to the Reconciliation screen.
6. If the Difference amount in the RECONCILIATION SUMMARY is now 0, your account is in balance. If not, return to Step 2 and continue looking for additional errors.

What if your account doesn't balance but the difference amount is small, and you don't want to spend any time tracking it down? You can ignore the difference and have Quicken make an adjustment for you. You'll learn how to do this in the next section. Remember that I strongly advise against this course of action. You may save a little time now, but you will introduce inaccuracies into your account that may cause trouble in the future.

CHECK YOURSELF

To ensure that you understand the reconciliation procedure, you should now reconcile the Smiths' account. This exercise assumes that you have been entering information for the Smiths' account in previous Check Yourself exercises, including the checks that were written to be printed. The Smiths' bank statement includes the following information:

Opening balance:	$1,255.46
Closing balance:	$4,444.58
Service charge:	$4.00
Interest earned:	$19.25

Reconciling Your Account

Checks cleared:

104, $56.65
107, $45.08
108, $25.00
1005, $180.45

Deposits cleared:

one for $3,500.00

As you reconcile this account, your screens should look like the ones presented earlier in this chapter.

ANSWER

1. Display the register for the Smiths' FNB checking account.
2. Select Activities, then select Reconcile from the pull-down menu.
3. In the window, enter the closing balance, service charges, and interest earned as obtained from the Smiths' bank statement.
4. Press **F10**.
5. Quicken displays a list of uncleared transactions. To mark a transaction as cleared, use the arrow keys to highlight the transaction and press **Spacebar**.
6. Mark as cleared all transactions that appear on the Smiths' bank statement.
7. Once all transactions have been marked, the Difference field in the lower-right corner of the screen should read 0.

Completing Reconciliation

When you have finished marking transactions as cleared, press **Ctrl+F10** from the Reconciliation screen. What happens next depends on the details of your reconciliation:

If Your Account Balances

If you did not change the Quicken opening balance and your account balances, then Quicken displays the message, Congratulations! Your account balances. You then have the option of printing a reconciliation report (which, to be honest, is not particularly useful!). Enter **Y** to print a report, **N** to decline. You are now finished with reconciliation. Cleared items are marked with an asterisk in the register. The closing balance from this reconciliation period will be used as the opening balance the next time you reconcile this account.

If Your Account Does Not Balance

If you press **Ctrl+F10** to end reconciliation with the account out of balance (in other words, Difference not 0), Quicken displays a message telling you that your account is not in balance. You then have two options:

- Press **Esc** to return to the register to find and correct the error that is causing the problem. This is the recommended course of action.
- Press **Enter** to have Quicken adjust for the discrepancy. The Adding Balance Adjustment Entry window is displayed (Figure 5.5). Enter **Y** to have Quicken add a transaction to the account and to adjust for the difference, then enter an optional category for the transaction. Remember, having Quicken adjust for an out-of-balance reconciliation may result in errors later.

If You Changed the Opening Balance

You should remember that at the start of the reconciliation procedure you compared Quicken's calculated opening balance with the opening balance on your bank statement. If the two differed, you changed the Quicken opening balance to match the bank statement opening balance. In this case, you need to account for the difference. When you press **Ctrl+F10** to end reconciliation, Quicken will display the Create Opening Balance Adjustment window (Figure 5.6). In this window, Quicken displays the amount of the discrepancy between the calculated opening balance and the bank statement opening balance. You have three choices:

Reconciling Your Account

▼ Figure 5.5. The Adding Balance Adjustment Window

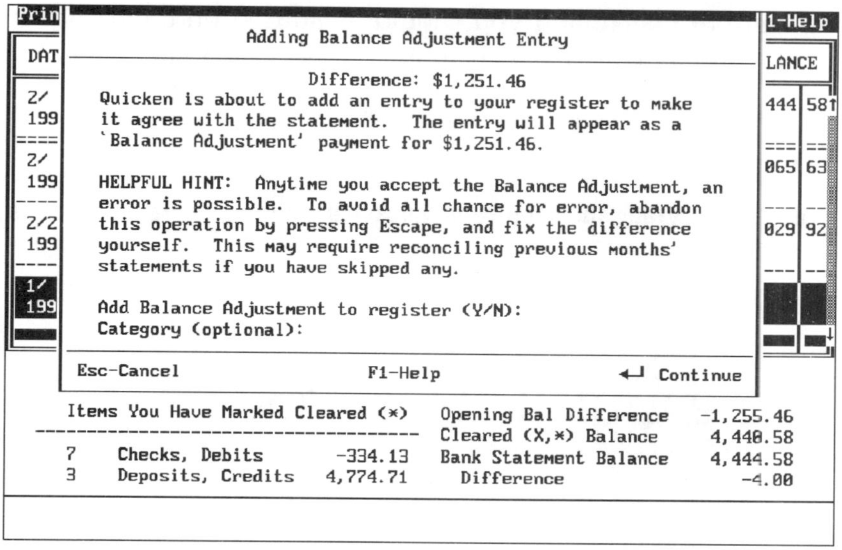

▲ Press **Esc** to return to reconciliation.

▲ Enter **Y** followed by an optional category to have Quicken create an opening balance adjustment to bring your Quicken account into agreement with your bank statement.

▼ Figure 5.6. The Create Opening Balance Adjustment Window

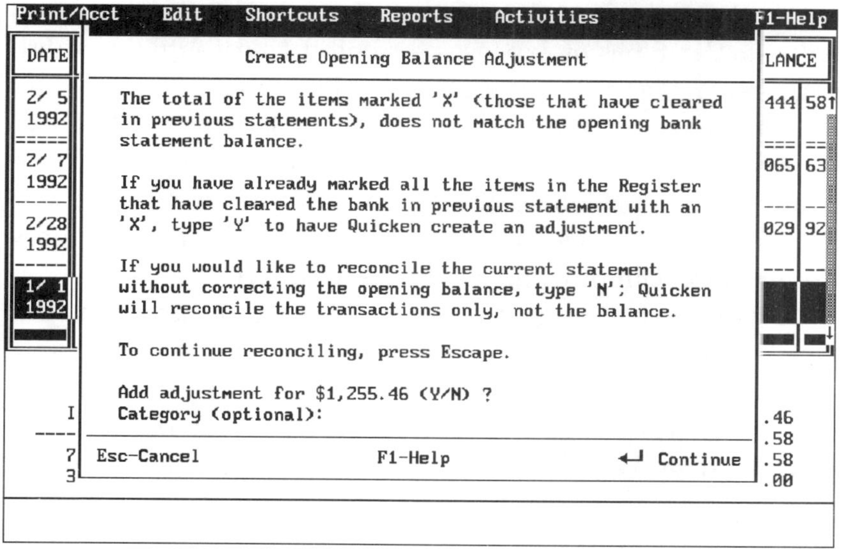

▲ Enter **N** to complete reconciliation without an opening balance adjustment. Your Quicken account and bank statement will not match, and you should be sure to find and correct the problem before reconciling your next bank statement.

TIP

To ensure accuracy and keep your Quicken account up to date, reconcile every month.

Using Quicken Classes

Classes are an additional method that Quicken provides for you to keep track of your income and expenses. Classes work in conjunction with categories. While categories tell you what a transaction is for, a class tells you the "where," "who," or "when" of a transaction. The following is an example.

What Are Classes For?

Imagine that you are lucky enough to own two homes, your regular home in the city and a vacation home at the shore. You have similar types of expenses for both homes—utilities, mortgage, repairs, and so on—but would like to keep expenses for the two properties separate. This is easily done by creating two classes. You could create the class City for the city home and Shore for the vacation home. Then, when a house-related transaction occurs, you would assign it to the appropriate category (for instance, Utilities) and also to the appropriate class.

Classes provide a great deal of additional flexibility to your Quicken data. A transaction can be assigned to a category, to a class, or (most frequently) to both. Using classes in conjunction with categories gives you two different ways of looking at your financial data. When creating reports, you can base the reports

Using Quicken Classes

on an account's categories, its classes, or both. Continuing the above example, you could easily determine:

- ▲ Total utility expenses for both houses.
- ▲ Repair expenses for the vacation house.
- ▲ Total expenses in all categories for the city house.

Perhaps the most common use for classes is when a single checking account is used for both personal and business purposes. You could set up two classes, Business and Personal, and assign transactions to one or the other, as appropriate. It would then be a simple matter to have Quicken provide detailed information on your business-related income and expenses separately from your personal transactions.

Creating Classes

Quicken does not come with a predefined list of classes, so you must create your own.

Here's how to create a list of classes:

1. From either the Register screen or the Write Checks screen, press **Ctrl+L** to display the Class List window (Figure 5.7).
2. Since you're setting up your first class, this list is empty except for the top selection <New Class>. Select this by pressing **Enter**.
3. The Set Up Class window is displayed. In the "Name" field, enter the name for the class. The name can contain as many as 15 characters, including spaces but not the characters /, :, [, or]. In the "Description" field, you can enter an optional description of the class, up to 25 characters long. If you enter a description, it will be used in place of the class name in report headings. Figure 5.8 shows the Set Up Class window with a class name and description filled in.
4. With the cursor on the "Description" field, press **Enter**. You are returned to the Class List window, with the newly cre-

▼ *Figure 5.7. The Class List Window*

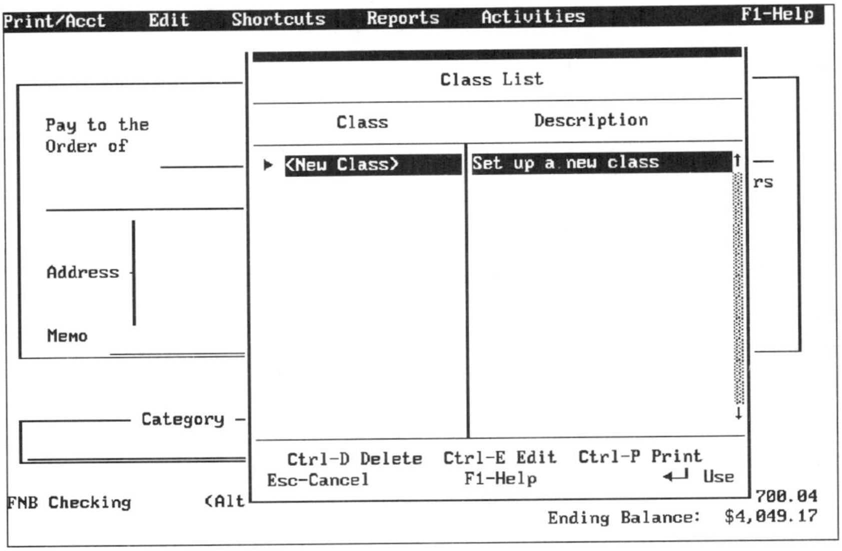

ated class and description listed. You can now press **Esc** to close the Class List window, or again select <New Class> to set up another new class.

▼ *Figure 5.8. The Set Up Class Window*

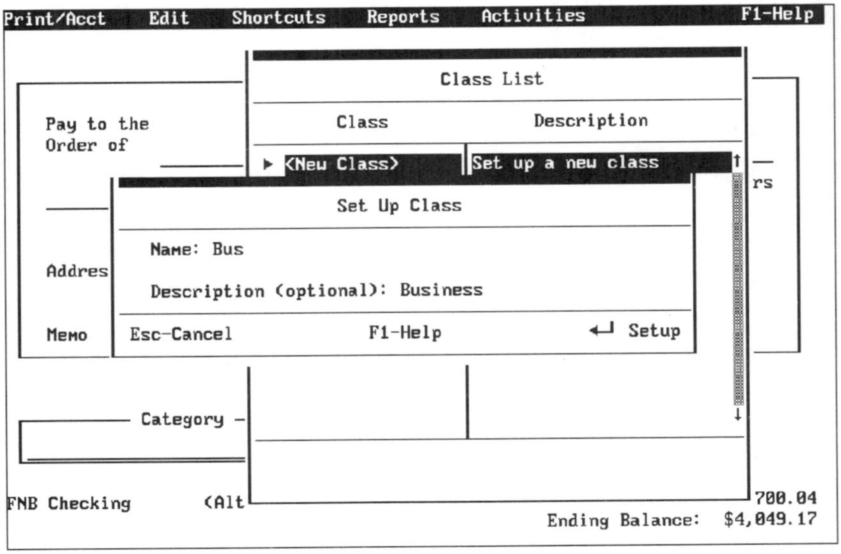

Using Quicken Classes

5. While the Class List window is displayed, you can perform several other actions:

   ▲ Press **Ctrl+P** to create a printout of the class list.

   ▲ Highlight a class name and press **Ctrl+E** to edit the class. You can change the class name and/or description. If you make changes in the class name, they are automatically made in all transactions that have been assigned to the class.

   ▲ Highlight a class name and press **Ctrl+D** to delete a class. It will also be deleted from all transactions.

Assigning Transactions to Classes

A transaction is assigned to a class in the same way it is assigned to a category. While you can assign a transaction to a class without also assigning it to a category, most often, you will use both.

Here's how to assign transactions to classes:

1. From either the Write Checks screen or the register, enter the transaction in the usual fashion.
2. In the CATEGORY field, enter the category (and subcategory, if you are using one) for the transaction.
3. Type / (forward slash). Do not press Enter.
4. Enter the class name. As with category names, there are several methods for entering the class name in the field:

   ▲ Type the full class name.

   ▲ Press **Ctrl+L** to display the class list, then highlight the desired class name and press **Enter**.

   ▲ Type the first few letters of the class name and press **Enter**. Quicken searches the class list and, if a single match is found, enters the full class name in the field. If no match, or more than one match, is found, you have the option of adding the new name to the class list or selecting an existing name from the class list.

5. Once the full class name is entered in the CATEGORY field, press **Enter** to continue with data entry.

CHECK YOURSELF

How do you assign a transaction to a class?

ANSWER

1. Enter the transaction in the usual fashion, up to the Category.
2. In the CATEGORY field enter the category for the transaction.
3. Immediately following the category name enter / followed by the class name.
4. Press **Enter**.

TIP

Classes are used to specify the "who," the "where," or the "when" of a transaction. Categories, however, are different; they specify the "what" of a transaction.

Memorizing and Recalling Transactions

One of Quicken's time-saving features is the ability to memorize transactions. This feature can be used with any transaction that occurs regularly—depositing your paycheck, the mortgage payment, or paying the utility bill. Once memorized, a transaction can be recalled with just a few keystrokes, saving you time and reducing the opportunity for errors.

Memorizing Transactions

Memorizing and Recalling Transactions

When you ask Quicken to memorize a transaction, you can fill in the entire transaction (payee, amount, address, category, and so on) or just a part of it (for instance, payee and category, or memo and address). Memorizing the entire transaction is useful for those transactions that occur regularly for the same amount—your monthly mortgage payment, for example. Memorizing only part of the transaction is useful for transactions that occur regularly but are for a different amount each time, such as the monthly utility bill.

To memorize a transaction:

1. You can memorize a transaction from either the register or from the Write Checks screen. Display one of these screens.
2. Enter the information you want memorized, and leave blank any fields you don't want memorized (those you will not be using at all, or those that change). For example, for the utility bill you would fill out all fields except Amount.
3. Press **Ctrl+M**, or select Shortcuts from the menu then select Memorize Transaction from the pull-down menu.
4. Quicken highlights the information that is about to be memorized. Press **Enter** to memorize, **Esc** to cancel.
5. The transaction is memorized and you are returned to either the Write Checks screen or the register (wherever you started from).
6. You now have the option of completing the transaction and adding it to the register (if you're working in the register) or to the list of checks to print (if you're working in the Write Checks screen). Simply complete typing in the transaction information in the usual fashion, then press **Ctrl+Enter**.
7. You also can clear the transaction without adding it to the register or the checks to print list. To do so, press **Ctrl+D** then verify that you want the transaction deleted. This clears the information from the screen but does not affect the memorized transaction.

TIP

To memorize a transaction that you already entered, highlight the transaction in the register, then press *Ctrl+M.* All information except the date and check number is memorized.

CHECK YOURSELF

How do you memorize a transaction?

ANSWER

1. In the register or the Write Checks screen, enter the transaction details you want memorized.
2. Press **Ctrl+M**.
3. Press **Enter**.

Recalling a Memorized Transaction

You can recall any memorized transaction while working in the Write Checks screen or in the register.

To recall a memorized transaction:

1. From the Main Menu, select Use Register to display the register, or select Write/Print Checks to display the Write Checks screen.
2. Press **Ctrl+T**, or select Shortcuts from the menu then select Recall Transaction from the pull-down menu.
3. Quicken displays a list of all memorized transactions (Figure 5.9).
4. The transactions are listed alphabetically. Press the **Up** arrow and **Down** arrow to highlight the desired transaction, then press **Enter**.
5. The memorized information is entered in the fields in the register (if you're working in the register) or in the blank check (if you're working in the Write Checks screen).

Memorizing and Recalling Transactions

▼ ***Figure 5.9. The Memorized Transactions List Window***

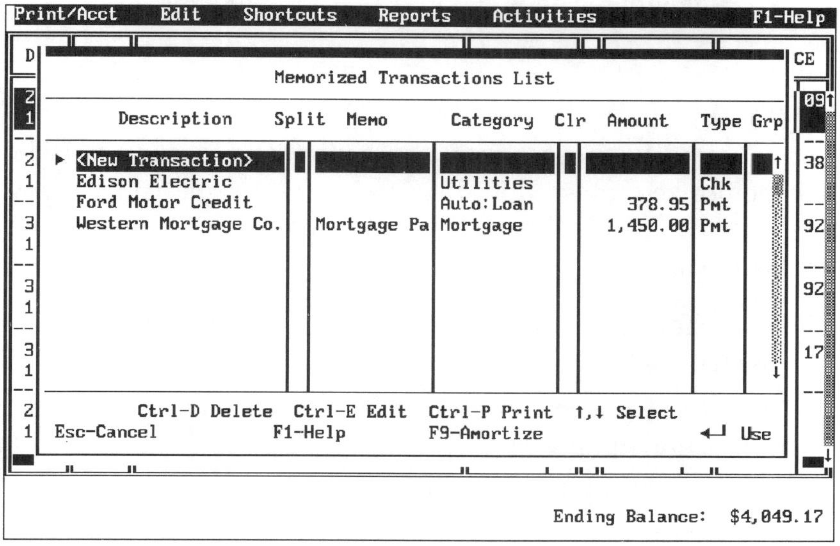

6. Make any necessary changes or additions to the information, then record the transaction by pressing **Ctrl+Enter**.

TIP

To save time, type the first few letters of the payee name in the PAYEE field, then press *Ctrl+E*. Quicken fills in the information for the matching memorized transaction. If there's more than one memorized transaction that matches, Quicken displays the Memorized Transactions List window from which you can select.

CHECK YOURSELF

How do you recall a memorized transaction?

ANSWER

1. Move the cursor to a blank transaction in the register or the Write Checks screen.

2. Press **Ctrl+T**. A list of memorized transactions is displayed.
3. Highlight the desired transaction and press **Enter**.

Changing Memorized Transactions

You can modify a memorized transaction, and you can also delete memorized transactions that you are no longer using.

To change a memorized transaction:

1. From the register or the Write Checks screen, press **Ctrl+T** to display the Memorized Transactions List window.
2. Press the **Up** arrow and **Down** arrow keys to highlight the transaction of interest.
3. Press **Ctrl+D** to delete the transaction.
4. Press **Ctrl+E** to edit the transaction. An editing window opens. In this window you can add new information, and modify or delete existing information from the transaction. With the cursor on the last field, press **Enter** to terminate editing.

QUICK COMMAND SUMMARY

To reconcile your account with your bank statement:

1. Have your latest bank account statement available.
2. From the register or the Write Checks screen, select Activities then select Reconcile Account.
3. Verify that the opening balance calculated by Quicken matches the amount on your statement. If not, type the correct amount (from the statement) into the field.
4. Enter the ending balance, service charge, and interest information from your statement into the corresponding fields.
5. Quicken displays a list of all uncleared transactions. Mark as cleared all transactions that appear on your bank statement.

6. When all transactions on your statement have been marked as cleared in Quicken, the Difference field in the RECONCILIATION SUMMARY should read 0. If not, check your work for mistakes.
7. Press **Ctrl+F10** when reconciliation is complete. If you adjusted the opening balance, account for it now.

To create a new Quicken class:

1. From the register or the Write Checks screen, press **Ctrl+L**.
2. Select <New Class>. Enter the name and description of the class, then press **Enter**.

To assign a transaction to a class:

1. Enter the transaction in the normal fashion, up to and including the category (but don't press Enter yet).
2. With the cursor at the end of the CATEGORY field, type /. Then type the class name, or press **Ctrl+L** and select from the class list.
3. Press **Enter**.

To memorize a transaction:

1. In the register or the Write Checks screen, enter the transaction information you want memorized.
2. Press **Ctrl+M**. Quicken highlights the information to be memorized.
3. Press **Enter**. The transaction is memorized.
4. Complete the transaction, or press **Ctrl+D** to delete it.

To recall a memorized transaction:

1. From the register or the Write Checks screen, press **Ctrl+T**.
2. A list of memorized transactions is displayed. Highlight the desired transaction and press **Enter**.

PRACTICE WHAT YOU'VE LEARNED

Reconciliation is an important aspect of using Quicken bank accounts. To ensure that Quicken is reporting accurate account balances, you must reconcile regularly. It's impossible to "practice" reconciliation because you need a real account and a real account statement. I suggest, however, that after you start a Quicken account for your checking account, you perform the reconciliation steps as soon as you get your next statement, and then regularly thereafter.

Other topics that you learned in this chapter can be practiced, using your "dummy" account if desired:

- ▲ Set up two classes to permit your transactions to be classified as "business" or "personal."
- ▲ Create memorized transactions for some of your recurring payments or deposits. For example, your rent or mortgage payment and your paycheck are good candidates.
- ▲ Practice recalling your memorized transactions. How much time did you save?

6

Using Quicken for a Home Budget

This chapter shows you how to use Quicken to set up and use a budget. With a budget you plan your expenses, category by category, to match your available income. A budget can help you avoid over-spending, and can make it easier to meet certain financial goals. In this chapter you'll learn

- **What a budget is**
- **How to set up budget amounts and categories**
- **How to have Quicken set up a budget based on your past income and expenses**
- **How to print your budget or save it to disk for transfer to other programs**

What Is a Budget?

The term *budget* means different things to different people. To some, "being on a budget" simply means being careful about expenditures—passing up that new pair of shoes until you really need them. In the world of finance, however, the term has a more specific meaning. A budget is when you divide your expenses into categories and assign a spending limit to each category.

For example, imagine that your monthly take-home pay is $2,500. You could set up a budget as follows:

Expense	Limit
Mortgage	1,250
Loan payments	350
Groceries	400
Clothing	100
Entertainment	150
Savings	150
Miscellaneous	100
Total	2,500

Looking at this budget, you can see that $150 per month is budgeted for entertainment. This means that you are limited to $150 per month for going to movies, eating out, and so on. If you spend the entire $150 by the second week, it's eating at home and watching TV for the rest of the month! On the other hand, if you have spent only $75 by the 29th of the month, you know it's okay to splurge $75 at that fancy French restaurant.

Planning for Your Budget

Many people cringe at the thought of using a budget. And it's certainly true that using a budget is not necessary or even desirable for everyone. But for many, a budget can be an invaluable

Planning for Your Budget

financial tool. By matching expenses to income, a budget can tell you exactly what you can spend—and more importantly, cannot spend—in a given period. To be really useful, however, a budget has to be carefully planned to suit your own individual or family needs.

The first and most important step in planning a budget is to know what your financial goals are. The most common reason that people use a budget is to limit spending in certain areas so they will have more money left for other areas. A common financial goal is to increase savings, perhaps for a house down payment or the children's college education (or both). Another goal might be to decrease or eliminate charge card purchases. In any case, for a budget to be useful it must be tailored to your goals.

Establishing Budget Categories

As you probably could guess, a Quicken budget makes use of categories. In it, you specify how much you can spend in each category. You then enter checks and other expenses into Quicken, assigning them to the proper categories. At any time, you can ask Quicken to produce a budget report. This report lists totals for each category and lists the differences between the budgeted amount and actual expenditures. You can quickly see how you're doing and how much money, if any, is left to spend in each category.

TIP

Always include a "miscellaneous" category in your budget for those transactions that don't belong in any other category.

While one of the most important uses of a budget is to keep track of expenditures, it can also be used to monitor income. This is not a particularly useful feature for people who have a fixed income, but some individuals, such as sales people who work on commission, have a variable income. In this situation, it can be useful to "budget" a certain amount of commission income each month, then enter the actual amount when you deposit your monthly commission check. Your Quicken budget can then tell you how much your actual commission income differs from the budgeted income, and you can adjust expenditures accordingly.

When planning your budget, you need to decide exactly what needs to be included in it. You may decide to include everything in your budget, so that every dollar that passes through your hands is accounted for. You may decide that only certain areas need budgeting, such as expenses for clothing or entertainment. Again, remember that the budget must fit *you*. Also, remember that you can always change the budget later if you find that the initial setup isn't ideal.

Before you can set up your budget, you must establish the categories that it will use. A budget can also make use of subcategories and classes. Quicken's default category list will contain many, if not all, of the categories that most people will need. If you've been using Quicken for your checking account for a while, you probably have already set up any specialized categories that you'll need. If not, start Quicken now and, using the techniques you've learned in earlier chapters, set up any additional categories and subcategories that you may need.

A Quicken budget can operate on a monthly, quarterly, or yearly basis. It can also be set up to deal with items that occur biweekly. A monthly budget is usually most appropriate and will be used in this chapter's examples.

Setting Budget Amounts

Perhaps the most difficult part of setting up a budget is deciding on the amounts for each category. It's essential that you arrive at realistic figures and that total expenses do not exceed total income. Determining budget amounts usually requires that you spend some time with your financial records, a pencil, paper, and a calculator. If you've been using Quicken to keep track of expenses for a while, you can also use the program to help determine budget amounts. Both of these methods are explained below.

Setting Budget Amounts

Determining Budget Amounts Manually

The first step in setting your budget amounts is determining your income. For those of you with regular paychecks this is a simple matter. If you have an irregular income, such as commissions, you should determine the average income per month.

The next step is getting some idea of how much you've been spending, and on what. Expenses fall into two general categories:

- *Non-discretionary* expenses are those that you have little choice about and whose amounts are fixed, such as your mortgage or rent payment and loan payments.
- *Discretionary* expenses are all others. Note that some expense categories are more "discretionary" than others. You certainly have to spend some money on groceries, for example, but the amount you spend is under your control to some extent. Money spent on, say, concert tickets is another matter and could be cut out altogether if necessary.

First, list all your monthly non-discretionary expenses and add them up. Subtract this total from your total monthly income. The difference is the amount you have available for discretionary expenses.

Next, list estimated amounts for your discretionary expenses. If you have records of expenditures for the past few months, you can use them to get an idea of what you have been spending in each category. Add all of these amounts, and compare the sum to the amount available for discretionary expenses. If the total is greater than the amount available, you'll have to make changes, decreasing the amount in some categories and possibly deleting some categories altogether. Continue modifying and totaling the discretionary budget amounts until the total is equal to the amount available for discretionary expenses.

Look over the amounts you have budgeted for each category. Are they realistic? Just because your total budgeted expenses do not exceed your income does not mean it's a good budget. If you budgeted $20 a month for groceries and $750 for clothing, you're just fooling yourself!

You now have a preliminary budget. The next step is to enter the budget information into Quicken, then try it out for a few months. You'll probably have to make adjustments later, but that's no problem.

Entering Your Budget into Quicken

To enter your budget amounts into Quicken, first display the register. Next, select Activities from the menu and Set Up Budgets from the pull-down menu. The Budget screen is displayed (Figure 6.1).

When you first display this screen, all of the amounts are 0 because you haven't established a budget yet. Take a look at the screen and note its parts:

▲ Each column holds data for a single month. Only four months are visible on the screen at one time; the other months are

▼ *Figure 6.1. The Budget Screen*

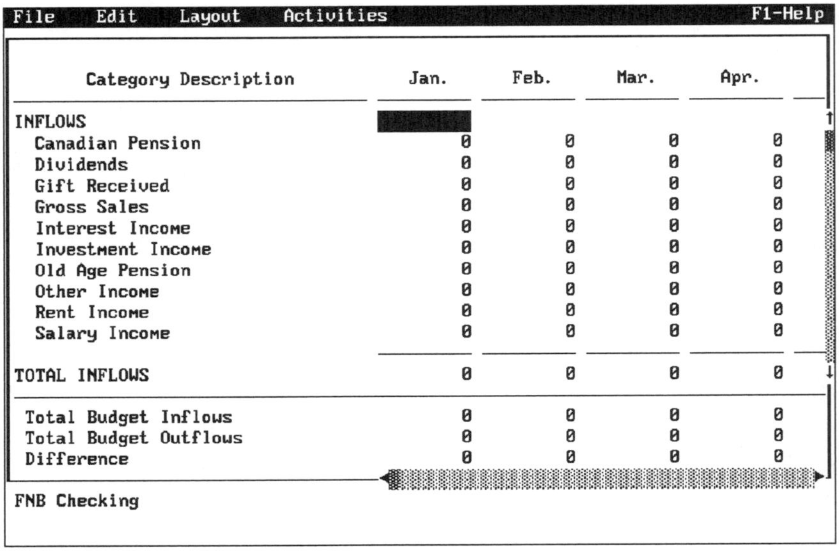

out of view but can be displayed by scrolling with the keyboard or the mouse.

- ▲ The column to the far right on this screen holds yearly totals for each row. The column is not visible in Figure 6.1; it's to the right of the December column.
- ▲ In the upper section of the screen, each row holds data for a single category. Category names are listed along the left edge of the screen. There are too many categories to display at once. In Figure 6.1, the Inflow categories are visible. Other categories are located below, and can be displayed by scrolling.
- ▲ The bottom three lines of the screen hold totals for each month: Total Budget Inflows, Total Budget Outflows, and Difference. Once you start entering information into your budget, these rows will display the monthly totals.

Setting Budget Amounts

Here's an overview of how the Budget screen is used. In the field at the intersection of each month column and each category row, you enter your budget amount for that category for that month. Both income (inflows) and expenses (outflows) must be budgeted. As you enter amounts, the total fields at the bottom of the screen will instantly calculate total inflows, total outflows, and the difference between them. A difference of less than 0 means your budgeted outflows exceed your budgeted inflows. As discussed earlier in this chapter, a balanced budget is one where budgeted outflows equal budgeted inflows, and the difference is 0.

There are two general approaches to setting up a budget:

- ▲ Budget the same amount in each category for every month of the year. This method is most appropriate for individuals whose income and expenses are fairly regular from month to month.
- ▲ Budget different amounts for each month in some or all categories. This method is appropriate for individuals whose income and/or expenses vary significantly from month to month.

The first method, budgeting equal amounts each month, is appropriate for most people. This method is perfectly capable of handling special situations, as will be explained later.

Navigating the Budget Screen

To efficiently use the Budget screen, you need to be able to move around in it. Like many Quicken screens, this screen contains fields that hold information. The actions of some keys depend on the type of field the cursor is in at that moment. There are two types of fields on the Budget screen:

- An *editable* field is one where you can enter and modify information. There is an editable field at the intersection of each month row and category column.
- A *calculated* field is one where Quicken displays the result of a calculation. You can move the cursor to some calculated fields, but you cannot enter or change data there. The Total and Difference fields at the bottom of the screen are calculated fields.

The following keys can be used to move around the Budget screen:

Press	To Move:
Left arrow	Left one character in an editable field; Left one column in a calculated field.
Right arrow	Right one character in an editable field; Right one column in a calculated field.
Ctrl+Left arrow	Left one column.
Ctrl+Right arrow	Right one column.
Tab	To next month in the same row.
Shift+Tab	To previous month in the same row.
Up arrow	Up one row in the same column.
Down arrow	Down one row in the same column.
Page Up	Up one page in the same column.
Page Dn	Down one page in the same column.

Setting Budget Amounts

Press	To Move:
Home	To the first character in an editable field; To the first field in a row of calculated fields.
End	To the last character in an editable field; To the last field in a row of calculated fields.
Home-Home	To the first field in a row of editable fields; from a calculated field, to the upper-left corner of the screen.
End-End	To the last column in a row of editable fields; from a calculated field, to the lower-right corner of the screen.
Home-Home-Home	From an editable field to the upper-left corner of the screen.
End-End-End	From an editable field to the lower-right corner of the screen.

The mouse can be quite useful when working in the Budget screen:

- ▲ Click in any visible field to move to it.
- ▲ Click on the arrows on the horizontal scroll bar to move left or right one column.
- ▲ Click on the arrows on the vertical scroll bar to move up or down one column.
- ▲ Click above or below the scroll box on the vertical scroll bar to move up or down one page.

In an editable field, the Quicken editing keys work in the usual fashion.

Budgeting for Different Periods

By default, the Budget screen is set up for a monthly budget, which is appropriate for most people. Quarterly and yearly budgets are also possible; these time periods are more appropriate for certain business uses.

To change the budget period:

1. From the Budget screen, select Layout.
2. From the pull-down menu, select Month, Quarter, or Year.
3. The Budget screen changes to reflect the newly selected budget period.

Entering Budget Data

Entering your budget data is a simple matter of transferring amounts from your paper-and-pencil calculations to the Quicken budget screen. You can also use the screen to help develop your budgets.

Here are the steps to enter budget data:

1. Display the Budget screen. If you are creating a budget for the entire year, move the cursor to the January column. If you are creating a budget for only part of the year, move the cursor to the column for the first budget month.
2. Press the **Up** arrow and **Down** arrow keys to move between categories. Enter your monthly budget amount for each inflow and outflow category. You will, of course, enter amounts only for those categories that your budget uses. Many categories will be left with an entry of 0.
3. Once all of your budget amounts have been entered, check the totals at the bottom of the column. The totals for inflow and outflow should be the same. If they are not, go back and check the amounts entered for each category, making adjustments until the budget balances.
4. If you are budgeting different amounts in some categories for each month, move the cursor to the columns for other months and return to Step 2 to enter category amounts for each month in the budget.
5. If some or all of your categories will have the same amount budgeted from month to month, you can use the following special keys and commands to copy budget amounts between months:

Setting Budget Amounts

- With the cursor in an editable field, press ' to copy the amount from the field immediately to the left into the current field.
- From the Edit menu, select Fill Right to copy the amount from the current field to all months to the right in the current row.
- From the Edit menu, select Fill Columns to copy the amounts from all rows in the current month to the corresponding rows in all months to the right.

6. Check the inflow and outflow totals for each month, verifying that they're the same. Make any necessary adjustments to bring the budget into balance.

Budgeting Biweekly Items

Even if you're using a monthly budget, there may be individual items that you need to budget on a biweekly basis. For example, if you receive your paycheck every two weeks, you will get 26 paychecks per year. In most months you'll receive 2 checks, but there will be two months each year when you receive three checks. For Quicken to accurately budget, you must inform it of any biweekly items that need to be included.

To inform Quicken of biweekly items:

1. On the Budget screen, move the cursor to the row of the category to be budgeted biweekly.
2. Select Edit from the menu, then select Two Week from the pull-down menu.
3. The Set Up 2 Week Budget window is displayed (Figure 6.2).
4. In the "Enter the amount:" field, enter the amount of the biweekly budget item.
5. In the "Every 2 weeks starting:" field, enter the first date that the biweekly item will occur on (for instance, your next payday).
6. Press **Enter**. Quicken determines when the biweekly event will occur in the future and enters the appropriate totals in the category for each budget month to the right of the cursor.

▼ *Figure 6.2. The Set Up 2 Week Budget Window*

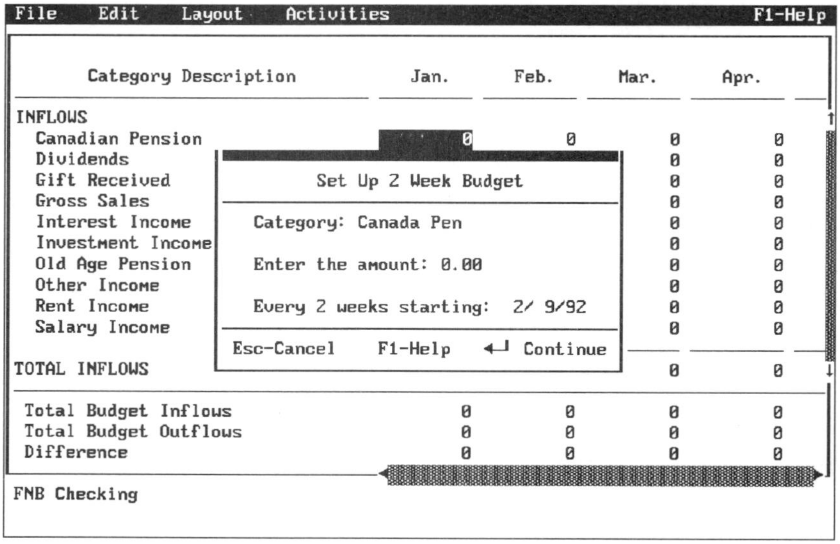

CHECK YOURSELF

Now that you have read about the most important steps in setting up a budget, you should try to set up a budget for yourself. If you feel a bit unsure about the process, you should set up a budget for the Smiths.

ANSWER

1. From the Register screen, select Activities, then select Set Up Budgets.
2. If necessary, press the **Left** and **Right** arrow keys to move the cursor to the column for the first budget month.
3. Press the **Up** and **Down** arrow keys to move between budget categories.
4. Enter the monthly budget amount for each inflow and outflow category that your (or the Smiths') budget will use.
5. Check the totals at the bottom of the column. The totals for inflow and outflow should be the same. If they are not, go back and check your entries.

Setting Budget Amounts

6. If you are budgeting different amounts in some categories for each month, move the cursor to the columns for other months and return to Step 3 to enter category amounts for each month in the budget.
7. Press **Esc** to save the budget.

Determining Budget Amounts with Quicken's Help

If you have already been using Quicken to keep track of your finances for a while, you can use it to help establish your budget amounts. Quicken does this by determining your actual expense and income amounts per category for past months, up to a maximum of 12, then transfers these amounts to the corresponding categories in the budget. You can use these amounts for your budget or, more likely, as a basis for establishing actual budget amounts.

When Quicken calculates budget amounts for you, it uses data from all accounts in the current file. Presently, you may only be using Quicken for a single account, your checking account. For Quicken to obtain reasonably accurate figures for your income and expenses, you must be using Quicken for all your accounts—credit cards, cash, checking, and so on. If you are not using Quicken for all your financial transactions, you may not want to have Quicken calculate budget amounts for you. Rather, you should do these calculations by hand. Or, you can wait until you have read more of this book and have started using Quicken for all your accounts, then return to this section to complete your budget.

To have Quicken set up budget amounts for you:

1. From the Register screen, select Activities from the menu then select Set Up Budgets from the pull-down menu. The Budget screen is displayed (Figure 6.1).
2. Select Edit from the menu, then select Autocreate from the pull-down menu. The Automatically Create Budget window is displayed (Figure 6.3).

▼ *Figure 6.3. The Automatically Create Budget Window*

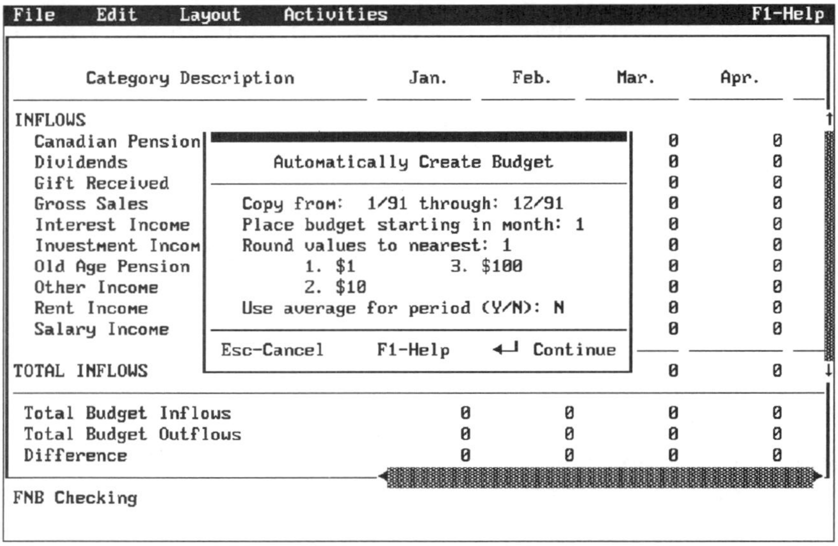

3. The first line in the window lists the date range that Quicken will use to set up budget amounts. Change these dates if desired. Enter only a month and a year for each date, as Quicken works on a month-by-month basis.
4. In the "Place budget starting in month:" field, enter the number (1 through 12) of the first budget month in which you want values placed. For example, if the date range you entered is 1/91 through 6/91, and you want these values placed in the budget months July through December, enter **7**.
5. The "Round values to nearest:" field lets you specify how Quicken is to round off the budget amounts. The default is rounding to the nearest dollar. You can round to the nearest $10 or $100 if you prefer.
6. In the "Use average for period:" field, enter **Y** if you want Quicken to calculate monthly income and expense averages for the period that you specified in Step 3, then enter these averages in the budget month you specified in Step 4. If you enter **N**, Quicken will calculate actual income and expense amounts for each of the months in the date range from Step

3 and enter the actual amount for each month in individual budget months starting with the month specified in Step 4.

7. Press **Enter** and Quicken will begin its calculations, then enter the amounts in the corresponding budget categories. You can now use the keys that you learned earlier in the chapter to view different parts of the Budget screen and make any necessary modifications to the budget.

Setting Budget Amounts

CHECK YOURSELF

Create a budget, but this time have Quicken calculate budget amounts for you. Note that this method will work only if you have been using Quicken for a while to keep track of your finances.

ANSWER

1. From the Register screen, select Activities, then select Set Up Budgets.
2. Select Edit, then select Autocreate.
3. Enter the date range that Quicken should use to set up budget amounts.
4. In the "Place budget starting in month:" field, enter the number (1 through 12) of the first budget month in which you want values placed.
5. Specify how Quicken is to round off the budget amounts.
6. In the "Use average for period :" field, enter **Y** to calculate monthly income and expense averages, or enter **N** to calculate actual monthly income and expense amounts.
7. Press **Enter**. Quicken will perform its calculations, then enter the amounts in the corresponding budget categories.
8. Check the Budget screen and make any necessary modifications.
9. Press **Esc**.

Using Your Budget

At this point, you have set up a budget and are ready to start using it. How do you actually "use" your budget? Remember, a budget is nothing more than a plan, or a goal, that tells you how much money you can spend each month on various types of expenses. To use your budget, you must be able to determine how you are doing—in other words, to compare your actual income and expense amounts with the budgeted income and expense amounts. You do this with a budget report, which you'll learn about in the next chapter.

Printing Your Budget

You can print a copy of your budget, which can be useful when you have to modify it. You can also save the budget in a disk file, then transfer it to a spreadsheet or word-processing program.

To print your budget:

1. From the Budget screen, press **Ctrl+P**. You can also select File from the menu then select Print Budgets from the pull-down menu. The Print Budget window is displayed (Figure 6.4).
2. In the "Print to" field enter **1**, **2**, or **3** to specify the printer to use. (You'll usually use the report printer to print budgets) Or, enter **4** to save the budget in an ASCII file (appropriate for reading into word-processing programs) or **5** to save the budget in a Lotus 1-2-3 worksheet file (appropriate for reading into Lotus and most other spreadsheet programs).
3. Press **Enter** to begin printing. If you specified 4 or 5 in the "Print to" field you will be prompted for the name of the file to save the budget in. Enter a file name, including disk and/or path information if desired, then press **Enter**.

Printing Your Budget

▼ ***Figure 6.4. The Print Budget Window***

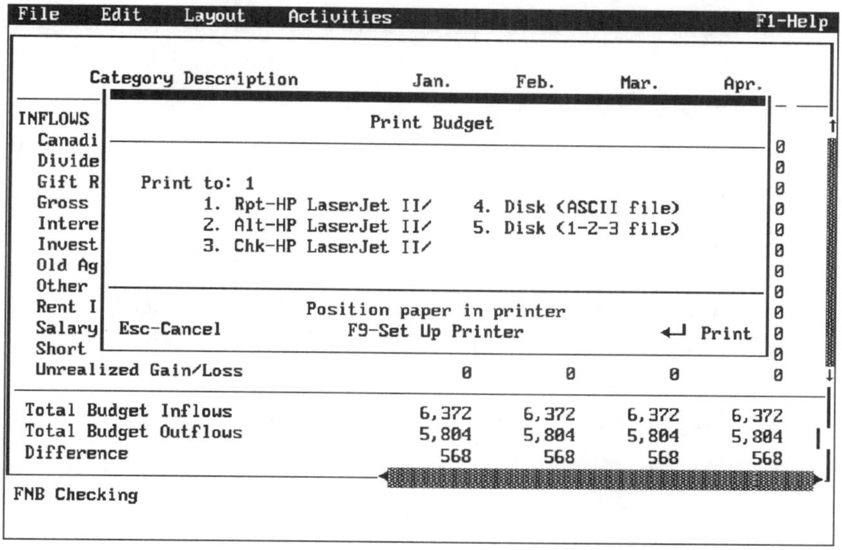

Exiting the Budget Screen

When you're finished working on the budget, you can press **Esc** or **Ctrl+R** to close the Budget screen and return to the register. You can also press **Ctrl+W** to go directly to the Write Checks screen. The budget is saved automatically as part of your Quicken data file.

QUICK COMMAND SUMMARY

To set up a budget manually:

1. Using paper and pencil and your recent financial records, determine the budget categories you'll need and a reasonable monthly amount for each category. Be sure total monthly expenses are equal to total monthly income.
2. Start Quicken. From the register select Activities, then select Set Up Budgets.

3. On the Budget screen, enter monthly amounts in each category you are using. Use the same budget amounts for each month, or enter different amounts for some months. Use Quicken's special commands to copy amounts from column to column.
4. Look at the Totals fields at the bottom of the Budget screen to verify that budgeted inflows equal budgeted outflows for each month.
5. When the budget is complete, press **Esc** to return to the register. The budget is saved automatically. You can always repeat the above steps to make modifications.

To have Quicken calculate budget amounts:

1. From the Register screen, select Activities. Then, select Set Up Budgets to display the Budget screen.
2. Select Edit, then select Autocreate.
3. In the window that is displayed, specify the period from which Quicken is to take its data, and specify other options for the budget creation process.
4. Press **Enter** and Quicken scans your transactions for the specified period, entering amounts for each category into the budget.
5. If necessary, modify the budget amounts Quicken has entered to create the final budget.

PRACTICE WHAT YOU'VE LEARNED

Try to set up a budget for yourself. Even if you're not ready for a "real" budget, you can set up a practice budget to become familiar with how the process works. If you have entered sufficient financial data into Quicken, you can have Quicken calculate budget amounts for you.

7

Savings Accounts, Transfers, and Tax-related Categories

This chapter covers some of the other activities that you will do with Quicken accounts. The emphasis is on Quicken bank accounts, but some of these activities are also applicable to other account types, such as credit card and investment accounts. You'll learn about these other account types in later chapters. In this chapter you'll learn how to

- **Use Quicken for a savings account**
- **Transfer money between accounts**
- **Locate and modify transfer transactions**
- **Use tax-related categories**

Using Quicken for a Savings Account

After a checking account, the most common type of account that people have is a savings account. A savings account is not much different from a checking account except that you cannot use it to write checks. With a savings account, you make deposits and withdrawals, earn interest, and in some cases, pay bank fees.

To use Quicken for a savings account, you follow the same procedures that you have learned for setting up and using a checking account. Reconciliation follows the same procedures as well, although reconciling a savings account is usually quicker than reconciling a checking account because there are fewer transactions.

TIP

A savings account is set up and used in the same way as a checking account, except that you don't write checks from it.

CHECK YOURSELF

Set up a savings account for the Smiths. This will check your knowledge of how to set up a savings account and will also provide a second account for the Smiths that you can use later in this chapter. Call the account "FNB Savings," then give it the description "Joint savings" and a balance of $1,500 as of January 1, 1992.

ANSWER

1. From the Main Menu, select Select Account.
2. Highlight <New Account> and press **Enter**.
3. Enter **1** for account type.

4. Enter **FNB Savings** for the account name.
5. Enter **1500** for the balance, and **1/1/92** for the date.
6. Press **Ctrl+Enter**.

Using Quicken for a Savings Account

Transferring Money between Accounts

When your Quicken file contains two or more accounts, it's easy to transfer money from one account to another. Quicken's transfer feature will save you time and help ensure that the transactions are recorded accurately. Examples of account transfers include:

- ▲ Transferring money from your savings account to your checking account.
- ▲ Writing a check for a payment on your credit card account.
- ▲ Obtaining a cash advance on your credit card and depositing the money in your checking account.

When you enter a transfer into Quicken, there are always two accounts involved. The "from" account is where the money is coming from, and the "to" account is where the money is going to. The amount transferred appears in the PAYMENT field in the "from" account and in the DEPOSIT field in the "to" account. You need to enter the transfer in only one of the accounts, and Quicken automatically makes the corresponding entry in the other.

Transfer transactions cannot be assigned to a category, subcategory, or class. This is because when you transfer money from one account to another, you are not spending the money nor is there any income. There is no inflow or outflow and, therefore, nothing to assign to a category or class.

Basic Transfer Steps

The steps required to make a transfer are not much different from entering a regular transaction.

To make a transfer:

1. Make the "from" account current, and display the Register screen. If the "from" account is a checking account and you want a check printed, you can use the Write Checks screen.
2. Enter the transaction information as you normally would up to, but not including, the CATEGORY field. The transfer amount is entered in the PAYMENT field.
3. In the CATEGORY field, enter the name of the account to which the money is being transferred.
4. Press **Enter**. Quicken encloses the *to* account name in the CATEGORY field with square brackets (Figure 7.1). These brackets identify the transaction as a transfer rather than a regular expenditure. Quicken also enters the parallel transaction in the "to" account's register, with the "from" account name enclosed in brackets in the CATEGORY field (Figure 7.2).

▼ Figure 7.1. Transfer Transaction Entered into Savings Account Register

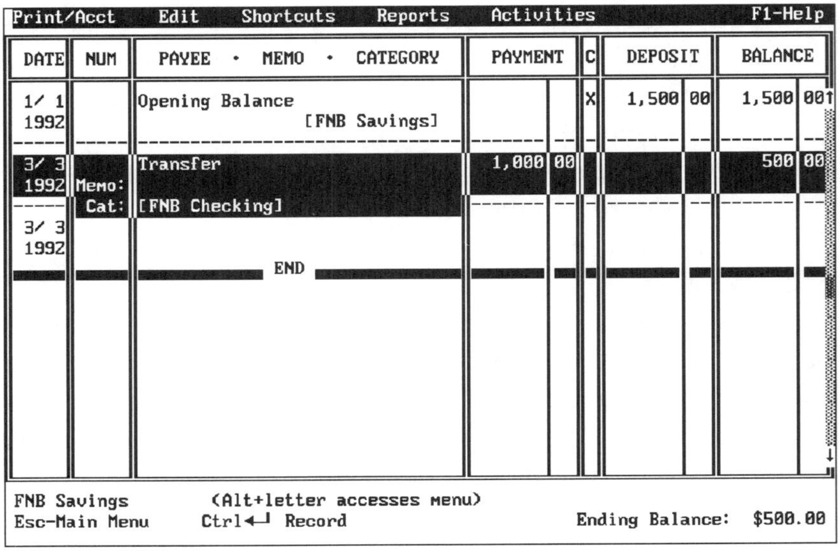

▼ ***Figure 7.2. Corresponding Transaction Made in Checking Account Register***

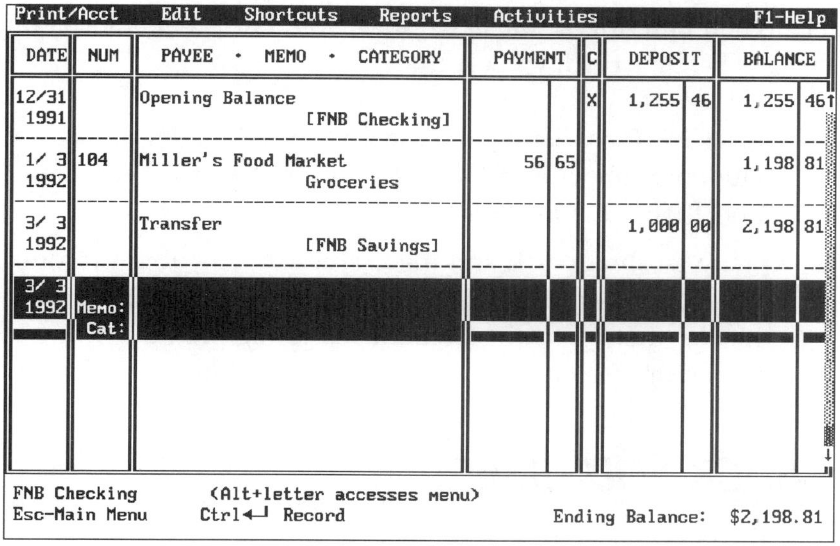

Transferring Money between Accounts

Figure 7.1 shows a transaction entered in the Smiths' savings account register for a transfer of $1000 to their checking account. Note that the CATEGORY field reads [FNB Checking], which is the name of the *to* account. Figure 7.2 shows the corresponding transaction that Quicken automatically made in the Smiths' checking account register.

When you are entering a transfer, you can also make your entry in the "to" account's register by entering the amount in the DEPOSIT field and the name of the "from" account in the CATEGORY field. Quicken will automatically make the corresponding entry in the "from" account register, entering the transfer amount in the PAYMENT field and the "to" account name in the CATEGORY field.

Entering Account Names in Transfer Transactions

From the above description of entering transfer transactions, you can see that account names are used in the same fashion as category names. In fact, Quicken lets you use some of the same shortcuts to enter an account name that are available for category names. Account names are kept as part of the category list. When entering a transfer transaction, and the cursor is on the CATEGORY field, you can:

- ▲ Press **Ctrl+C** to display the category list. Account names are included at the end of this list. Scroll to the desired account name, then press **Enter**.
- ▲ Enter a left bracket ([) and the first few letters of the account name, then press **Ctrl+C**. Quicken displays the category list with the first matching account name highlighted. You can accept it or scroll to another account name, then press **Enter**.

CHECK YOURSELF

You should now be able to enter a transfer transaction of your own. Suppose the Smiths wrote a $500 check from their checking account, payable to CASH and deposited the money in their savings account. Enter this transfer transaction in the checking account, then switch to the checking account to verify that the corresponding transaction has been properly entered by Quicken.

ANSWER

1. From the Main Menu, select Select Account.
2. Highlight FNB Checking, then press **Enter**.
3. Enter the date, number, payee (Cash), and amount (500) of the check.
4. In the CATEGORY field, enter **FNB Savings**, then press **Enter** and record the transaction.
5. Press **Esc** to return to the Main Menu.
6. Choose Select Account.
7. Highlight FNB Savings, then press **Enter**.

8. Verify that a transaction has been entered for the $500 transfer from FNB Checking.

Transferring Money between Accounts

Splitting Transfer Transactions

There may be times when a transfer is part of a split transaction. For example, suppose you are depositing $1,500 in your checking account ($1,000 transferred from your savings account and your $500 bonus check). This is easily handled using the Split Transaction window. You simply enter the transfer account name in the Category column, as shown in Figure 7.3.

Modifying Transfer Transactions

Remember, transfer transactions exist in pairs—one in the *to* account and one in the *from* account. Quicken maintains a link between the transactions that are part of a transfer so that changes are accurately reflected in both.

▼ ***Figure 7.3. The Split Transaction Window***

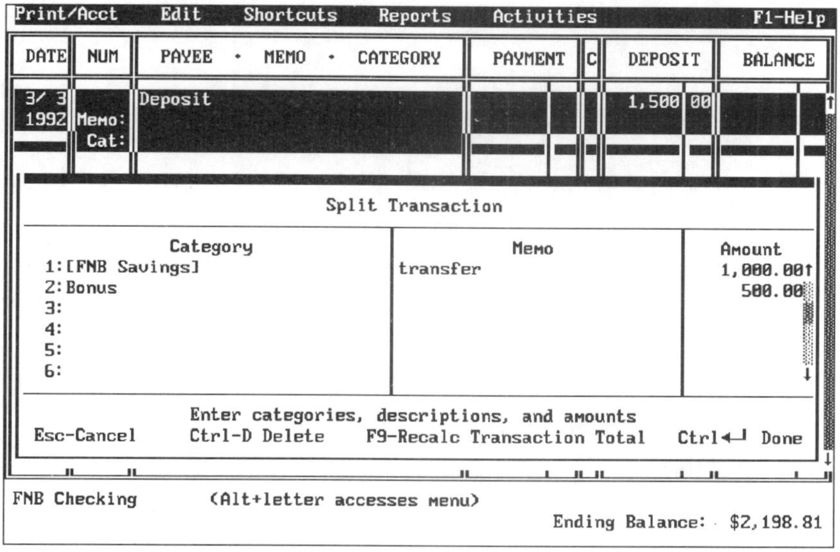

Remember:

- ▲ If you change the date or amount of a transfer transaction, it is changed in both accounts.
- ▲ If you delete a transfer transaction, it is deleted in both accounts.
- ▲ If you change the name of an account, it is automatically changed in all transfer transactions involving the account.

One exception is when a transfer is part of a split transaction in the "from" account. In this case, if you modify the transaction in the "to" account, it will not automatically be changed in the "from" account. You must display the original transaction and make the changes manually. See the next section for a quick way to locate the second in a pair of transfer transactions.

Finding the Parallel Transfer Transaction

Quicken makes it easy to find the second in a pair of transfer transactions. This technique can be used when you want to see the second transaction created by the transfer. It is also useful when you need to make modifications to a transfer transaction that originated with a split transaction (as explained in the last section).

To display the parallel transfer transaction:

1. In the register, select the transfer transaction. This can be in either the "to" or the "from" account.
2. If the transaction is split, press **Ctrl+S** to display the Split Transaction window, then move the cursor to the item to be transferred.
3. Select Edit, then select Go to Transfer, or press **Ctrl+X**. Quicken opens the register for the transfer account and highlights the corresponding transaction.
4. To return to the original account and transaction, repeat Step 3.

Using Tax-related Categories

Using Tax-related Categories

One of the most painful tasks many people face is tax preparation. Quicken can help with taxes by keeping your finances organized. You can make things even easier by making use of Quicken's tax-related category setting.

Every category and subcategory in Quicken is either tax-related or non tax-related. This is true of both income and expense categories. You can see this by displaying the category list, as shown in Figure 7.4. (From the Register screen, press **Ctrl+C**.) The right-most column in this window, labeled Tax, contains a bullet if a category is tax-related, or is blank if the category is non tax-related.

The benefit of using tax-related categories comes when you are creating reports at tax time. You'll learn about reports in the next chapter. For now, it's enough to know that a *report* is a summary of financial information. By using the tax-related des-

▼ Figure 7.4. The Tax Column in the Category List

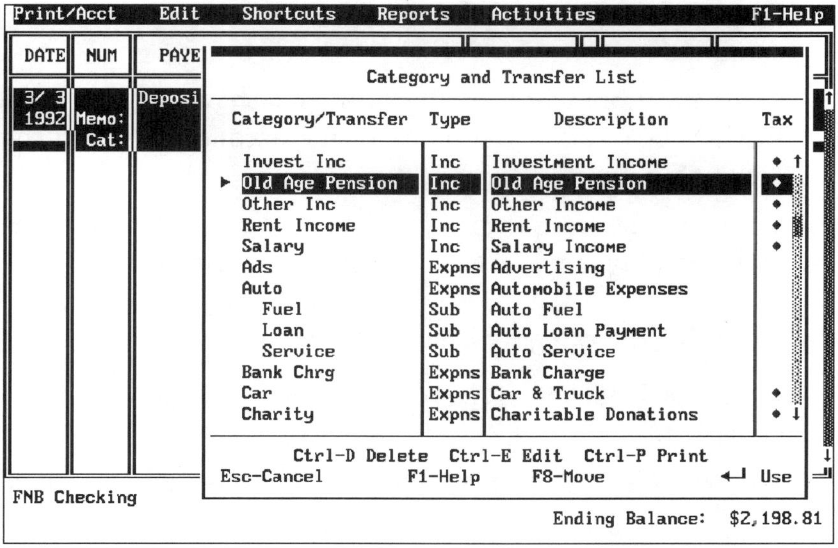

ignation for categories, you will easily be able to create reports that include only the information you need for tax preparation.

When you create your own new categories and subcategories (as you learned in Chapter 2), you can make them tax-related. In the Set Up Category window, there is a field labeled Tax Related. Enter **Y** if the category is tax-related, **N** if it is not.

To change the tax-related status of an existing category:

1. From the Register screen, press **Ctrl+C** to display the category list.
2. Use the arrow keys to highlight the desired category, then press **Ctrl+E** to edit it.
3. The Edit Category window is displayed. Press **Tab** to move the cursor to the Tax-related field, then enter **Y** or **N**.
4. Press **Ctrl+Enter** to return to the category list, then press **Esc** to return to the register.

QUICK COMMAND SUMMARY

To transfer money between Quicken accounts:

1. Display the register for the account from which the money is coming.
2. Enter the transaction in the normal fashion. In the CATEGORY field, enter the name of the account to which the money is going.
3. Complete the transaction. Quicken automatically enters the corresponding parallel transaction in the other account.

To determine if a category is tax-related:

1. From the Register screen, press **Ctrl+C** to display the category list.
2. If necessary, scroll the list until the desired category is visible.
3. Look in the Tax column. If a bullet is displayed, the category is tax-related.

Changing a category's tax-related status:

1. From the Register screen, press **Ctrl+C** to display the category list.
2. Highlight the desired category, then press **Ctrl+E**.
3. In the Edit Category window, press **Tab** to move the cursor to the Tax-related field, then enter **Y** or **N**.
4. Press **Ctrl+Enter**.

PRACTICE WHAT YOU'VE LEARNED

1. Set up a savings account for yourself.
2. Transfer money between your savings and checking accounts.
3. Set up some tax-related categories.

8

Reports

This chapter introduces you to Quicken reports. A report is a summary or compilation of the information in your Quicken Accounts. Quicken offers a wide range of report types, allowing you to examine your financial data from many different angles and to extract exactly the information you need. Quicken's report capabilities are quite sophisticated, but once you know the basics they are relatively easy to use. In this chapter you'll learn

- **What a report is**
- **Report basics**
- **How to use Quicken's preset reports**
- **How to customize reports**
- **How to memorize and recall report settings**

What Is a Report?

What is a report and why might you need it? Isn't it enough to have Quicken keep track of your account balances? You can, in fact, use Quicken only to keep your balances up to date, and ignore reports altogether. However, if you do so, you'll be missing many of the benefits that Quicken can bring to your financial organization.

Quicken can create a wide variety of reports, allowing you to examine your finances from many different angles. For example, Quicken reports can:

- Tell you how much you spent on entertainment last month.
- Total all deductible expenses at tax time.
- Determine how successful you have been at sticking to your budget.
- Provide complete details of your cash flow over the last six months.

Quicken offers two general types of reports. *Preset* reports are already built into Quicken. They are predefined, and you can use them easily with a minimum of preparation. *Customized* reports are designed by you to meet specific needs not covered by the preset reports.

Quicken's preset reports are very powerful, so most users will rarely, if ever, need to create a customized report. It is a good idea to become familiar with the preset reports before attempting to create a customized report.

Categories of Reports

Quicken's preset reports fall into three categories: *personal*, *business*, and *investment*. There are seven preset personal reports that are used to summarize information about your personal finances:

What Is a Report?

- Cash flow report
- Monthly budget report
- Itemized categories report
- Tax summary report
- Net worth report
- Missing check report
- Tax schedule report

There are eight preset business reports that are useful when you are using Quicken to keep track of small business finances:

- Profit and loss statement
- Cash flow report
- Accounts payable by vendor
- Accounts receivable by customer
- Job/Project report
- Payroll report
- Balance sheet
- Missing check report

There are five investment reports that are applicable when you are using Quicken to keep track of investments:

- Portfolio value report
- Investment performance report
- Capital gains report
- Investment income report
- Investment transactions report

This chapter covers Quicken's personal reports. Investment reports are covered in a later chapter. Because this book is aimed at individuals using Quicken for personal finances, business reports are not covered.

Personal Reports

This section explains the information presented by each type of preset personal report and gives examples of when and why you might want to create each report type. First, the basic steps you must follow to create a report are explained.

Basic Report Procedure

The following steps are common to all personal reports:

1. Make sure that the file containing the account(s) you want the report based on is current.
2. From the Main Menu, select Create Reports, or from the register or the Write Checks screen, select Reports.
3. Another menu is displayed. From this menu select Personal Reports.
4. Yet another menu is displayed listing the seven types of preset personal reports. Select the desired report type.
5. Quicken displays a setup window for the report you have selected. For example, Figure 8.1 shows the setup window for the Cash Flow report. In this window, you enter details about how the report is to be created. All report types let you specify an optional report title, which will be displayed and printed at the top of the report. If you do not specify a title, Quicken uses the report name as the title. Most of the preset personal reports require that you enter dates for the period to be covered by the report. You enter a start month/year and a stop month/year, and the report will cover all transactions in that period (inclusive).
6. After you fill in the required setup information, Quicken creates the report and displays it on your screen. You can scroll around to view different parts of the report by using the **Up** arrow, **Down** arrow, **PgUp**, and **PgDn** keys. For example, Figure 8.2 shows part of a cash flow report displayed on the Reports screen.

Personal Reports

▼ *Figure 8.1. The Cash Flow Report Setup Window*

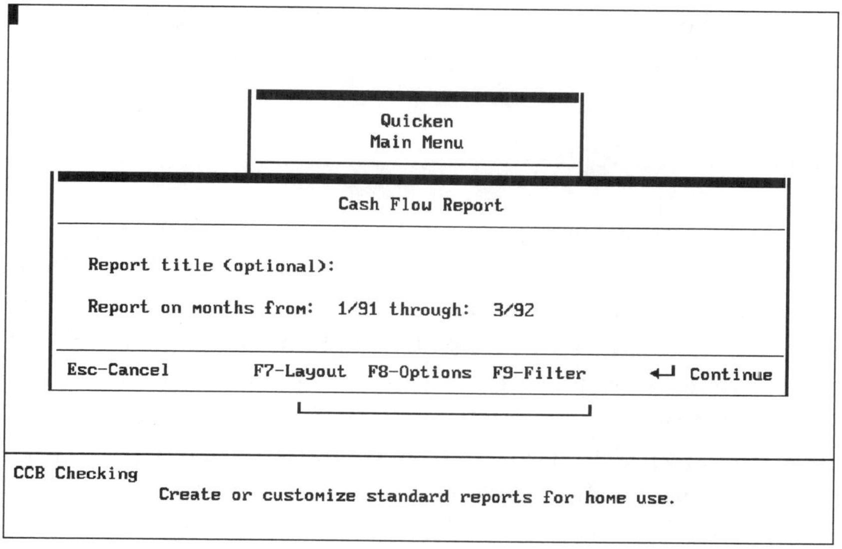

7. While the report is displayed on the screen, you can print it by pressing **Ctrl+P** or by selecting File/Print then selecting Print Report.

▼ *Figure 8.2. A Cash Flow Report*

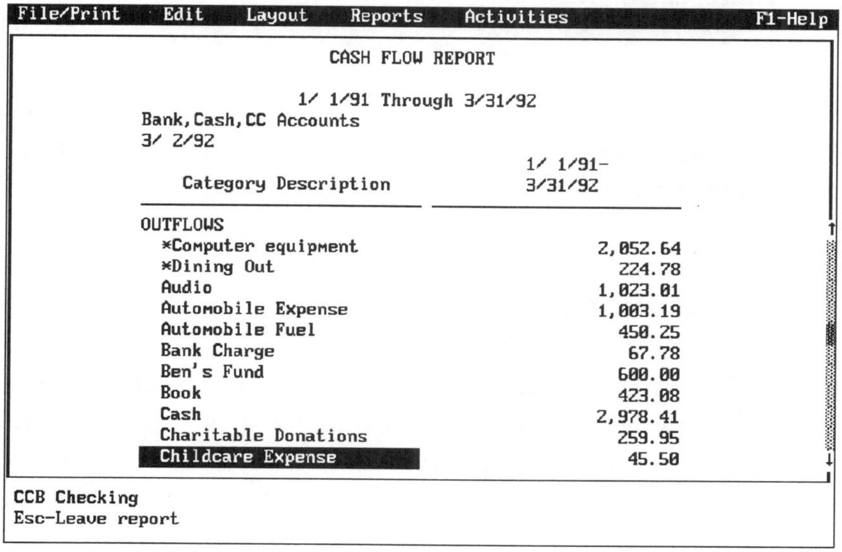

8. Press **Esc** to close the report and return to the report setup window. From this window, you can modify the setup and redisplay the report, or press **Esc** to close the setup window and return to what you were doing originally.

Cash Flow Report

The cash flow report tells you where your money is coming from and where it's going. This report summarizes transactions in your bank, cash, and credit card accounts. It does not include transactions in investment, asset, or liability accounts (although it does include transfers to and from those account types). The amounts reported are totals per category and subcategory—individual transaction information is not provided in a cash flow report. Figure 8.2 shows part of a cash flow report.

A cash flow report divides amounts between *inflows* and *outflows*. Inflows consist of all income categories (for instance, salary and interest income), as well as transfers of funds from investment, asset, or liability accounts into bank, cash, or credit card accounts. Outflows include all expense categories as well as transfers of funds from bank, cash, or credit card accounts into investment, asset, or liability accounts. Transfers between bank, cash, and credit card accounts are not included because they cancel each other out.

TIP

Use a cash flow report to see how much you have spent in each category over a certain period.

Monthly Budget Report

A monthly budget report calculates your actual income and expenses for a specified period and compares them with the budgeted amounts for the same period. You can create a budget report only if you have set up a budget, as was described in

Personal Reports

▼ Figure 8.3. A Monthly Budget Report

File/Print Edit Layout Reports Activities F1-Help

MONTHLY BUDGET REPORT

1/ 1/91 Through 12/31/91

Bank,Cash,CC Accounts
3/ 2/92

Category Description	9/ 1/91 Actual	- Budget	9/30/91 Diff	10/ 1/91 Actual	- Budget
Automobile Expense	59	80	-21	48	80
Automobile Fuel	34	40	-6	67	40
Bank Charge	0	10	-10	0	10
Ben's Fund	0	50	-50	0	50
Book	0	40	-40	29	40
Cash	338	250	88	350	250
Charitable Donations	100	20	80	0	20
Clothing	471	70	401	0	70
Duke Travel	-80	-10	-70	0	-10
Education	0	370	-370	0	370
Entertainment	39	20	19	18	20
Federal tax paid	0	610	-610	0	610

CCB Checking
Esc-Leave report

Chapter 6. A budget report includes transactions from your bank, cash, and credit card accounts, but not from investment, asset, or liability accounts.

A monthly budget report calculates and displays the actual amount in each income and expense category, and also displays the difference between actual and budgeted amounts. You can quickly see which categories are overspent, which are under spent, and which are on-budget. Figure 8.3 shows a portion of a monthly budget report.

Itemized Categories Report

The itemized categories report lists individual transactions, grouped and subtotaled by category and subcategory. This type of report includes transactions from all of your account types, and includes transfers and balances. Figure 8.4 shows part of an itemized categories report.

Be aware that the itemized category report lists *every* transaction in your accounts for the specified period. This can create

▼ *Figure 8.4. An Itemized Categories Report*

File/Print Edit Layout Reports Activities F1-Help

ITEMIZED CATEGORY REPORT

1/ 1/91 Through 12/31/91

All Accounts
3/ 2/92

Date	Acct	Num	Description	Memo	Category	Clr	Amount
	Clothing						
8/ 2	CCB Che	678	Sears		Clothing	X	-19.28
2/25	Credit	4726	L.L. Bean		Clothing	X	-111.00
3/ 9	Credit	4743	S&K		Clothing	X	-125.95
9/25	Amex Ca		Nowell's		Clothing		-47.70
9/25	Amex Ca		Jos A. Bank		Clothing		-366.92
7/ 8	CCB Mas		L.L. Bean		Clothing		-57.50
7/22	CCB Mas		L.L. Bean		Clothing		-35.00
9/ 7	Citiban		Eno Traders	Shoes	Clothing		-56.18
	Total Clothing						-819.53

CCB Checking
Esc-Leave report

a very long report. This report is generally most useful when you filter it to include only a subset of your transactions. You'll learn how to filter a report later in this chapter.

TIP

Use an itemized categories report to obtain information on individual transactions.

Tax Summary Report

The tax summary report is an itemized transactions report that has been filtered to include only transactions that have been assigned to tax-related categories (as you learned in Chapter 7).

Net Worth Report

As you might have guessed, the net worth report calculates your net worth. *Net worth* is defined as your total assets minus your

Personal Reports

total liabilities. Rather than covering a specified time period, the net worth report calculates your net worth as of a specific date. This report lists totals for all asset accounts grouped by account type (cash and bank accounts, investment accounts) and for all liability accounts (credit cards, loans). Figure 8.5 illustrates a portion of a net worth report.

The net worth report includes all of your Quicken accounts. Please note, however, that the total net worth figure in this report will be accurate only if you have created Quicken accounts for all of your assets and liabilities. Since for many people equity in their home is a major component of their net worth, it will be necessary to create an Other Asset account for your home's current value and an Other Liability account for the amount owed on your mortgage. You'll learn how to do this in Chapter 15.

TIP

Use a net worth report to determine current balances in all of your accounts.

▼ ***Figure 8.5. A Net Worth Report***

```
File/Print   Edit   Layout   Reports   Activities                F1-Help

                        NET WORTH REPORT

                          As of 3/ 2/92
          All Accounts
          3/ 2/92
                                                      3/ 2/92
                           Acct                       Balance
          ------------------------------------      ----------
          ASSETS
            Cash and Bank Accounts
              Amex Money Mkt                          4,056.83
              CCB Checking                            3,332.86
              CCB Savings                             1,134.00
              Credit Union                              560.00
              Petty Cash                                469.86
              Signature                                 688.49
                                                    ----------
            Total Cash and Bank Accounts             10,242.04

                                                    ----------
CCB Checking
Esc-Leave report
```

▼ *Figure 8.6. A Missing Check Report*

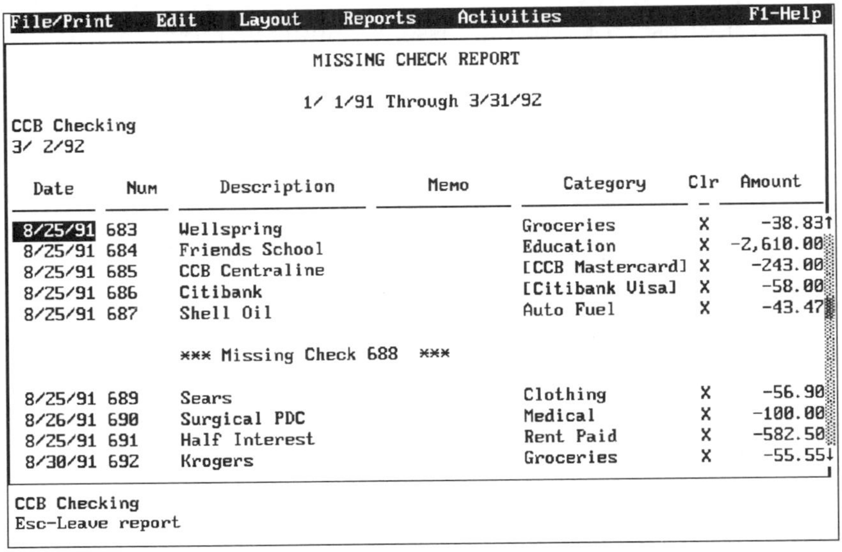
File/Print   Edit   Layout   Reports   Activities   F1-Help

MISSING CHECK REPORT

1/ 1/91 Through 3/31/92

CCB Checking
3/ 2/92

Date	Num	Description	Memo	Category	Clr	Amount
8/25/91	683	Wellspring		Groceries	X	-38.83
8/25/91	684	Friends School		Education	X	-2,610.00
8/25/91	685	CCB Centraline		[CCB Mastercard]	X	-243.00
8/25/91	686	Citibank		[Citibank Visa]	X	-58.00
8/25/91	687	Shell Oil		Auto Fuel	X	-43.47
		*** Missing Check 688 ***				
8/25/91	689	Sears		Clothing	X	-56.90
8/26/91	690	Surgical PDC		Medical	X	-100.00
8/25/91	691	Half Interest		Rent Paid	X	-582.50
8/30/91	692	Krogers		Groceries	X	-55.55

CCB Checking
Esc-Leave report

Missing Check Report

The missing check report lists all payments, sorted by check number. It includes only transactions from the current account and is relevant, of course, only to checking accounts. Use the missing check report to spot missing check numbers and duplicate check numbers. A missing check report is shown in Figure 8.6.

Tax Schedule Report

The tax schedule report provides information on account transactions and transfers that you have assigned to a tax schedule. You can display and print the report, and can also save it on disk in a format that can be read by certain tax preparation programs.

CHECK YOURSELF

Create an itemized categories report covering the current year.

Personal Reports

ANSWER

1. From the Main Menu, select Create Reports, or from the register or the Write Checks screen, select Reports.
2. Select Personal Reports.
3. Select Itemized Categories.
4. Enter a report title, then enter the dates the report should cover. For example, enter January of this year as a start date, and the current month as the stop date.
5. Press **Enter**.

Customized Reports

You can create a customized report when one of Quicken's preset reports does not meet your needs. All customized reports are, in fact, based upon one of the preset reports. You start with the predefined report then modify it to meet your needs. You can then memorize the customized report definition for repeated use.

The extent to which a report can be customized depends to some extent on the type of report from which you are starting. For example, the itemized categories report is very flexible, whereas the missing checks report can be customized only slightly. This section explains the most important report customization options.

Report Organization

The Quicken program contains four basic types of reports:

- The *transaction report* lists individual transactions from one or more accounts.
- The *summary report* summarizes transactions, subtotaling by category or other criteria. A summary report does not list individual transactions.

▲ The *budget report* compares actual income and expenses with budgeted income and expenses.

▲ The *account balances report* lists total balances for your accounts.

These basic report types are never used "as is." Rather, they serve as templates on which the Quicken reports that you actually use are based. Each of Quicken's preset reports is a customized version of one of the four basic report types. For example, the itemized categories report is based on the transaction report, and the net worth report is based on the account balances report. When you need to create a customized report, you have two ways to proceed:

▲ Select one of Quicken's preset reports, then modify it to meet your needs.

▲ Start from scratch with one of the four basic report types, and design your report from the ground up.

The second method is rarely needed by most Quicken users. It is required only when you need to create a report that is significantly different from one of the preset reports. When you select Create Reports from the Main Menu or Reports from either the register or the Write Checks screen, you'll see the four basic report types listed at the bottom of the pull-down menu (Figure 8.7). To create a customized report, select the desired base report type from this menu. Quicken then leads you through the customization steps. Because this method of report customization is rarely needed, it will not be covered further in this book. However, once you become familiar with customizing the preset reports (the subject of the remainder of this chapter), you will probably be able to work your way through customizing a basic report.

TIP

Create a customized report when one of Quicken's preset reports does not meet your needs.

Customized Reports

▼ ***Figure 8.7. Reports Pull-down Menu with Four Basic Report Types***

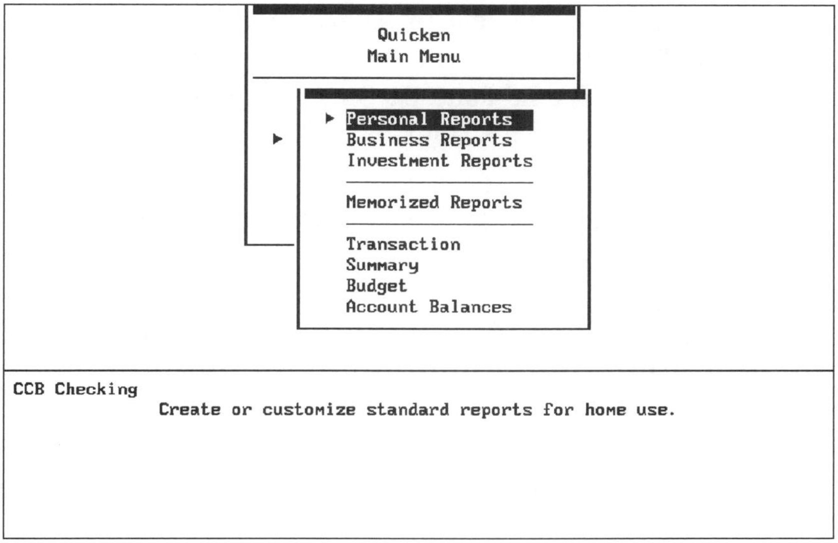

Basic Customization Steps

Here are the basic steps involved to customize a report:

1. Make sure that the file containing the account(s) you want the report based on is current.
2. From the Main Menu, select Create Reports; or from the register or the Write Checks screen, select Reports.
3. Another menu is displayed. From this menu select Personal Reports, Business Reports, or Investment Reports.
4. Yet another menu is displayed listing the available preset reports. Select the desired report type.
5. Quicken displays the setup window for the selected report. At the bottom of the setup window F7-Layout, F8-Options, and F9-Filter are displayed. These are keys you can press to display various customization windows (discussed below). You can also access these windows later in the process. For now, enter the basic setup information (Title, dates, and so on) for the report, then press **Enter**.

6. Quicken creates the report and displays it on your screen. Remember, you view different parts of the report by pressing the **Up** arrow, **Down** arrow, **PgUp**, and **PgDn** keys. Note that the Reports screen (shown in Figure 8.6) has a menu across the top. The Edit and Layout commands on this menu can be used to customize the report.
7. While the report is displayed on the screen, you can print it by pressing **Ctrl+P** or by selecting File/Print then selecting Print Report. Press **Esc** to close the report and return to the report setup window.

As you have seen, there are two ways to access the report customization features: from the report setup window before the report is displayed, or from the menus on the Reports screen while the report is displayed. Generally, you will find that the second method is more convenient because you view the report before making changes, then when you make a change the report is redisplayed with the changes in effect. Both methods are equivalent and provide access to the same features. The remainder of this chapter explains how to customize reports from the Reports screen.

Filtering Your Report

When you *filter* a report, you tell Quicken to limit the report to only those transactions that meet a certain criterion. For example, you could filter a report to include only transactions assigned to a certain category or class, payments to a specific payee, or transactions that have cleared. You can also limit a report to a subset of categories or classes, or to one or more accounts in your file.

Filtering by Category or Class

You can filter a report by category or by class, selecting those categories or classes to be included in the report and excluding all others. You have compete control over which categories or classes are included or excluded.

Customized Reports

To filter a report by category or class:

1. Display the preset report as described earlier in this chapter.
2. From the Reports screen, select Edit. From the pull-down menu, select either Categories or Classes. The remainder of this section describes filtering by categories, but the procedure is essentially identical for classes.
3. From the next menu, choose Selected. A list of all categories is displayed (Figure 8.8).
4. The Select Categories To Include window lists all categories alphabetically. Income categories are listed first, followed by expense categories and transfer categories (or account names). The right-most column in the window indicates whether each category is currently included in the report.
5. Press the **Up** arrow, **Down** arrow, **PgUp**, **PgDn**, **Home**, and **End** keys to move the highlight bar in the category list. Press **Spacebar** to toggle the highlighted category between included and excluded. Press **F9** to toggle all categories between included and excluded.

▼ *Figure 8.8. The Select Categories to Include Window*

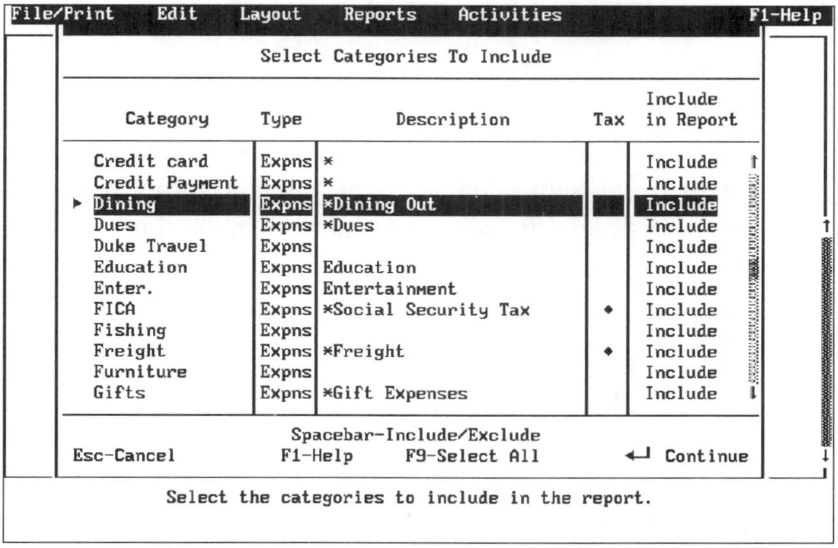

6. When all of the desired categories are marked, press **Enter**. Quicken regenerates the report using only the included categories and displays it on the screen.

TIP

You can have both category and class filters in effect at the same time.

Quicken will remember the categories that you selected to include and exclude from the report. They will be in effect the next time you display a report with the Edit Categories Selected command active (as indicated by a check mark on the menu next to the command). To return to a report that includes all categories, select Edit Categories All from the Reports screen.

Filtering by Account

Quicken's default is to use information from all accounts in a file to create a report (or all accounts of a certain type). This is fine for most reporting situations, but at times you may want to limit a report to transactions from one or more selected accounts. To do this, you filter the report by account.

These are the steps to filter a report by account:

1. Use the steps described above to create the preset report that you want to customize.
2. From the Reports screen, select Edit, then select Accounts. Another pull-down menu is displayed that offers three options (the option with the check mark displayed next to it is currently in effect):
   - ▲ Current restricts the report to transactions from the current account.
   - ▲ All (the default) includes all accounts of the appropriate types in the report.
   - ▲ Selected lets you specify which accounts are to be included in the report.

3. If you choose Current or All, the report is immediately displayed based on your selection. If you choose Selected, a window opens displaying all accounts in the current file. Press the **Up** arrow, **Down** arrow, **PgUp**, **PgDn**, **Home**, and **End** keys to move the highlight bar in the account list. Press **Spacebar** to toggle the highlighted account between included and excluded. Press **F9** to toggle all accounts between included and excluded.
4. When all of the desired accounts are marked as included, press **Enter**. The report is redisplayed using information from the selected accounts.
5. Quicken remembers the accounts you have selected and will use them the next time you create the report with the Selected option in effect. If the Selected option is on, Quicken displays the Select Accounts To Use window as soon as you exit the report setup window. You can modify the account selection or press **Enter** to display the report using the remembered account selection.

Customized Reports

The Filter Transactions Window

In addition to filtering transaction by category, class, or account (as described above), you can use the Filter Transactions window to create a more detailed filter for your report. The Filter Transactions window is shown in Figure 8.9.

The entries in this window are used as follows:

▲ The first four fields are used to enter criteria that will be used to select transactions to be included in the report. You can enter match criteria for one or more of the "Payee contains:", "Memo contains:", "Category contains:", and "Class contains:" fields. The report will be restricted to only those transactions that contain the criteria characters in the corresponding field(s). You can also use Quicken's special match characters to limit the search.

▲ In the "Tax-related categories only:" field, enter **Y** to restrict the report to transactions that have been assigned to a tax-related category. Enter **N** (the default) to include all categories.

▼ Figure 8.9. The Filter Transactions Window

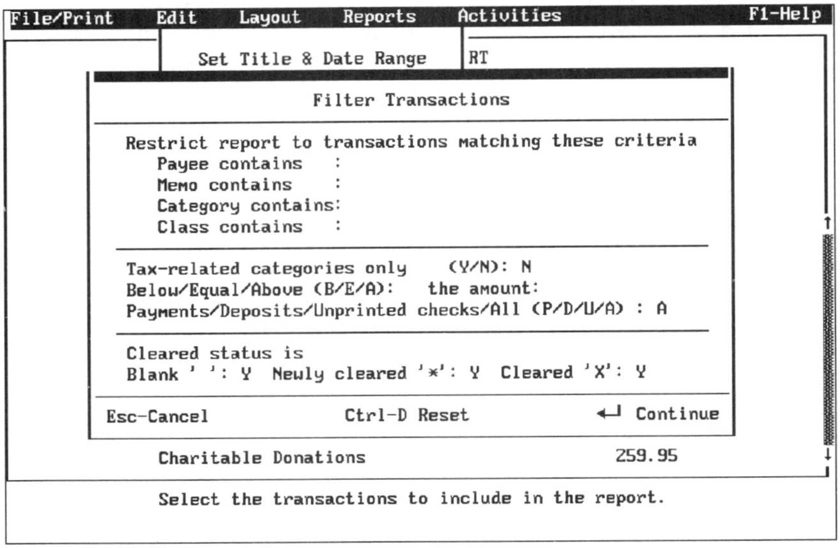

▲ The next line in the window lets you include or exclude transactions by amount. In the "the amount:" field enter the dollar and cents amount. In the "Below/Equal/Above:" field enter **B**, **E**, or **A** to match transactions where the amount is below, equal to, or above the specified amount.

▲ In the "Payments/Deposits/Unprinted checks/All:" field specify the type of transactions to include. **P** restricts the report to payments, **D** restricts the report to deposits, **U** restricts the report to unprinted checks, and **A** (the default) includes all transaction types.

▲ The next section of the window lets you include or exclude transactions based on their cleared status. Enter **Y** next to each cleared status to include transactions with that status: Use Blank for transactions that have not been marked cleared; Use "Newly cleared" for transactions that have been marked cleared in the register but have not yet been reconciled; Use Cleared for transactions that have been cleared and reconciled with your account.

You can press **Ctrl+D** at any time to reset all entries in this window to their default settings.

Customized Reports

To use the Filter Transaction window, follow these steps:

1. Using the steps described earlier in the chapter, create the preset report.
2. From the Reports screen, select Edit then select Filter Transactions.
3. The Filter Transactions window is displayed. Make entries in this window as described above.
4. With the cursor on the last field in the window, press **Enter**; or with the cursor on any field, press **Ctrl+Enter**. The report is redisplayed using the filter settings you have entered.

CHECK YOURSELF

Now that you understand how to filter reports, you should give it a try.

ANSWER

1. Display a report on the screen.
2. Select Edit.
3. Select Filter Transactions.
4. Enter the desired filter information.
5. Press **Ctrl+Enter**.

Cautions when Using Filters

When using filters, especially when creating an important report, you want to be sure that your filters are set properly. It's not uncommon, particularly for those with relatively little experience using Quicken, to apply filters incorrectly. Check the filtered report to be sure that it includes (and excludes) the correct transactions.

Also, keep in mind that Quicken "remembers" your filter settings, and uses them the next time you create a report. If you forget that you had been using a filter, you may inadvertently use the filter for your next report. Quicken indicates when a filter is in effect by displaying "(filtered)" at the top of the report set up window, and also in the lower-right corner of the Reports screen.

To disable all filters:

1. Display the Filter Transactions window and press **Ctrl+D** to reset all fields to their defaults.
2. From the Reports screen, select Edit Accounts. Be sure the All option is selected.
3. Repeat Step 2 with the Edit Categories and Edit Classes commands.

Report Layout

The Layout selection on the Reports screen menu is used to modify the way a report is organized. Unlike the Edit menu selection, which is used to control what information is included in the report, the Layout selection is used to control how the information is arranged.

When you select Layout from the Reports screen, a pull-down menu is displayed, which is shown in Figure 8.10. Its menu commands are explained below. Be aware that some of the commands on this menu are applicable only to certain report types. Quicken will not allow you to apply a layout command to an inappropriate type of report.

The Hide Cents command lets you suppress the display of cents in a report. Quicken rounds all amounts to the nearest dollar. For example, $12.86 will be displayed as $13. When Hide Cents is active, the menu command will read Show Cents, which you select to return to the display of cents amounts.

The Hide Split/Show Split command determines whether split transaction information is included in the report. When Show Split is active, the report will include the details of split transactions. When Hide Split is active, the report will not in-

Report Layout

▼ Figure 8.10. The Layout Pull-down Menu

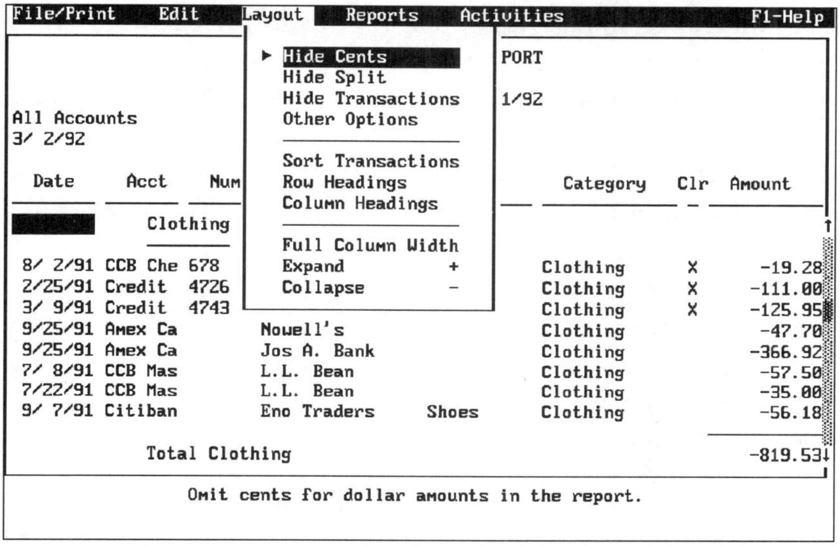

clude this information, but only the overall total for each transaction. These commands are applicable only to non-investment transaction reports.

The Hide Transactions/Show Transactions command determines whether a transaction detail is hidden or displayed in the report. When Hide Transactions is active, the report shows only the total dollar amount of transactions in each category. When Show Transactions is active (the default), the report lists all individual transactions. These commands are applicable only to non-investment transaction reports.

The Other Options command is used to modify how information is organized in an investment or a customized report. For example, you can choose between cash flow or income and expense organization, specify whether transfers and unrealized gains should be included, and control the display of memo, category, and subcategory information. Some options are available only for certain report types.

The Sort Transactions command lets you specify the order in which transactions are listed in the report. Transactions can be sorted by account, date, check number, or amount. Sort order is applicable only to non-investment transaction reports.

The Row Headings command is used to specify the headings that are used for rows in the report. For summary reports, you can choose to base the report on categories, classes, payees, or accounts. For transaction or investment reports, you can choose how to group transactions or investment data. Non-investment transactions can be grouped and subtotaled by time period, category, class, payee, or account. Investment transactions can be grouped by time period, account, category, security, security type, or investment goal.

The Column Headings command is used to specify the items that will be used as column headings in the report. Summary reports can include a separate column for each time period, category, class, payee, or account. For budget reports, you can specify the time period (weekly, biweekly, monthly, and so on) that will be used for each column. Account balances reports let you specify the interval at which your net worth will be calculated.

The Full Column Width/Half Column Width is used only with transaction reports. This command lets you select the column width to be used in the report.

The Expand and Collapse commands are applicable only to non-investment summary, budget, and account balances reports. The Collapse command hides the details associated with a report row heading while keeping the report totals the same. The Expand command redisplays the detail that was hidden with the Collapse command. To collapse or expand a row heading, double-click on it with the mouse. With the keyboard, highlight the heading, then select Layout Collapse (or press the minus key) to collapse, or select Layout Expand (or press the plus key) to expand.

Using QuickZoom

Quicken's QuickZoom command provides a quick method of investigating specific items in reports. For example, the cash flow report in Figure 8.11 reports total Dining Out expenses of

▼ *Figure 8.11. The QuickZoom Command Used in a Cash Flow Report*

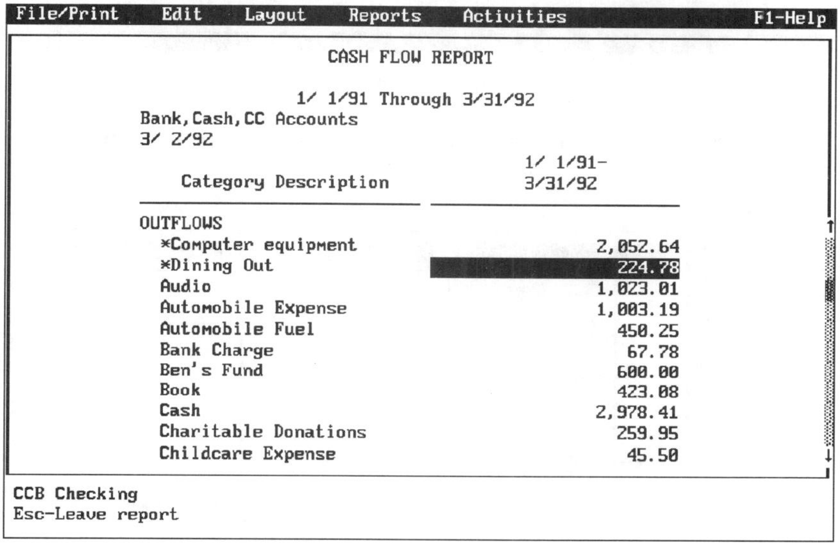

Using QuickZoom

$224.78. If you wanted to look at the individual transactions that are summarized in that amount, you would use QuickZoom. Note that QuickZoom is available only in non-investment summary, transaction, and budget reports.

To investigate a report item:

1. Display the report, then use the arrow keys to highlight the desired amount (for example, the Dining Out amount in Figure 8.11).
2. Press either **Ctrl+Z** or **Enter**. Quicken searches the registers and displays a list of all the transactions that are summarized in the report amount. For example, Figure 8.12 shows the transactions for the Dining Out amount from Figure 8.11.
3. To return to the report, press **Esc**. If you need more information on a specific transaction, use the arrow keys to highlight the transaction and press **F9** to display that transaction in the register.

▼ *Figure 8.12. The Transaction List Displayed by the QuickZoom Command*

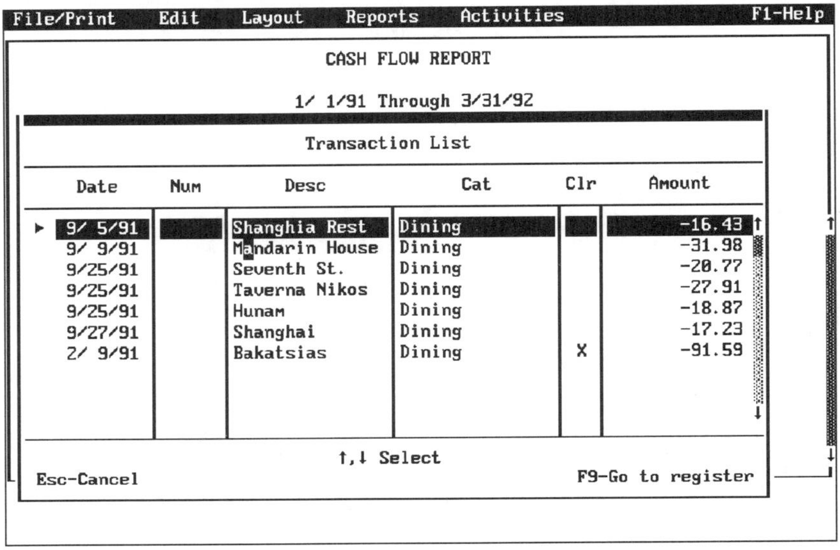

TIP

To QuickZoom with a mouse, double-click the amount of interest on the Reports screen.

Once you go to the register from the QuickZoom transaction list, you cannot return directly to the report. If you want to view the report again, you must re-create it. Therefore, before using QuickZoom, you may want to memorize your report, as described in the next section.

CHECK YOURSELF

Use the QuickZoom feature to view details about a report amount.

ANSWER

1. On the Reports screen, use the arrow keys to highlight the amount of interest.

2. Press **Ctrl+Z**.
3. Press **F9** to view the register, or press **Esc** to return to the report.

Using QuickZoom

Memorizing and Recalling Custom Report Settings

Quicken lets you memorize report settings then recall them later to re-create the same report. This is particularly useful when you have created a custom report with several filter and layout settings. When you memorize a report, Quicken records all details of it except the date range, budget amounts, and printer.

To memorize a report:

1. Create the report as you learned previously.
2. With the report displayed, press **Ctrl+M**. Quicken displays the Memorizing Report window and prompts you for the report title.
3. If you specified a title for the report in the setup report window, that title is entered here. You can accept this title or modify it. If you did not specify a title, the field is blank and you must enter one now.
4. Press **Enter**. The report settings are memorized. If the specified title is used by another memorized report, you are given the option of replacing the original with the new report, or entering a new title.

To recall a memorized report:

1. From the Main Menu, select Create Reports; or from the register or the Write Checks screen, select Reports. The Reports menu is displayed.

2. Select Memorized Reports. Quicken displays a list of all memorized report titles. Use the arrow keys to highlight the name of the report you want to use, then press **Enter**.
3. A memorized report window is displayed. This is similar to the set up window you learned about earlier. In this window, you can change the report title and specify the range of dates the report is to cover.
4. Once the memorized report is displayed, you have available all of Quicken's report customization features. You can view/print the report as it is, or further customize it. If you change the report, you can memorize it under the original name or a new name.

CHECK YOURSELF

Memorizing and recalling report settings can be a great time-saver, particularly if you create heavily customized reports. Now, create a customized report and have Quicken memorize it.

ANSWER

1. Display a customized report.
2. Press **Ctrl+M**.
3. Enter a title for the memorized report.
4. Press **Enter**.

QUICK COMMAND SUMMARY

To create a preset personal report:

1. Make the Quicken file that you want the report based on current.
2. From the Main Menu, select Create Reports, then select Personal Reports.

3. From the next menu, select the type of report you want.
4. In the setup window, enter a report title, then enter the date range the report is to cover.
5. The report is displayed on the screen. Scroll around the report by pressing the **Up** arrow, **Down** arrow, **PgUp**, and **PgDn** keys.
6. Press **Ctrl+P** to print the report. Press **Esc** to leave the report.

To create a customized report:

1. Display the preset report that you want to customize.
2. From the Reports screen, use the commands on the Edit menu to filter the report, controlling what information is included in the report.
3. From the Reports screen, use the commands on the Layout menu to modify the report organization and layout.

To investigate a specific report amount:

1. Highlight the desired amount.
2. Press **Enter** or **Ctrl+Z**. Quicken displays a list of all transactions that are summarized in the amount.

To memorize the settings for a customized report:

1. Display the customized report.
2. Press **Ctrl+M**, then enter a title for the report (or accept the existing title).
3. Press **Enter**. The report settings are memorized under the specified title.

To recall a memorized report:

1. From the Main Menu, select Create Reports.
2. Select Memorized Reports.
3. Select the desired report.

PRACTICE WHAT YOU'VE LEARNED

While an important feature of Quicken, reports can be a bit complicated. You should practice creating and working with reports until you are comfortable with the various procedures.

1. Display Quicken's various preset reports.
2. Try customizing the preset reports in different ways, such as using a filter.
3. Use QuickZoom to view details of a report.
4. Memorize a report setting.
5. Recall a memorized report setting.

9

Credit Card Accounts

Almost everyone has at least one credit card, and these cards are being used more and more every day. To maintain a complete picture of your finances, you will have to keep track of the credit card transactions you make. Quicken is ideal for this task. In this chapter you will learn

- **How to set up a Quicken credit card account**
- **How to record credit card charges and payments**
- **How to reconcile your credit card account**
- **When you can use your Quicken checking account to keep track of credit cards**

Setting Up a Credit Card Account

The first step you must take to use Quicken to track credit card use is to set up a credit card account. Quicken offers a special account type for keeping track of credit cards. As with all Quicken account types, you must first set the account up before you can start using it. To introduce you to credit card accounts, we will go though the process of setting up an account for the Smiths' MasterCard.

When setting up a credit card account, you must decide how far back the account will go. If you want the Quicken account to contain information about your charges for the past six months, you will have to dig out your old credit card statements and enter information from them into Quicken. For most people, it is sufficient to start with current information.

To set up a credit card account:

1. Be sure the correct file is current. Then, choose Select Account from the Main Menu. A list of existing accounts is displayed.
2. Use the arrow keys to scroll to the top entry in the list, which reads <New Account>, then press **Enter**.
3. The Set Up New Account window is displayed (Figure 9.1). In this window, you enter information about the account you are setting up. The process for a credit card account is similar to the process of setting up a checking account, which you learned in Chapter 1. Remember, when you're entering information in a window you press **Tab** to move to the next field, and **Shift+Tab** to move to the previous field.
4. Enter **2** in the "Account Type:" field to specify that this will be a credit card account.
5. In the "Name for this account:" field, you enter the account name. For the Smiths' account, enter **MasterCard**.
6. In the "Balance:" field, you enter the closing balance from your most recent credit card statement. In the "as of:" field,

▼ *Figure 9.1. The Set Up New Account Window*

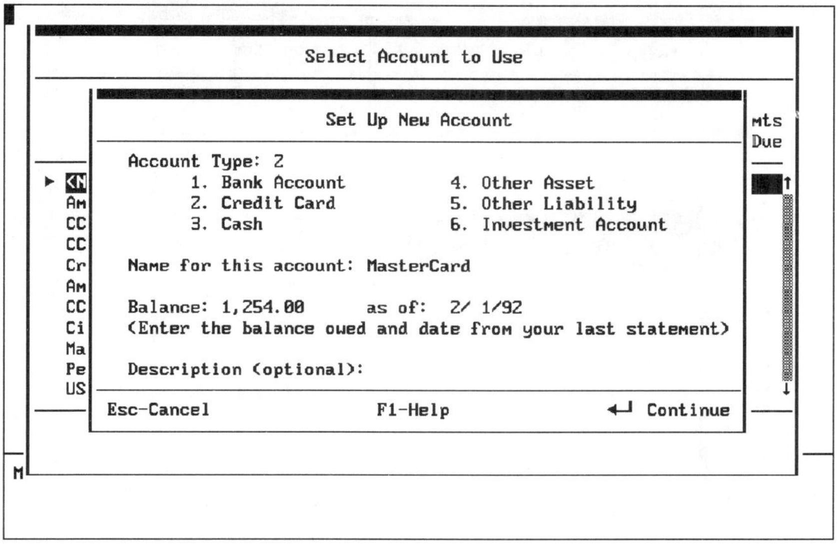

Setting Up a Credit Card Account

you enter the date of that statement. For the Smiths' account, enter **$1254** and **2/1/92**.

7. In the "Description:" field, enter a description for the account, then press **Enter**.
8. Next, Quicken displays a window asking you to enter the credit limit for the account. This is optional. If you enter your credit limit, Quicken will be able to calculate and display the account's available credit (which is the credit limit minus the account balance). For the Smiths' account, enter a credit limit of $5000, then press **Enter**.
9. Quicken adds the new credit card account to the list of accounts, which is again displayed. To view the register for the account, move the highlight to the account name and press **Enter**. The register for the Smiths' MasterCard account is shown in Figure 9.2.

Take moment to examine the credit card account register. Generally, it is similar to the register for bank accounts, but there are some differences. Fields that are the same for the two account types are the DATE, PAYEE, MEMO, CATEGORY, and

▼ ***Figure 9.2. The Register for a Credit Card Account***

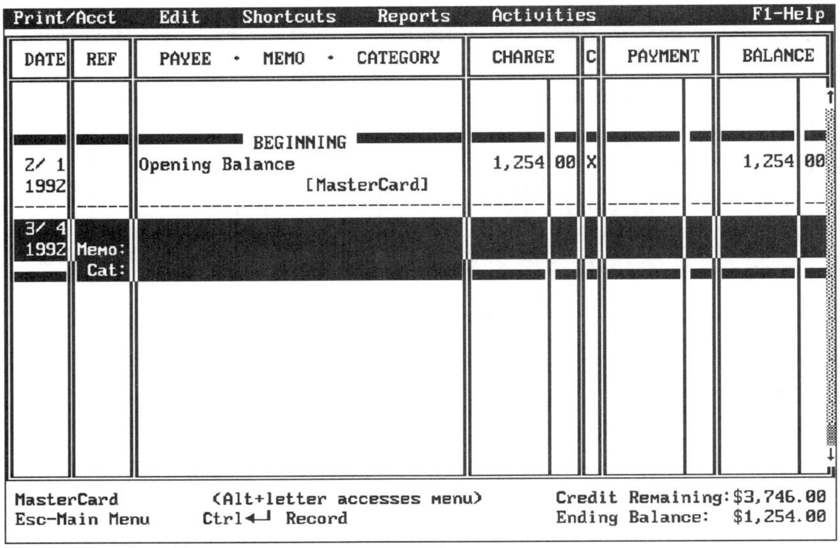

BALANCE fields. In a credit card account, these fields are used in exactly the same way as they are used in a checking account. The differences between bank account and credit card account registers are:

- ▲ In a credit card register, there is no NUM "check number" field. This field is called REF, but it is not used in a credit card account.
- ▲ The CHARGE field is used to enter the amount of transactions that increase the amount you owe on the account—charges, interest charges, and annual fees.
- ▲ The PAYMENT field is used to enter the amount of transactions that decrease the amount you owe on the account—payments you make, credits for returned merchandise, and so on.
- ▲ In the lower-right corner of the credit card register, the ending balance is displayed. This is the amount you owe on the account, based on all the account transactions that have been entered.

▲ If you specified a credit limit when you set up the account, the "Credit Remaining:" field displays the amount of credit that is available on the account.

Setting Up a Credit Card Account

CHECK YOURSELF

Now that you understand the procedure for setting up a credit card account, you can set up your own (assuming you use a credit card). First, find your most recent credit card account statement.

ANSWER

1. From the Main Menu, choose Select Account.
2. Highlight <New Account>, then press **Enter**.
3. Enter **2** in the "Account Type:" field.
4. Enter the account name in the "Name for this account:" field.
5. Enter the closing balance from your most recent credit card statement in the "Balance:" field.
6. Enter the statement date in the "as of:" field.
7. Press **Ctrl+Enter**.
8. Enter the credit limit for the account.
9. Press **Enter**.

Basics of Using a Credit Card Account

Before getting to the details of using a credit card account, take a look at the general outline of the procedure. There are three aspects to using a credit card account:

- You enter charge transactions (purchases and cash advances) into the account. As you'll see below, you have several options when it comes to entering charges. Credit card transactions are assigned to categories, subcategories, and/or classes (just like bank account transactions), including splitting transactions.
- You record payments that you make to the account. Since you will usually pay your credit card bill from your checking account, you'll use a transfer between accounts to record the payment.
- You reconcile your account. When you reconcile, you verify that the information on the credit card statement provided by your bank matches the information in your Quicken account. If your account is accruing interest charges, you also enter these amounts during reconciliation.

Entering Charges

There are several different approaches you can take toward entering charges into your Quicken credit card account. Which approach you use will depend on the information you want Quicken to provide, and your own personal preferences.

The first choice you have is *when* to enter charges:

- You can enter charges as they occur throughout the month, using information from the charge slips that the merchant gives you after your purchase. This method can be inconvenient, because it requires you to run Quicken and make entries frequently. Its main advantage is that Quicken will report correct amounts for account balance and available credit at all times.
- You can enter the month's charges all at once at the end of the month, using information from your monthly statement. This method is certainly more convenient, but it means that Quicken may not report accurate amounts for account balance and available credit at all times.

Entering Charges

The second choice you have to make is *which* charges to enter:

- ▲ If you want to keep track of the details of all your charges, you must enter each and every charge as a separate transaction.
- ▲ If you need the details of only some of your credit card charges, you can save yourself some time by doing the following: Enter only those charge transactions for which you want to keep a detailed record. Then, create a single transaction to cover all the charges for which you don't want individual records. For this lump transaction, you can create a category such as "Misc. chgs."

Entering Credit Card Transactions

The procedure for entering credit card transactions is essentially identical to that for bank account transactions.

To enter credit card transactions:

1. From the Main Menu, choose Select Account.
2. On the list of accounts that is displayed, move the highlight to the desired credit card account name, then press **Enter.** The register for that account is displayed, with the cursor in the DATE field of a blank transaction.
3. Obtain the transaction information from either the credit card statement or the charge slip. Enter the transaction date in the DATE field. Remember, you can use Quicken's special date keys (explained in Chapter 2) to change the date.
4. Press **Tab** twice to move the cursor to the PAYEE field, then enter the name of the payee.
5. Press **Tab** to move to the CHARGE field, then enter the amount of the charge.
6. Press **Tab** three times to move to the MEMO field, then enter memo for the transaction. Remember, a memo entry is only

for your own benefit—Quicken does not use this information in any way.

7. Press **Tab** again to move to the CATEGORY field. There are several options available when entering a category:

   - ▲ Type in the entire category name.
   - ▲ Type the first few letters of the category name, then press **Enter**. If the letters match only a single category name, Quicken fills in the CATEGORY field with that name. If they match two or more category names, you are given the option of either selecting from the category list or adding to it.
   - ▲ Press **Ctrl+C** to display the category list. Then, highlight the desired category and press **Enter**.

8. Once you have filled in the CATEGORY field, review your entry to be sure all the fields are correct. If you need to make a correction, press **Tab** and **Shift+Tab** to cycle among fields, then make the necessary corrections.
9. Once you have verified the entry, press **Enter** (with the cursor in the CATEGORY field) or **Ctrl+Enter** (with the cursor in any field) to record the transaction. The recorded transaction, with updated "Ending Balance:" and "Credit Remaining:" fields, is shown in Figure 9.3.

Making Payments on a Credit Card Account

When you make a payment on your credit card account, you must record the payment to keep your account balance correct. There are several ways to do this:

- ▲ When you reconcile your credit card account, you have the option of letting Quicken automatically write a check to pay your credit card bill. This is explained further below.

▼ ***Figure 9.3. The Credit Card Transaction Has Been Entered***

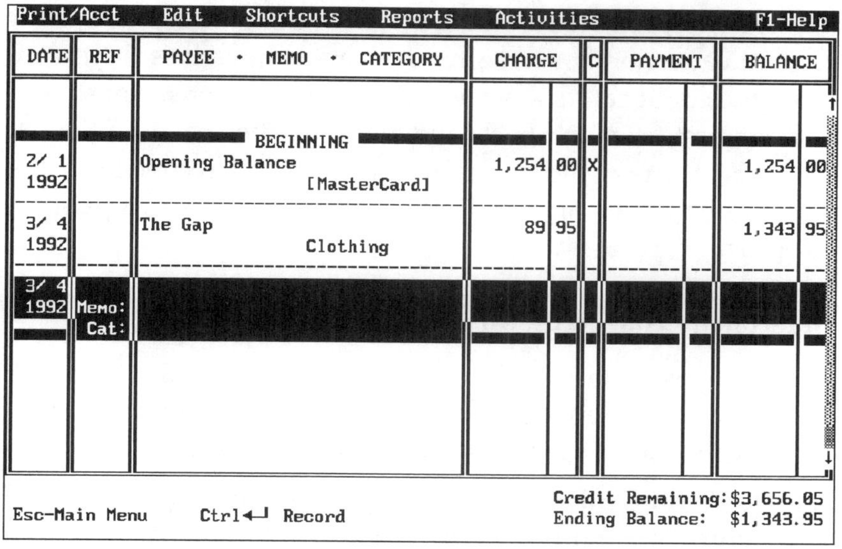

Making Payments on a Credit Card Account

- ▲ If you pay your credit card bill from a Quicken bank account, use an account transfer (as you learned in Chapter 7). When you write the check to pay the bill or enter the check transaction in the checking account register, enter the name of the credit card account as the category. Quicken will automatically create the corresponding payment transaction in the credit card account.
- ▲ If you pay your credit card from somewhere other than a Quicken account, you must enter the transaction directly in the credit card register. Enter the transaction as usual, placing the payment amount in the PAYMENT field and assigning the transaction to whatever category is appropriate.

Reconciling Your Credit Card Account

Reconciling your credit card account is just as important as reconciling your checking account. It's during reconciliation that you verify your transaction entries against the bank's credit card statement, and it's also where you enter any interest charges that have accumulated on the account. You should reconcile your account each month, soon after the statement arrives. If you are using the credit card statement to enter transactions, you should do that first, then go back and perform the reconciliation. It might be tempting to enter transactions and reconcile in the same step, but you are less likely to make errors if you perform these tasks separately.

To reconcile your credit card statement:

1. Have your latest credit card statement available. From the credit card register, select Activities. Then, from the pull-down menu, select Reconcile/Pay Credit Card.
2. The Credit Card Statement Information window is displayed (Figure 9.4). In this window you will enter information from your credit card statement.
   - ▲ In the "Charges, Cash Advances:" field, enter the total amount of new charges and cash advances appearing in the statement.

▼ ***Figure 9.4. The Credit Card Statement Information Window***

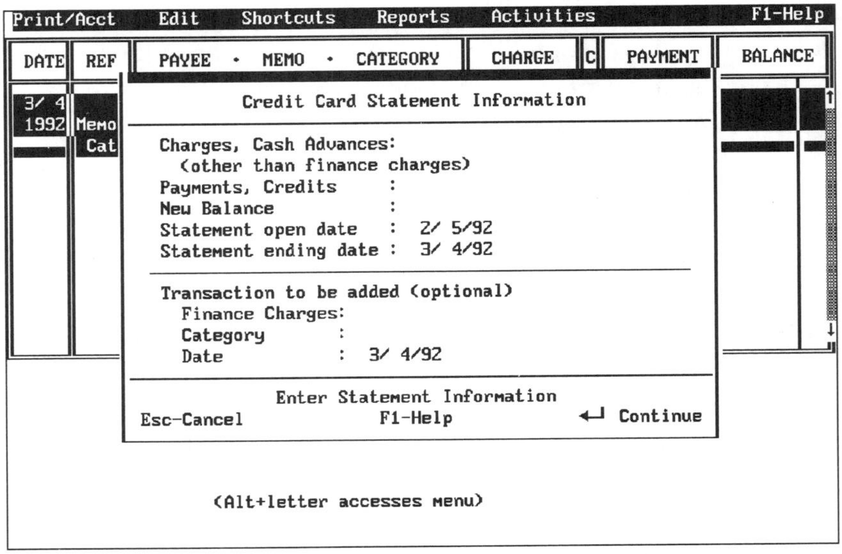

Reconciling Your Credit Card Account

- ▲ In the "Payments, Credits:" field, enter the total of new payments and credits that appear in the statement.
- ▲ In the "New Balance:" field, enter the new account balance.
- ▲ Change or enter the statement dates, if necessary.
- ▲ If there are any interest charges on the account, enter the amount in the "Finance Charges:" field and the category they should be assigned to (usually "Int Paid," for Interest Paid). Quicken will automatically create a transaction for this amount.
- ▲ The "Date:" field shows today's date. Change this if necessary, then press **Enter**.

3. Quicken displays a list of uncleared transactions (Figure 9.5), plus any finance charge transaction, which is already marked as cleared (as indicated by an asterisk next to the transaction).
4. Mark each transaction in the list as cleared if it appears in your credit card statement. To mark a transaction as cleared, use the arrow keys to move the highlight to the transaction,

▼ ***Figure 9.5. List of Uncleared Credit Card Transactions and a Cleared Finance Charge Transaction***

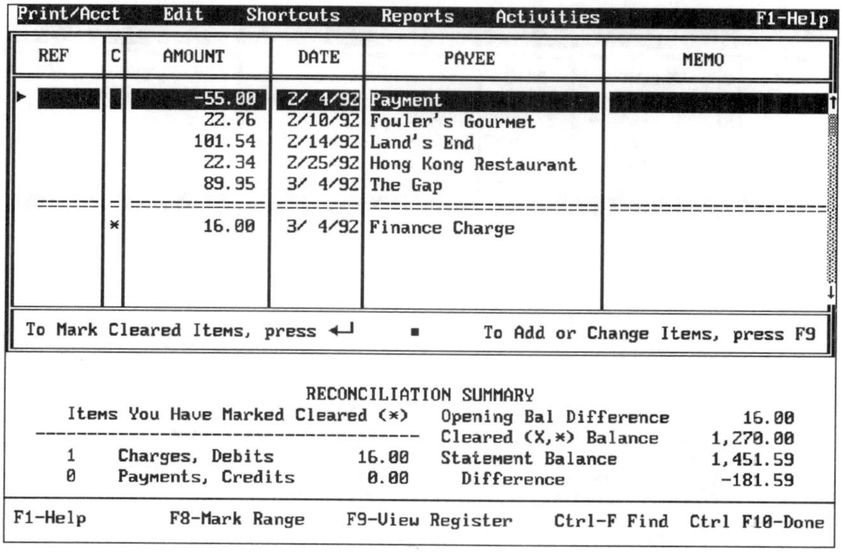

then press **Spacebar**. Press **Spacebar** again if you need to remove the "cleared" mark from the transaction.

5. As you mark transactions as cleared, the balances in the lower-right corner of the screen keep track of your progress. Once you have cleared all transactions that appear in your statement, the Difference field should read 0.00, as shown in Figure 9.6. This means that your account balances. In this case, proceed to Step 7.

6. If the Difference field does not read 0.00, your account does not balance. There are several possible causes for this:

   - ▲ You made an error entering the amount for one or more transactions.
   - ▲ You forgot to enter one or more transactions that appear in your statement.
   - ▲ You made a mistake entering the balance or finance charge amount from your statement.

   To look for errors, press **F9** to return to the register. Check for missing transactions and incorrect entries, and make the necessary corrections. Then, return to Step 1 to complete the reconciliation process.

▼ Figure 9.6. Balanced Account with Difference Field Displaying 0.00

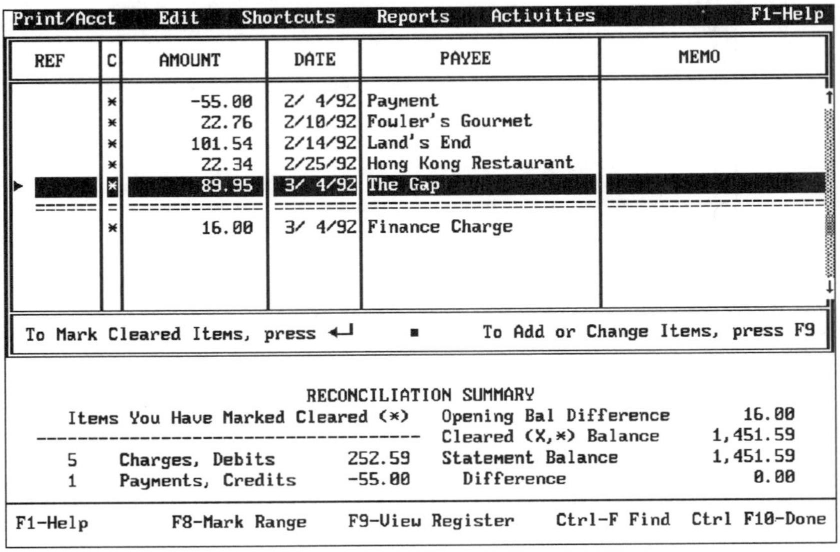

Reconciling Your Credit Card Account

7. Once the Difference field reads 0.00, press **Ctrl+F10**. Quicken displays the Make Credit Card Payment window, as shown in Figure 9.7. If you do not want to make a credit card payment at this time, press **Esc**. You are finished with reconciliation.
8. To make a credit card payment, fill in the two fields in the Make Credit Card Payment window:
   - ▲ In the "Bank Acct:" field, enter the name of the checking account that you want to use for the payment. If you don't remember the name of the account, press **Ctrl+C** to see a list of accounts.
   - ▲ In the "Hand-written check:" field, enter **N** if you want Quicken to print a check, **Y** if you will be hand-writing the check.
9. Press **Enter**. Quicken takes you to the Write Checks screen (if you specified a printed check) or the checking account register (if you specified a hand-written check). Finish filling in the information for the check. Quicken automatically makes the check amount equal to your entire credit card account balance. If you want to make only a partial payment at this time, change the check amount.

▼ Figure 9.7. The Make Credit Card Payment Window

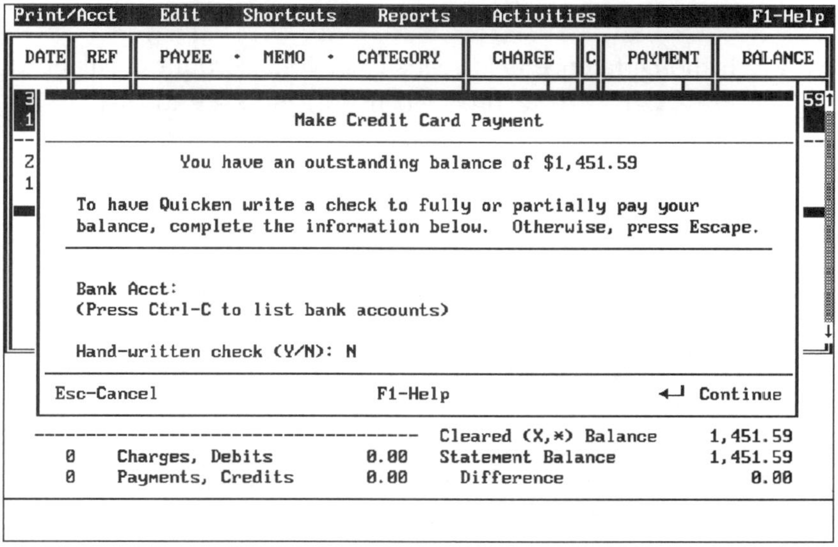

10. Once the check information is complete, press **Ctrl+Enter** to record it. Remember to either write out the hand-written check, or print the Quicken check. If you entered payee, memo, and/or address information for the check, Quicken remembers it and will automatically insert it the next time you make a credit card payment on this account.

CHECK YOURSELF

If you've been entering credit card transactions and have received a new statement, you can reconcile your account.

ANSWER

1. Display the register for the account.
2. Select Activities.
3. Select Reconcile/Pay Credit Card.
4. Enter the information from your most recent credit card statement.
5. Press **Enter**.
6. Use the arrow keys to move the highlight bar, then press **Spacebar** to mark as cleared each transaction that appears in your credit card statement.
7. If the Difference field reads 0.00, your account is balanced. Press **Ctrl+F10** to proceed. If not, press **F9** to display the register and check for mistakes, then return to Step 2.

Tracking a Credit Card with Your Checking Account

Under some circumstances, you may find it easier to keep track of your credit card transactions with your Quicken checking account. This method is feasible if you pay your full credit card balance each month and if you usually don't have a large number of charge transactions.

Tracking a Credit Card with Your Checking Account

The general procedure is: each month, when you receive your credit card statement, write a check to pay the full balance of the credit card account. Use the split transaction feature to assign the individual charges to the proper categories.

To track a credit card with your checking account:

1. Display the register or the Write Checks screen for the checking account you want to use to pay the credit card bill.
2. Write a check for the full amount of the credit card bill. In the CATEGORY field, press **Ctrl+S** to display the Split Transaction window.
3. Using information from your credit card statement, enter a split transaction for each individual charge. Figure 9.8 shows split transactions entered for three charges.
4. Once all charges have been entered, close the Split Transaction window and finish entering the payment transaction.

▼ *Figure 9.8. The Split Transaction Window*

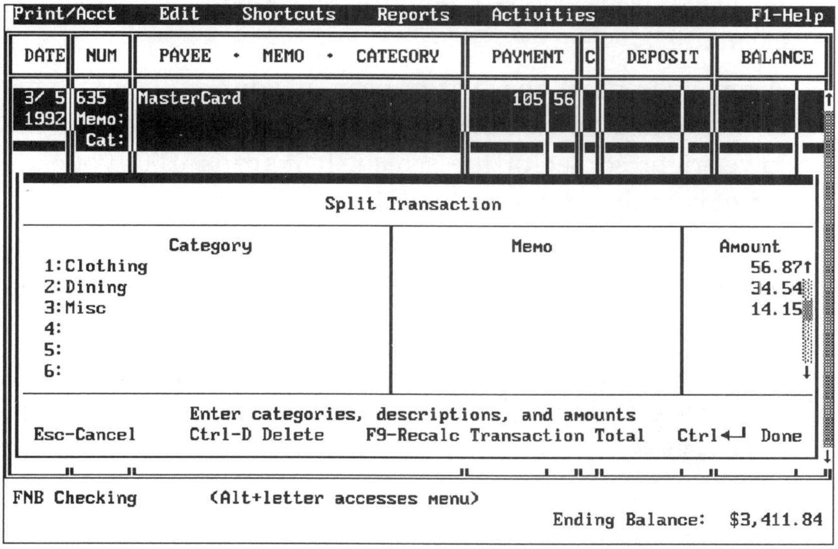

QUICK COMMAND SUMMARY

To set up a new credit card account:

1. Make sure the desired file is current.
2. From the Main Menu, choose Select Account, then select <New Account>.
3. Enter **2** in the "Account Type:" field, then enter a name for the account.
4. Enter the balance and date from your most recent credit card statement, then enter a description for the account. Press **Enter**.
5. Enter the account's credit limit, then press **Enter**.

To reconcile a credit card account:

1. Display the register for the account.
2. Select Activities, then select Reconcile/Pay Credit Card.
3. In the Credit Card Statement Information window, enter the information from your most recent credit card statement. From the Date field, press **Enter**.
4. Compare Quicken's list of uncleared transactions with your credit card statement. Use the arrow keys to highlight any uncleared transactions, then press **Spacebar** to mark them as cleared.
5. After all transactions that appear in your statement have been marked as cleared, check the Difference field in the lower-right corner of the screen. If it reads 0.00, your account is balanced. Press **Ctrl+F10** to proceed.
6. If the Difference field does not read 0.00, your account is not balanced. Press **F9** to display the register and check for mistakes, then return to Step 2.
7. The Make Credit Card Payment window is displayed. If you do not want to make a payment at this time, press **Esc**. You are finished.

8. To make a payment, enter the payment information in the Make Credit Card Payment window. Then, complete the payment transaction in either the register or the Write Checks screen.

PRACTICE WHAT YOU'VE LEARNED

Credit card accounts can be very useful, helping you keep track of charge expenses that tend to get out of hand. Practice what you've learned, using your own account or a dummy account.

1. Set up a credit card account.
2. Enter some credit card transactions.
3. Practice the reconciliation steps.

10

Cash Accounts

This chapter explains how to use a Quicken cash account. We all use cash for some of our transactions, even though checks and credit cards are becoming more prevalent. You use a cash account if you need to keep track of some or all of your purchases that are made with cash. By doing so, you enable Quicken to provide a complete picture of your financial situation. In this chapter you'll learn how to

- **Set up a cash account**
- **Enter cash transactions**
- **Transfer cash from other accounts**
- **Use a checking account to track cash**

Cash Account Versus Checking Account

Despite the increasing prevalence of checks and credit cards, some of your transactions will still involve cash. In fact, some people prefer to use cash. If you want to keep track of your cash transactions, Quicken offers you two options:

- ▲ If you have a significant number of cash transactions and you want to keep track of all or most of them, you can set up a separate Quicken cash account.
- ▲ If you need to keep track of only a few cash transactions, you can do so in your Quicken checking account.

Setting Up a Cash Account

The procedures for setting up a Quicken cash account are similar to those used for setting up other account types. As an example, you can set up a cash account for the Smiths.

To set up a Quicken cash account:

1. Make the desired file current (in this example, the Smiths' file), then from the Main Menu choose Select Account. Quicken displays a list of accounts in the file.
2. Use the arrow keys to highlight the selection <New Account> at the top of the list, then press **Enter**.
3. Quicken displays the Set Up New Account window. Make the following entries in this window (remember, to move forward and backward between fields, press **Tab** and **Shift+Tab**):

   - ▲ In the "Account Type:" field, enter **3** to specify a cash account.

Setting Up a Cash Account

- In the "Name for this account:" field, enter the account name. You can call it "Cash."
- In the "Balance:" field, enter the amount of cash you have on hand. For the Smiths, enter **$250**.
- The "as of:" field displays today's date, which you should accept.
- In the "Description:" field, enter an account description.

4. Once all fields in the Set Up New Account window are filled in, press **Ctrl+Enter** to set up the account. Quicken adds the new account to the list of accounts in the Select Account to Use window.

CHECK YOURSELF

You now know when a cash account is useful and how to set one up. If you plan to use a cash account, go ahead and set it up now.

ANSWER

1. From the Main Menu, choose Select Account.
2. Highlight <New Account>, then press **Enter**.
3. In the "Account Type:" field, enter **3**.
4. Enter the account name and the balance (the amount of cash you have on hand).
5. Accept today's date.
6. Press **Ctrl+Enter**.

Basics of Using a Cash Account

Like any account, a cash account has both inflows and outflows. An outflow, of course, is any transaction that decreases the amount of cash you have. Most outflows are expenditures, but you could also have an outflow if you deposit cash into a bank account. An inflow is any transaction that increases the amount of cash you have, such as cashing a check or making a withdrawal.

For complete accuracy, you must record every cash transaction. Unless you are extremely conscientious, however, this is impractical. It's also unnecessary. Few people need or want to keep track of every 50 cents they spend on coffee, chewing gum, or a newspaper. Such minor cash transactions can, as you'll see later, be lumped together in a category such as "Misc. cash."

It's the more significant cash transactions, such as $15 for a taxi or $20 for lunch, that you need to keep track of individually. Since you won't receive a convenient statement at the end of the month listing your cash transactions, you must keep track of them yourself.

TIP

To save time, record individual transactions for only your significant cash expenditures. All others can be lumped together in a "Misc. cash" category.

Entering Cash Transactions

To enter cash transactions, you must display the cash account register.

To display the cash account register:

1. From the Quicken Main Menu, choose Select Account.
2. The Select Account to Use window is displayed. Press the **Up** and **Down** arrow keys to highlight the name of the cash account, then press **Enter**.
3. The cash account register is displayed (Figure 10.1).

▼ *Figure 10.1. The Cash Account Register*

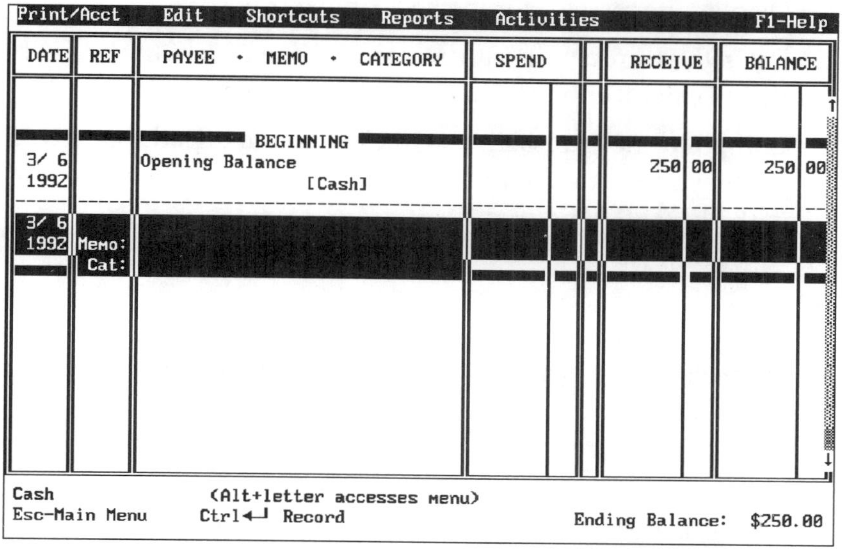

Entering Cash Transactions

Take a moment to look at the cash account register in Figure 10.1. The register components should look familiar to you. The DATE, PAYEE, BALANCE, MEMO, and CATEGORY fields are exactly the same as they are in other Quicken account types. In the SPEND field, you enter the amount of cash outflows; in the RECEIVE field, you enter the amount of cash inflows. In the lower-right corner of the screen, the "Ending Balance:" field shows the current balance—how much cash is currently on hand.

The procedure for entering a transaction in a cash account is no different from entering a transaction in any other kind of account. Cash transactions are assigned to categories, subcategories, and/or classes, just like other transactions. The following sections provide information on several specific situations you may run into that involve cash transactions.

Cashing a Check

When you cash a check, you are transferring money from your checking account to your cash account. This is exactly how you handle it in Quicken—as a transfer between accounts.

When you cash a check:

1. Display the register for the checking account.
2. Enter the transaction information for the check. In the CATEGORY field, enter the name of the cash account.
3. Complete the transaction. Quicken automatically creates a parallel transaction in the cash account with the check amount in the RECEIVE field.

TIP

An automatic teller machine withdrawal is handled the same way as a cashed check.

Getting Cash when Paying by Check

There are probably times when you get some cash as change when making a purchase by check. For example, you might purchase $45 worth of groceries, write a $65 check to the grocery store, and get $20 back in change.

To enter this type of transaction:

1. Display the register for the checking account.
2. Enter the transaction information for the check, placing the total check amount in the PAYMENT field. With the cursor in the CATEGORY field, press **Ctrl+S** to display the Split Transaction window.
3. Split the check transaction into two parts. One part should be for the items you purchased, assigned to the appropriate category (for instance, Groceries). The other part is for the cash you received in change. For this part, enter the cash account name in the Category column (see Figure 10.2).
4. Complete the transaction. Quicken will automatically create a parallel transaction in the cash account with the proper amount in the RECEIVE field.

▼ *Figure 10.2. A Split Check Transaction with Part of the Check Amount Being Transferred to a Cash Account*

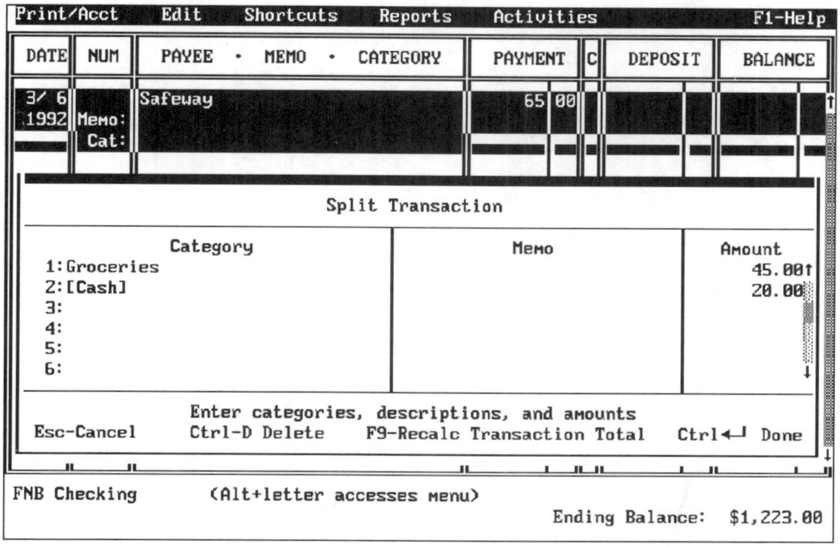

Getting Cash when Depositing a Check

When you take a check to the bank, you may elect to deposit part of the check and receive the balance back in cash. For example, you have received a $450 bonus check and want to deposit $400 in your checking account and receive $50 cash.

Here's how to get cash when depositing a check:

1. Display the register for the checking account.
2. Enter the transaction information for the check, placing the actual deposit amount, not the check amount, in the DEPOSIT field (in our example, $400). With the cursor in the CATEGORY field, press **Ctrl+S** to display the Split Transaction window.
3. Split the deposit transaction into two parts. The first part is for the entire amount of the check you deposited and is assigned to the appropriate category (in our example, $450 assigned to the Bonus category). The second part is for the amount of cash you got back and is a negative number. (Re-

▼ ***Figure 10.3. A Checking Account Deposit Is Split to Transfer a Portion of the Amount to a Cash Account***

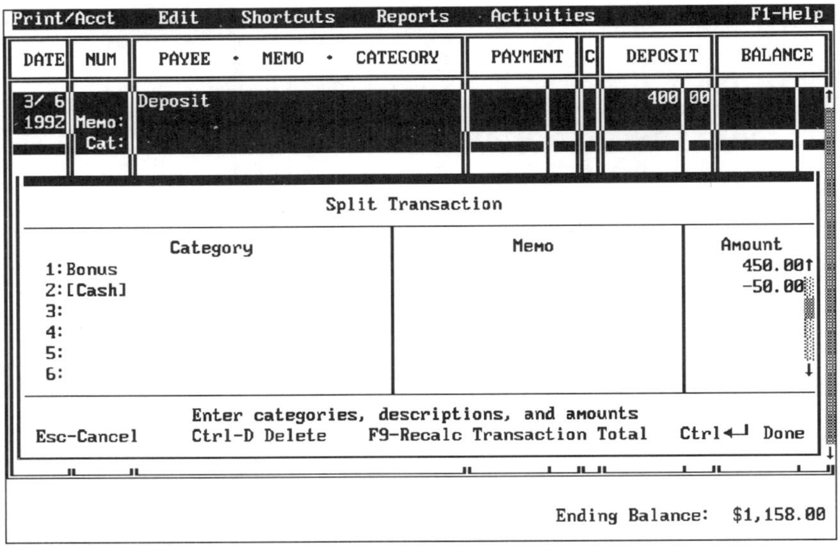

member, Quicken will calculate this automatically.) Figure 10.3 shows how this will look.

4. Complete the transaction. Quicken will automatically create a parallel transaction in the cash account with the proper amount in the RECEIVE field.

Using Your Quicken Bank Account for Cash Transactions

If you need to keep track of relatively few cash transactions, you may not need to set up a Quicken cash account. Rather, you can keep track of them in your checking account.

Here's how to go about it:

1. Create a category that you will use for miscellaneous cash transactions, such as "Misc. Cash."

Using Your Quicken Bank Account for Cash Transactions

2. Whenever you obtain cash, assign the cash amount to this category. The techniques to use are the same as described above, except instead of entering the name of your cash account in the CATEGORY field, you enter the name of your cash category (for instance, "Misc. cash").
3. If you later spend some of that cash on a significant transaction, keep the receipt or make a note of the transaction and its amount.
4. Later, start Quicken and find the original transaction for the cash withdrawal. Move the cursor to the CATEGORY field, then press **Ctrl+S** to display the Split Transaction window.
5. Split the transaction as desired, assigning part of it to the specific cash expenditures that you want to keep track of and the remainder to your Misc. cash category.

As an example, imagine that you cashed a $200 check. You entered the check into your Quicken checking account, assigning the entire amount to "Misc. cash." Over the next week you spent $65 on shoes, $49 taking the family to dinner, $30 on postage stamps, and the remainder on miscellaneous items. When you edit the transaction to split it, your screen will appear as in Figure 10.4.

TIP

If you need to keep track of only a few cash transactions, you can do so in your Quicken checking account.

Reconciling Your Cash Account

There is really no way to reconcile your cash account because there is no bank statement for you to compare your Quicken account to. Instead of reconciling, you adjust the balance of your cash account so that it agrees with the actual amount of cash you have on hand. If there's a discrepancy between these two

▼ Figure 10.4. Splitting a Transaction to Include Important Cash Expenditures

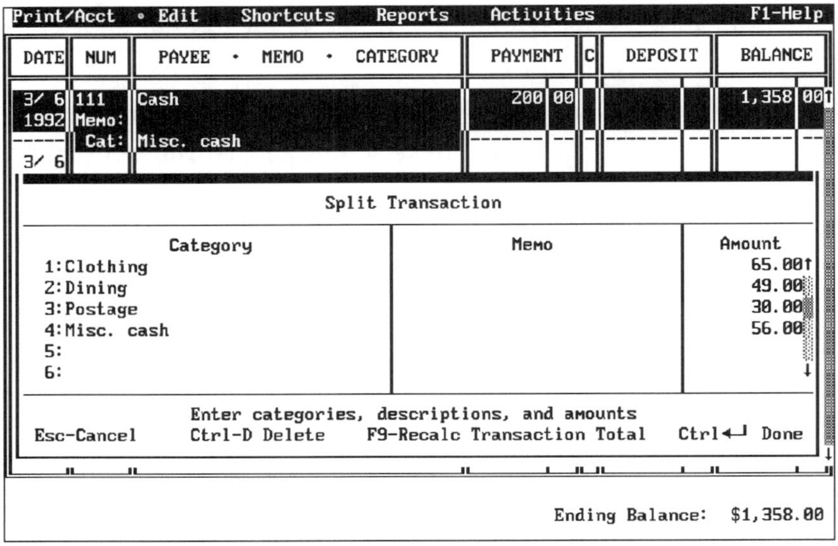

amounts, Quicken creates an account adjustment to bring things into balance.

Here's how:

1. Display the cash account register.
2. Select Activities, then select Update Account Balances from the pull-down menu.
3. The Update Account Balances window is displayed (Figure 10.5).
4. In the "Update this account's balance to:" field, enter the actual amount of cash you have on hand.
5. In the "Category for adjustment:" field, enter the category for the adjustment to be assigned to. Usually, you will use a category such as "Misc. cash" since the account discrepancy almost always represents small cash expenditures that you have not recorded individually.
6. Enter a date for the adjustment, then press **Enter**. Quicken enters an adjustment transaction in the account register to

▼ *Figure 10.5. The Update Account Balances Window*

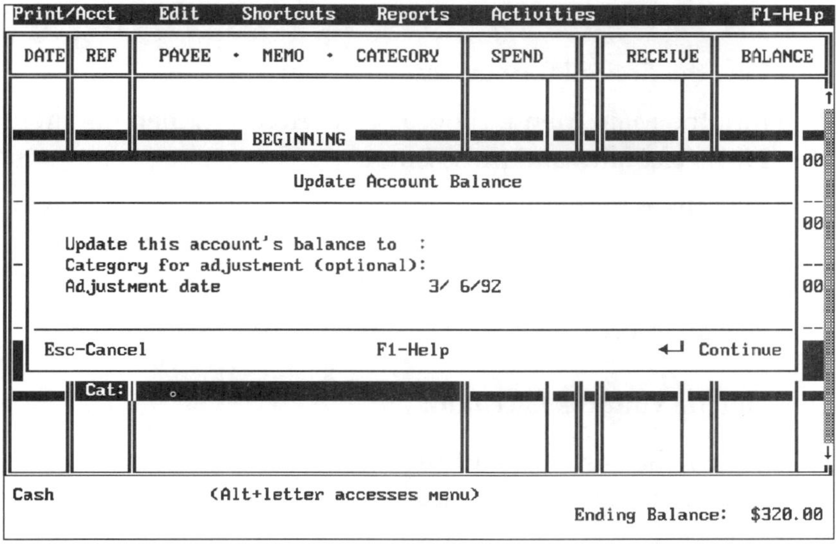

Reconciling Your Cash Account

bring the account balance into agreement with the actual amount of cash you have on hand (Figure 10.6).

▼ *Figure 10.6. Balance Adjustment Transaction Created by Quicken*

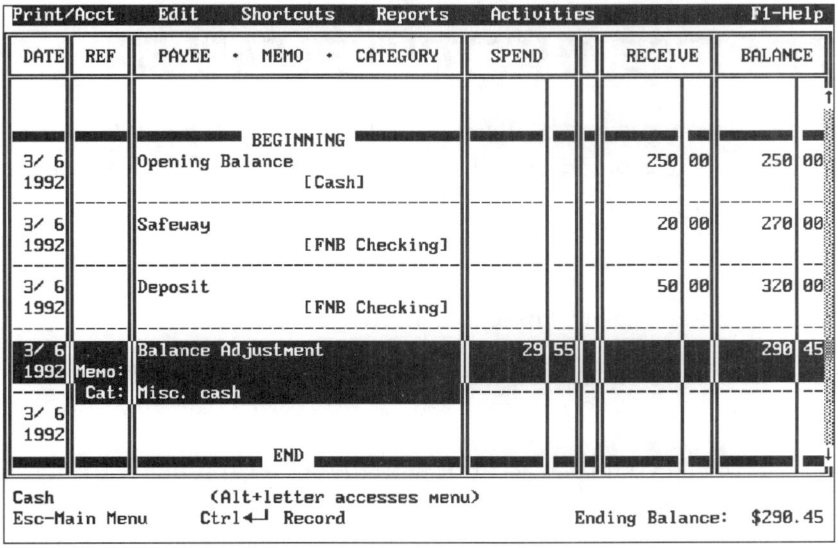

QUICK COMMAND SUMMARY

To set up a cash account:

1. Make the desired file current.
2. From the Main Menu, choose Select Account, then highlight <New Account> and press **Enter**.
3. Make the required entries in the Set Up New Account window. In the "Account Type:" field, enter **3**; for Balance, enter the amount of cash you have on hand.
4. Once all information has been entered, press **Ctrl+Enter**.

To reconcile your cash account:

1. Display the cash account register. Select Activities, then select Update Account Balances.
2. In the "Update this account's balance to:" field, enter the actual amount of cash you have on hand.
3. In the "Category for adjustment:" field, enter the category for the adjustment to be assigned to.
4. Enter a date for the adjustment, then press **Enter**. Quicken enters an adjustment transaction in the account register to bring the account into balance.

PRACTICE WHAT YOU'VE LEARNED

A cash account is handy when you want to keep track of your cash expenses. These practices will help you become familiar with using a cash account:

1. Set up a cash account.
2. Enter some cash transactions in the account.
3. Transfer some money from your checking account to the cash account.
4. Reconcile your cash account with the actual amount of cash you have on hand.

11

Investment Accounts

These days more and more people have investments. It's important to keep accurate investment records, both to make wise investment decisions and to provide information needed at tax time. Quicken is ideal for this task. This chapter introduces you to Quicken investment accounts and how to use them. You will learn

- **What an investment account is**
- **When you should use an investment account**
- **The differences between Quicken's two types of investment accounts**
- **Three approaches to starting an investment account**
- **How to set up a mutual fund investment account**
- **How to set up a regular investment account**

What Is an Investment Account?

As you probably know, an investment is something that you purchase in the hope that its value will increase, allowing you to sell it for a profit. Quicken investment accounts are specially designed to keep track of investments. Specifically, investment accounts are intended to keep track of investments that fluctuate in price.

For example, suppose you have invested in the stock market as a way of saving for your children's college expenses. When you purchase or sell stocks, you pay a commission to your broker. Stocks you own may pay dividends and will certainly fluctuate in price. All of these factors influence the value of your stock investment, determining how much it has increased or decreased in value. If you were entering all your investment transactions into a Quicken investment account, you would have instant access to all pertinent information about your account. You could quickly determine your account's current value, its percent gain or loss, and so on. With this information, you would be better able to make wise decisions about your investments.

An Investment Term Glossary

When discussing investments, there are some specialized terms that you should be familiar with. This section provides brief definitions of some of the most frequently used investment terms. If you are going to use Quicken to track your investments, you should become familiar with them. You'll see these terms when you start working with investment accounts and reports:

Security: A single investment that has a value and, in most cases, a specific share price (for instance, a stock, mutual fund, or bond).

Investment account: A group of one or more securities that you track together.

An Investment Term Glossary

Current market value: The total value of a security at its current price (or the most recently updated price).

Cost basis: The total cost of a security you purchased. The cost basis includes the price of the security as well as commissions, fees, and mutual fund loads. Cost basis also refers to all purchases, including reinvestment of capital gains distributions and dividends. It excludes the cost of shares that you have sold.

Average cost per share: The cost basis of a security divided by the total number of shares you own.

Unrealized gain or loss: The difference between the current market value of a security and its cost basis. If the current market value is greater than the cost basis, you have an unrealized gain; if the current market value is less than the cost basis, you have an unrealized loss. The term *unrealized* means that the gain or loss is on paper only, since you have not actually sold the security.

Realized gain or loss: The difference between the selling price of a security and its cost basis. If the selling price was greater than the cost basis, you have a realized gain; if the selling price was less than the cost basis you have a realized loss. The term *realized* means that the gain or loss is a real one, since you have actually sold the security.

Percent unrealized gain or loss: The unrealized gain for a security divided by its cost basis, then multiplied by 100.

Average annual total return: This is a percentage rate. It is equivalent to the interest rate on a bank account that would have been required to provide you with the same gain (or loss) on your investment over the same time period. Quicken's average annual total return calculations take into account all income from the security (interest payments, dividends, and capital gains distributions), as well as changes in share price.

Many people are confused by cost basis calculations when first working with investment accounts. Intuitively, you might think that "cost basis" would refer to the amount that you paid for a security, and that the difference between a security's cost basis and its current value would be equal to your profit (or loss) on the security. This is not the case, however, because cost basis includes the amounts paid for *all* shares of the security, even those purchased by reinvestment of dividends or interest. The following are two examples:

- ▲ You purchased 100 shares of a mutual fund at $10 a share, for a total expense of $1000. The fund paid $200 in dividends, which were reinvested to purchase another 20 shares at $10 a share. You now own 120 shares at $10 a share, and your investment is worth $1200—a gain of $200. The cost basis of this security is $1200, the total cost of shares purchased.
- ▲ You purchased 100 shares of a mutual fund at $10 a share, for a total expense of $1000. The fund paid no dividends, but its share price went up to $12. You now own 100 shares at $12 a share, and your investment is worth $1200—a gain of $200. The cost basis of this security is $1000, the total cost of shares purchased.

Keep these examples in mind when working with Quicken investment accounts. When viewing investment reports, remember that in many cases comparing cost basis with current value *does not* give a valid picture of your investment's performance.

When to Use an Investment Account

A Quicken investment account is ideal for many types of investments. Some investments, however, can be handled by either an investment account or by another type of account. The list below shows the type of account(s) recommended for different types of investments.

Type of Investment	**Quicken Account Type(s)**
Stocks or bonds	Investment
Mutual fund	Investment

When to Use an Investment Account

Type of Investment	Quicken Account Type(s)
Various stocks, bonds, and mutual funds in a brokerage account	Investment
Real estate investment trusts or partnerships	Investment
Unit trusts	Investment
IRA or Keogh accounts	Investment
Money market account with check writing	Bank
Cash management (checking account plus brokerage account)	Bank for checking, investment for rest
Fixed annuities	Investment or asset
CDs or treasury bills	Investment or asset
Employer retirement plans (pension, 401(k), 403(b), and so on)	Investment or asset
Real estate	Asset
Coins, stamps, and other collectibles	Investment or asset

Looking at this list, you'll see an *asset* account as an alternative for certain types of investments. You'll learn about asset accounts in Chapter 15. If you have an investment for which two types of Quicken accounts can be used, wait until you are familiar with both account types before making a choice.

Types of Investment Accounts

Quicken provides two types of investment accounts: mutual fund and regular. Each is suited for certain types of investments. You specify the account type when you first set up an investment account and, under certain circumstances, you can change an account from one type to another.

Mutual Fund Investment Account

The mutual fund investment account is designed specifically for mutual fund investments (which are currently very popular). This type of account:

- ▲ Can contain only a single security.
- ▲ Can contain security shares only; it cannot contain cash.
- ▲ Displays in the register the share balance and current market value for the single security.

Regular Investment Account

The regular investment account is used when you cannot, or do not want to, use a mutual fund investment account. A regular investment account:

- ▲ Can contain one or multiple securities.
- ▲ Can optionally contain a cash balance.
- ▲ Displays in the register the cash balance after every transaction and the current market value of all securities in the account (the pooled value).

Choosing an Account Type

The two types of Quicken investment accounts are similar in many ways: They both provide the same information about your investments and allow you to create the same types of investment reports. If your account will contain more than one security or will contain a cash balance, you have no choice but to use a regular investment account. For single security accounts, you can choose either account type. The difference between the two account types are:

Choosing an Account Type

- A regular investment account is more flexible. You can change the securities in it, add additional securities, and maintain a cash balance.
- A mutual fund investment account makes certain procedures a bit easier, particularly when transferring funds from a bank account to the investment account.

You can convert a mutual fund investment account to a regular investment account at any time. You can convert a regular investment account to a mutual fund investment account if the account contains only a single security and no cash balance.

Investment Account Options

Once you've decided on the type of investment account, you can start setting it up. You can, of course, create multiple investment accounts. In fact, it's a good idea to keep investments that have different purposes in different accounts. For example, you might have some investments for your children's college education and others for your retirement. You could even keep them in different files. Remember, however, that you cannot transfer money between accounts in different files, and you cannot create reports that summarize accounts in different files.

When you set up a Quicken investment account, you have three options as to how much historical information to include in the account. *Historical* information is a detailed record of your investment's past performance. Each option has advantages and disadvantages.

Setup with No Historical Information

The quickest way to set up an investment account is to simply enter the current status of your investments and ignore all historical information. This method lets you get started right away, and you always have the option of entering historical information at a later date if you decide it is necessary. When you use this method, you need the following information to start the Quicken account:

- The name of each security you own and its type (mutual fund, stock, and so on).
- The number of shares you own of each security.
- The current price per share of each security.
- Optionally, the cost basis for each security. (See the definition of cost basis earlier in this chapter.)

There are, however, several limitations that result if you omit all historical information:

- Because Quicken does not have complete information on your securities for the current year, it cannot produce reports for tax preparation purposes.
- You will have to wait at least several months before Quicken has enough data to calculate valid investment performance figures.
- If you do not enter the security's cost basis, Quicken will not provide accurate figures for average cost per share, percent gain, realized gain (if you sell), and unrealized gain (since these figures all depend on the cost basis of a security).

Setup with All Historical Information

To enable Quicken to create a complete picture of your investment's past performance, you must enter all historical data for your securities when you set up the account. You will need the following information for each of your securities:

- The name and type of each security.
- The date and amount of your initial purchase, and the number of shares bought (or the price per share).

Investment Account Options

- All subsequent changes in holdings, including purchases, reinvestment of dividends, sales, stock splits, gifts, and return of capital.
- All non-reinvested interest, dividends, and capital gains for the current year.
- Optionally, the non-reinvested interest, dividends, and capital gains for earlier years. Entering this information allows Quicken to calculate a more accurate investment performance value for past years, but does not affect cost basis calculations.
- The current price per share, and the price per share at the end of each year.

The only disadvantage to entering complete historical data is the time and effort required to locate and enter all of it. As compensation for all that work, you'll have the advantage that your investment reports will be complete and accurate. You can confidently use them for tax preparation, investment analysis, and other purposes.

Setup with This Year's Information

As a middle ground between entering no historical information and entering all historical information, you can enter only data for the current year. To do so, you will need the following:

- The name and type of each security.
- The number of shares owned and the share price at the end of last year.
- Optionally, the cost basis of the shares you owned at the end of last year.
- Details of all transactions during the current year.
- The current price per share.

There are both advantages and disadvantages to using this method to start a Quicken investment account:

- ▲ It is usually not too difficult to locate and enter the required information.
- ▲ Reports on income, performance, and unrealized gains are accurate for time periods starting with the beginning of the year, but not for periods before that.
- ▲ If you do not enter the security's cost basis, Quicken will not provide accurate figures for average cost per share, percent gain, realized gain (if you sell), and unrealized gain (since these figures all depend on the cost basis of a security).
- ▲ The capital gains report does not give the correct purchase date if you sell the security.
- ▲ Quicken can accurately report investment income for the current year. This value can be used when preparing tax schedule B.

You now know the basics of Quicken investment accounts and should be able to decide on the account type suitable for you, as well as the amount of historical data you will be entering. The next section shows you the actual steps you need to take to set up a Quicken investment account.

Setting Up an Investment Account

By reviewing the information just presented, you should be able to decide which approach to take when starting your own Quicken investment account. You will probably want to use either the second or third approach, entering the historical information for this year or for the life of your investment. The first method—omitting all historical information—may seem like a time-saver now, but it places significant limitations on the investment reports you'll be able to create.

Setting Up an Investment Account

To begin setting up an investment account:

1. From the Main Menu, choose Select Account. Quicken displays the Select Account to Use window.
2. Press the **Up** arrow key to highlight <New account> at the top of the list, then press **Enter**. Quicken displays the Set Up New Account window (Figure 11.1).
3. In the "Account Type:" field, enter **6** to specify that you're setting up an investment account.

TIP

Remember, to move the cursor forward and backward between fields in a window, press *Tab* and *Shift+Tab*.

4. In the "Name for this account:" field, enter the account name. The name can be up to 15 characters long and can contain letters, numbers, and spaces (but not the characters [,], /, or :). Use a descriptive name such as "Mike's 403(b)" or "college fund." If the account will be for a single mutual fund, use the fund name for the account name.

▼ Figure 11.1. The Set Up New Account Window

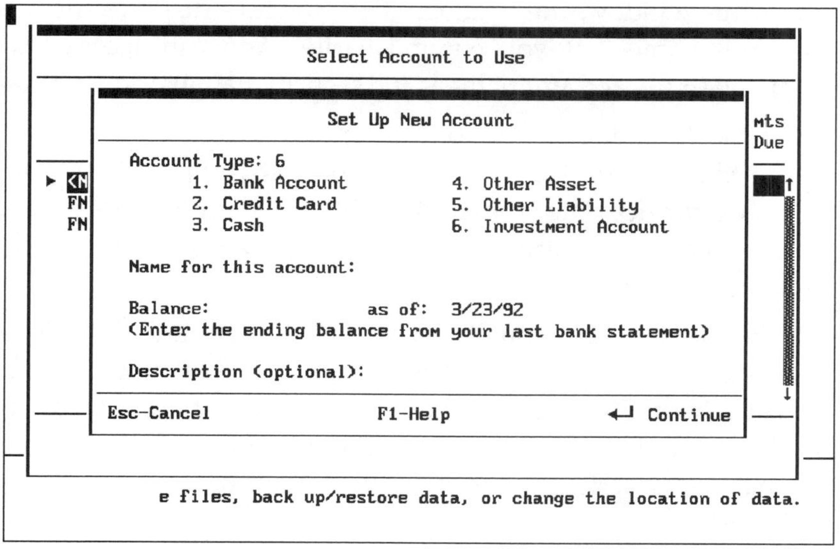

5. In the "Account is a single mutual fund:" field, enter **Y** to set up a mutual fund investment account, **N** to set up a regular investment account. Remember, a mutual fund account can contain only a single mutual fund, while a regular account can contain multiple securities.
6. In the "Description:" field, enter an account description. The description can be up to 21 characters long.
7. Check over the entries you have made in this window to ensure they are correct. Once you are satisfied that everything is okay, press **F10** to continue.

The next setup steps depend on the type of account you are setting up.

Mutual Fund Investment Account

If you're setting up a mutual fund investment account (that is, if you entered **Y** in Step 5 above), follow these steps to complete account setup.

1. When you press **F10** to leave the Set Up New Account window, Quicken displays the Set Up Mutual Fund Security window (Figure 11.2).
2. In this window, the "Name:" field initially displays the account name that you entered earlier. You can accept this name (if the account name is the security name) or change it.
3. In the "Symbol:" field, you can optionally enter the symbol for the security. This is necessary only if you plan to import security price data from a file, or if you want to track different lots of a security. Otherwise, you can leave this field blank.
4. The "Type:" field initially displays "Mutual Fund." If this is correct, accept it. If the account is for another type of security, press **Ctrl+L** (with the cursor in the "Type:" field) to display a list of security types (Figure 11.3). Select the type that best describes the security, then press **Enter**.

Setting Up an Investment Account

▼ *Figure 11.2. The Set Up Mutual Fund Security Window*

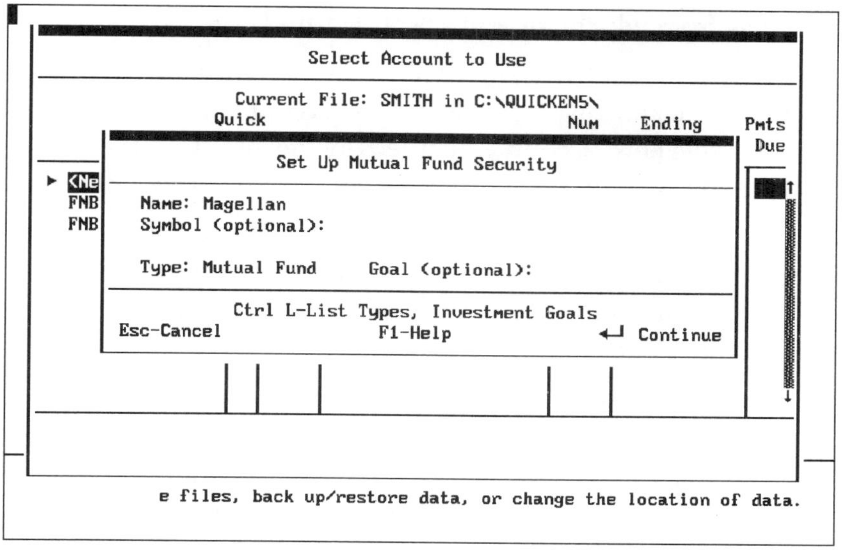

5. In the "Goal:" field, you can optionally enter a goal for this investment (for instance, college or retirement). If you enter goals for your investment accounts, Quicken can group data

▼ *Figure 11.3. The Security Type List*

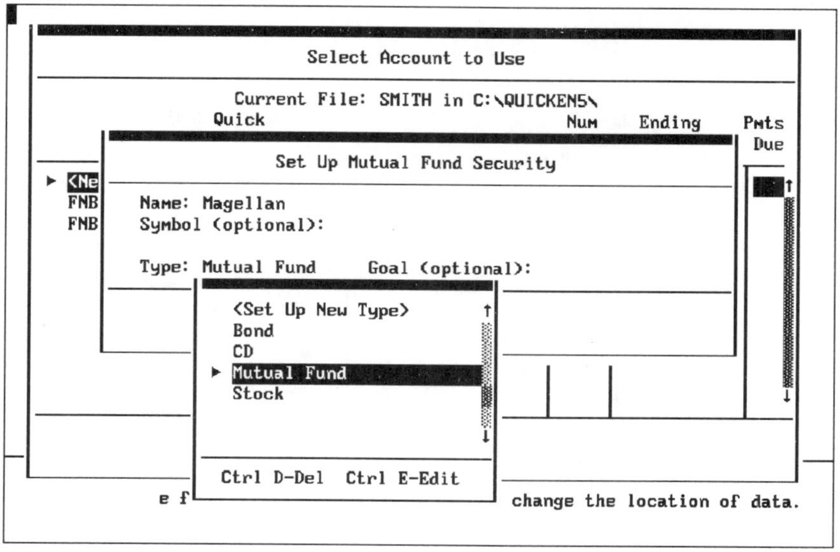

by investment goal in investment reports. Type in a goal or with the cursor in this field, press **Ctrl+L** to display a list of goals from which you can select (Figure 11.4).

6. Check your entries to be sure they are correct, then press **F10**. Quicken displays the Select Account to Use window with the new account included in the list. Use the arrow keys to highlight the new account name, then press **Enter**.
7. Quicken displays the Create Opening Share Balance window (Figure 11.5). The actions you take now depend on the amount of historical information you will be entering in the account. For example:
   - ▲ If you plan to enter full historical information for this account, *do not* make any entries in this window. Rather, press **Esc** to close the window and display the investment account register. Next, proceed with Step 3 under the section *Regular Investment Account,* later in this chapter.
   - ▲ If you are not entering any historical information into this account, enter today's date in the "Create Opening Balance as of:" field. Then, enter the number of shares

▼ *Figure 11.4. The Investment Goal List*

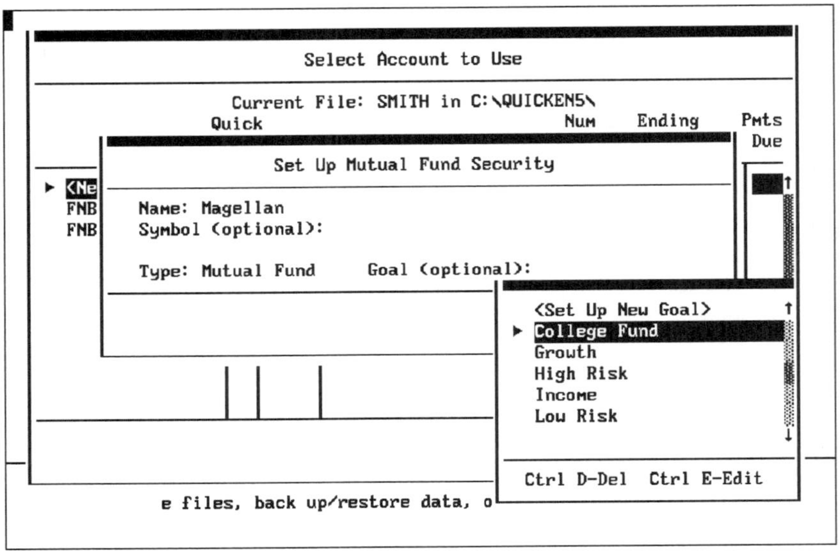

Setting Up an Investment Account

▼ *Figure 11.5. The Create Opening Share Balance Window*

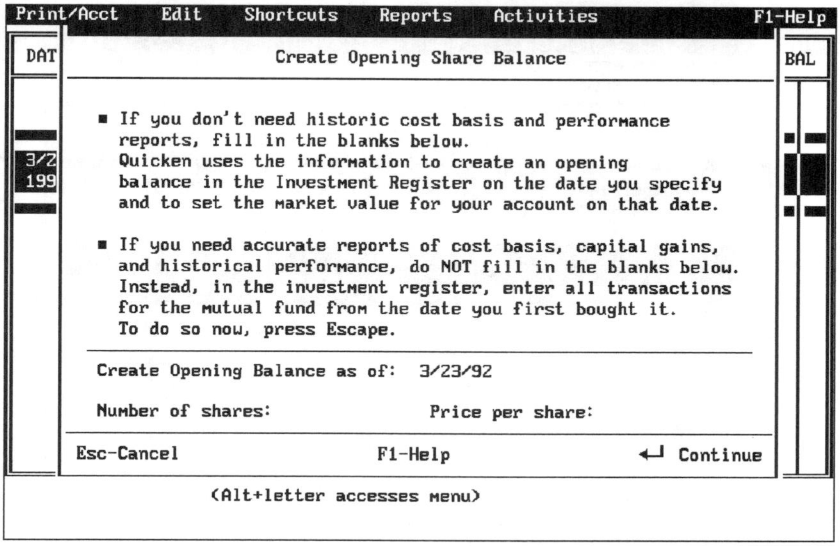

you own and the current price per share in the corresponding fields.

▲ If you plan to enter this year's historical information in the account, enter **12/31** of last year in the "Create Opening Balance as of:" field. Then, enter the number of shares you owned and the price per share at the end of last year in the corresponding fields.

8. After checking that your entries in the Create Opening Share Balance window are correct, press **F10**. Quicken displays the investment account register with the opening balance entered as the first transaction (Figure 11.6). Note that the register has a field named ACTION, and for the first transaction this field contains "ShrsIn." This is an abbreviation for "shares in," indicating that this transaction added security shares to the account. You'll learn more about the other parts of the mutual fund investment account register in Chapter 12.
9. If you are not entering historical information into the account, you are finished. Press **Esc** to close the account register. As future account transactions occur, you will enter them

▼ ***Figure 11.6. The Initial Share Balance, Displayed in the Account Register***

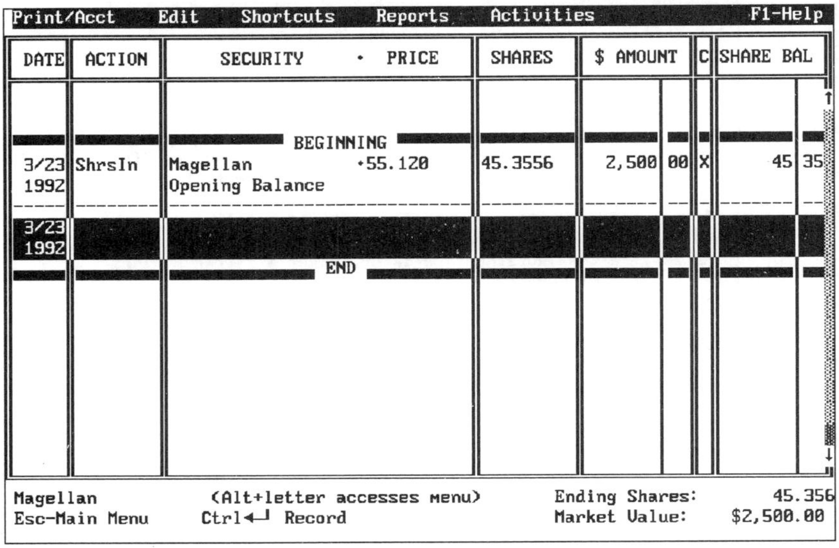

in the register. Entering investment transactions is covered in Chapter 12.

10. If you will be entering historical information for the current year, then the share price that you entered for your security was the price as of the end of last year. At this point, you can optionally update the account to reflect the current share price. To do so, select Activities from the Register screen, then select Update Prices from the pull-down menu. The Update Prices and Market Value screen is displayed (Figure 11.7). This screen lists all securities in the account (there will be only one security in a mutual fund investment account) and, in the Mkt Price field, the most recent price per share for the security. To update the price, move the cursor to the Mkt Price field and type in the current share price (obtained from your newspaper's business section or your most recent account statement). Then, press **Ctrl+Enter** to record the new price and **Esc** to return to the register.

11. As you've probably noticed, you still need to enter the historical information for this account. This is done by enter-

▼ ***Figure 11.7. The Update Prices and Market Value Screen***

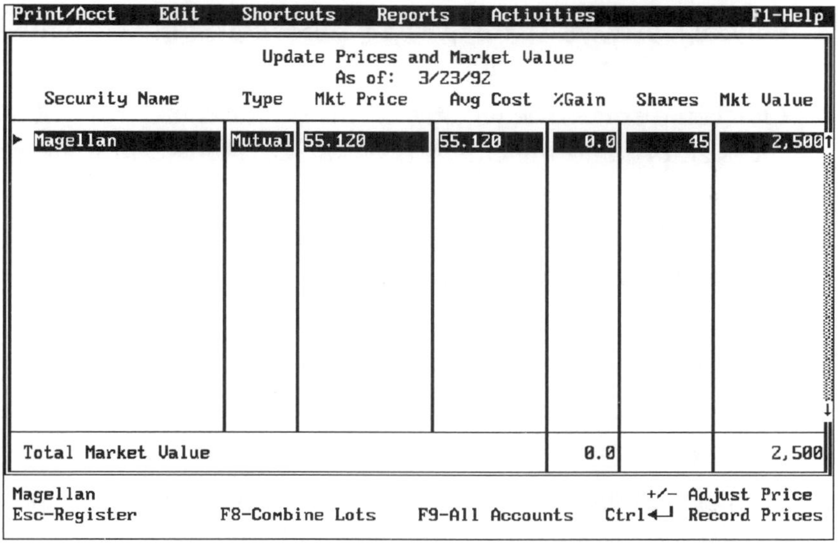

ing all of the account transactions that have occurred since January 1. You will learn the details of entering investment account transactions in Chapter 12. For now, press **Esc** to close the account register. Once you've completed this chapter and are ready to start the next, you can redisplay the account register and enter your historical transactions.

Regular Investment Account

The procedure for setting up a regular investment account involves making some entries in the account register, which is covered below. The complete details of working with an investment account register are presented in Chapter 12. If you feel unsure about following the steps below, you may wish to read Chapter 12 then come back to complete your account setup.

To complete setup of a regular investment account:

1. When you complete the final step in preliminary setup for a regular investment account (as detailed earlier in this chapter), Quicken displays the Select Account to Use window.

Use the arrow keys to highlight the name of the new account, then press **Enter**.

2. Quicken displays a message about first-time setup. Read this, then press **Enter** to continue.
3. Quicken displays the register for the new account. The register is empty, and the cursor is on the DATE field in the first transaction (Figure 11.8).
4. Enter a date in the DATE field according to the historical information option you have decided on:
   - ▲ For no historical information, enter today's date (which is already displayed in the field).
   - ▲ For this year's historical information, enter **12/31** of last year.
   - ▲ For complete historical information, enter the date of your earliest acquisition of any security in the account.
5. Once the date is entered, press **Tab** or **Enter** to move the cursor to the ACTION field. Type **ShrsIn**, then press **Enter** or **Tab**. "ShrsIn" is an abbreviation for "shares in," meaning

▼ ***Figure 11.8. The Account Register***

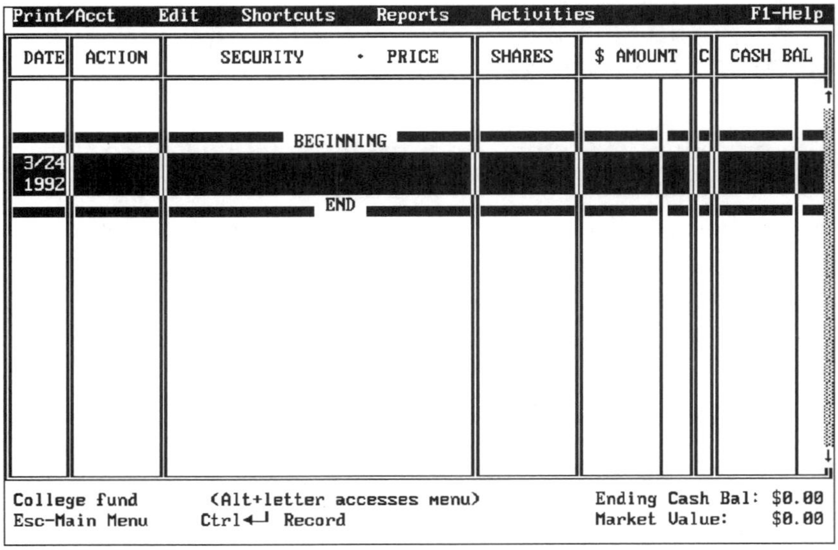

Setting Up an Investment Account

that this transaction added shares to the account. You'll learn more about the different account actions in Chapter 12.

6. With the cursor on the SECURITY field, enter the name of the security then press **Enter** or **Tab**. Quicken compares the security name with the list it maintains of all securities in your investment accounts. If the security name is found on the list, the cursor moves to the PRICE field, and you can continue with Step 11. If the name is not found, Quicken displays the Security Not Found window and gives you the choice of adding the security to the list or selecting from the security list. Select Add Security to List.
7. Quicken displays the Set Up Security window (Figure 11.9). In this window, the "Name:" field displays the security name that you entered in the register.
8. In the "Symbol:" field, you can enter the symbol for the security. This is necessary only if you plan to import security price data from a file, or if you want to track different lots of a security. Otherwise, you can leave this field blank.
9. In the "Type:" field, enter the type of security (stock, bond, and so on). You can enter the security type directly, or press **Ctrl+L**

▼ *Figure 11.9 Set Up Security Window*

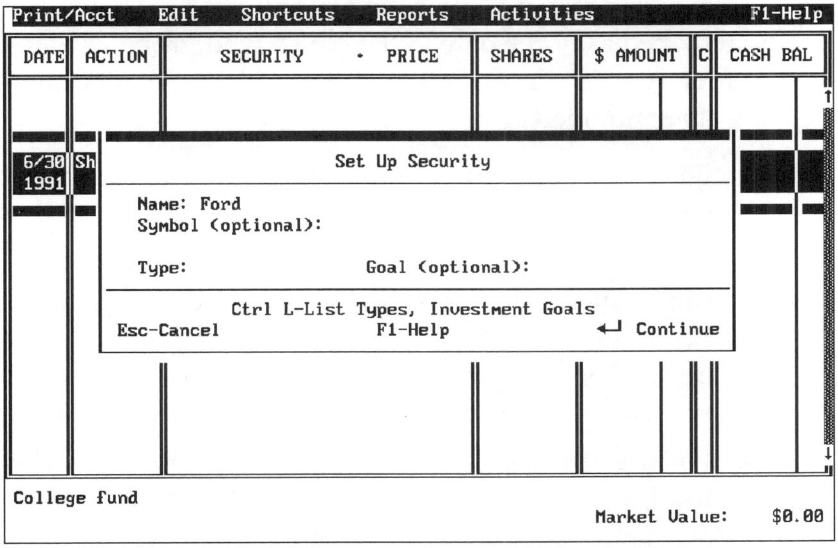

to display a list of security types (Figure 11.3) from which you select.

10. In the "Goal:" field, you can optionally enter a goal for this investment (for instance, college or retirement). If you enter goals for your investment accounts, Quicken can group data by goal in your investment reports. Type in a goal or, with the cursor on this field, press **Ctrl+L** to display a list of goals from which you can select (Figure 11.4). Press **Enter** to continue.

11. The PRICE field is for the price per share of the security. Make an entry in this field as follows:

    - If you're entering no historical information or one year's historical information, enter the cost per share (including commissions, loads, and fees) *if* you purchased all shares at one time. Otherwise, leave the price field blank.

    - If you're entering complete historical information, enter the cost per share (including commissions, loads, and fees) for your initial purchase of the security. You can leave the PRICE field blank and enter a total dollar amount in the $ AMOUNT field, and Quicken will calculate the proper share price for you (see Step 13).

12. In the SHARES field, enter the total number of shares that you owned as of the date in the DATE field, using as many as four decimal places. Follow these guidelines when entering share numbers:

    - For a stock or mutual fund, enter the actual number of shares.

    - For a bond, enter ten times the number of bonds owned (this matches the way that bond prices are quoted). Likewise, enter 0.01 times the total face value of the bonds. For example, if you own four bonds worth $4000, you would enter **40**.

    - For a certificate of deposit (CD) or a money market fund, enter the total dollar value. (In these types of accounts, one share = one dollar.)

Setting Up an Investment Account

- For precious metals, enter the number of ounces owned.
- For collectibles, enter **1**.

13. The $ AMOUNT field holds the total dollar cost of the transaction. Make an entry in this field as follows:
    - If you are entering no historical information or one year's historical information, leave this field blank.
    - If you are entering complete historical information, enter the total cost of the initial transaction, including commissions, fees, and so on.

TIP

For any investment transaction, the total cost is equal to the number of shares times the price per share. Expressed in terms of Quicken register fields, ($ AMOUNT) = (PRICE) x (SHARES). If you fill in any two of these fields, Quicken will automatically calculate the third and make the entry for you.

14. In the MEMO field, you can optionally enter a memo about the transaction.
15. Check your entries for accuracy, then press **F10**. Quicken records the transaction and updates the "Market Value:" field in the lower-right corner of the screen (Figure 11.10).
16. If the account will contain more than one security, repeat Steps 4 through 15 for each security.
17. If you are not entering any historical information, you are almost finished. Proceed to Step 19.
18. If you are entering historical information, you must enter all subsequent transactions for each security in the account. You will learn the details of entering investment account transactions in Chapter 12. For now, press **Esc** to close the account register. Once you've completed this chapter and are ready to start the next, you can redisplay the account register and enter your historical transactions, then proceed with Step 19.
19. At this point, your investment account should contain all of the relevant transactions, depending on the amount of

▼ *Figure 11.10. The "Updated Market Value:" Field*

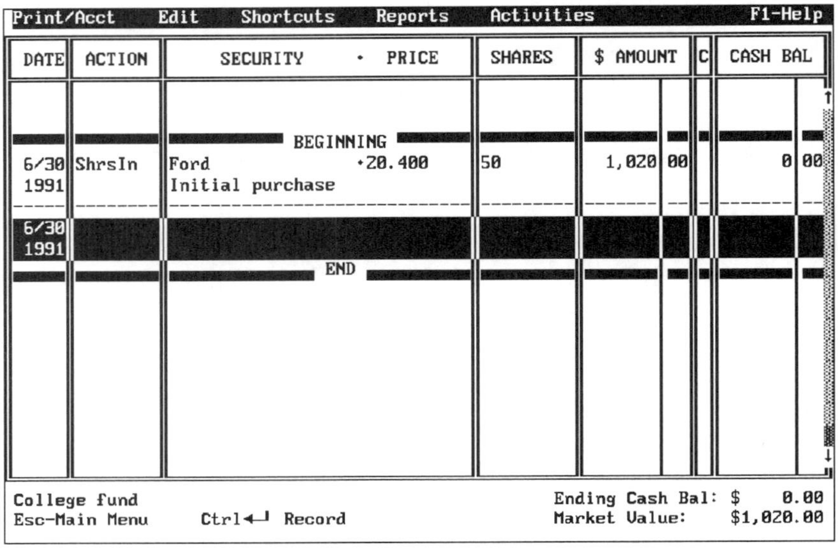

historical information you entered. You should now check the account balances against your most recent account statement(s) to verify that your Quicken account is accurate. You should check the share balances for each security and the cash balance. If everything checks out, you are finished and your investment account is set up. If not, check the following:

- ▲ If there is a discrepancy in a share balance for one or more securities, it is most likely due to your having made an error when entering transactions. Display the account register and review the transactions, correcting any errors you find.
- ▲ If there is a discrepancy in the account's cash balance, you need to make an adjustment. From the Register screen, select Activities, Adjust Balance, then Adjust Cash Balance. In the Adjust Cash Balance window (Figure 11.11), enter the correct cash balance for the account, then press **Enter** twice. Quicken creates a cash balance adjustment transaction in the register to bring the account's cash balance into balance (Figure 11.12).

Setting Up an Investment Account

▼ *Figure 11.11. The Adjust Cash Balance Window*

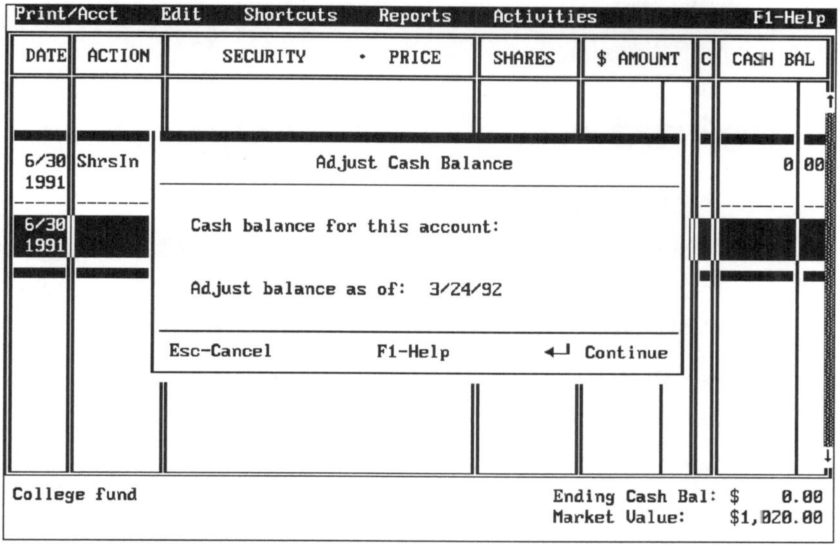

▼ *Figure 11.12. Balance Adjustment Transaction Added to the Account Register*

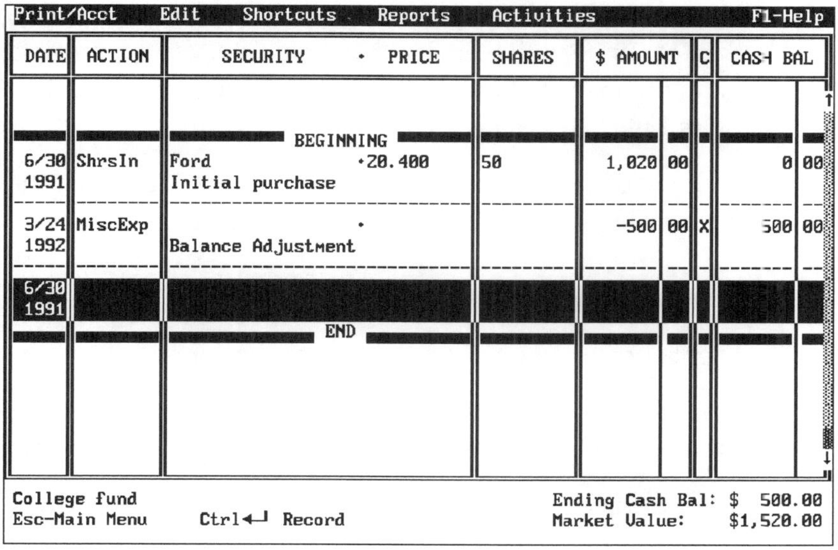

CHECK YOURSELF

Set up an investment account, using either your own account information or a fictional account.

ANSWER

1. Choose Select Account, then select <New Account>.
2. Fill in the needed account information. In the "Account is a single mutual fund:" field, enter **Y** to set up a mutual fund investment account, **N** to set up a regular investment account.
3. Press **F10**, then continue with the steps below, depending on the type of account you are setting up.

For a mutual fund account:

4. Enter the name and type of the account security, then enter the security symbol and the account's investment goal (if desired).
5. Press **F10**.
6. Highlight the name of the new account, then press **Enter**.
7. If you plan to enter complete historical information, press **Esc**, then continue with Step 8. Otherwise, enter the appropriate date, number of shares, and share price information, then press **F10**.
8. Quicken displays the investment account register. Enter the historical information transactions, if necessary.

For a regular investment account:

4. Highlight the name of the new account, then press **Enter** twice.
5. Enter the first transaction for one security. If necessary, enter information about the security in the Set Up Security window.
6. Enter the necessary historical transactions for the security.
7. Repeat Steps 4 through 6 for all other securities in the account.

Updating Share Prices

Updating Share Prices

The account market value that Quicken calculates is based on the most recent share prices that you entered. To obtain an accurate market value, you must enter the current share price for each security in the account. To do so, display the account register then press **Ctrl+U**, or select Activities, then select Update Prices. Quicken displays the Update Prices and Market Value screen (shown earlier in Figure 11.7). In this window, enter the current price per share for each security in the Mkt Price field, then press **Ctrl+Enter**. Quicken records the updated prices and recalculates the account's market value accordingly.

QUICK COMMAND SUMMARY

To start setting up an investment account of either type:

1. From the Main Menu, choose Select Account, then select <New Account>.
2. Fill in the needed information in the window that is displayed. In the "Account Type:" field, enter **6** to specify an investment account. In the "Account is a single mutual fund:" field, enter **Y** if you're setting up a mutual fund investment account, **N** if you're setting up a regular investment account.
3. When all data in the window is complete, press **F10**, then continue with the appropriate steps for the type of account you are setting up.

To complete setting up a mutual fund investment account:

1. After pressing **F10** (Step 3 above) another window is displayed. In the corresponding fields in this window, enter the name and type of the account security, and optionally enter the security symbol and the investment goal for the account. When you are finished, press **F10**.
2. The Select Account to Use window is displayed. Highlight the name of the new account, then press **Enter**.

3. Quicken displays the Create Opening Share Balance window. If you plan to enter complete historical information, you do not need to make any entries here. Press **Esc**, then continue with Step 4. Otherwise, enter the appropriate date, number of shares, and share price information, then press **F10**.
4. Quicken displays the register for the investment account. If you are entering historical information for the account, enter the transactions now.

To complete setting up a regular investment account:

1. After pressing **F10** (Step 3 above) Quicken displays the Select Account to Use window. Highlight the name of the new account, then press **Enter**.
2. Read the message that is displayed, then press **Enter** again.
3. The account register is displayed. Enter the first transaction for one security. The exact information you enter will depend on the amount of historical information you plan to enter.
4. If the security name is new to Quicken, enter information about the security in the Set Up Security window.
5. If you are entering historical information, enter the appropriate transactions for this security.
6. Repeat Steps 3 through 5 for all other securities in the account.

PRACTICE WHAT YOU'VE LEARNED

This chapter has shown you how to set up the two types of Quicken investment accounts. Practice setting up a Quicken account for your own investments. Don't worry about making mistakes because you can always correct them later.

12

Using Investment Accounts

Now that you have been introduced to the basics of Quicken investment accounts, you're ready to start learning the details. This chapter covers the most important investment account activities. You will learn

- **The components of the investment account register**
- **The types of investment account actions and how to enter them**
- **How to enter a security in a transaction**
- **How to work with the security list**
- **How to deal with commissions and fees**
- **How to enter transactions that involve transfers**

The Investment Account Register

Some components of the investment account register will be familiar to you because they are also found in the Quicken bank account register. Other components are new. Remember that Quicken offers two types of investment accounts: the mutual fund account and the regular account. These two investment account types have slightly different registers, as shown in Figures 12.1 and 12.2.

Remember, the differences between these two investment account types are:

- ▲ A mutual fund account can contain only a single security and cannot contain a cash balance.
- ▲ A regular account can contain multiple securities and can contain a cash balance.

▼ *Figure 12.1. The Regular Investment Account Register Screen*

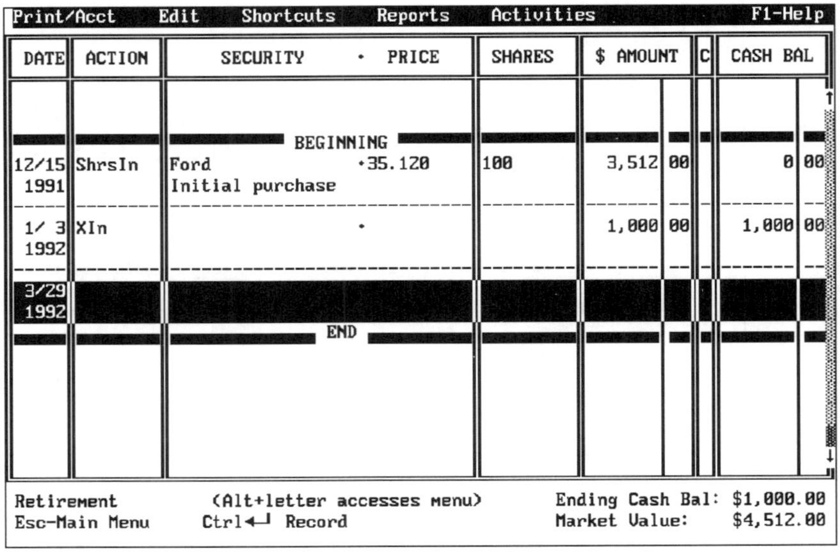

The Investment Account Register

▼ *Figure 12.2. The Mutual Fund Investment Account Register Screen*

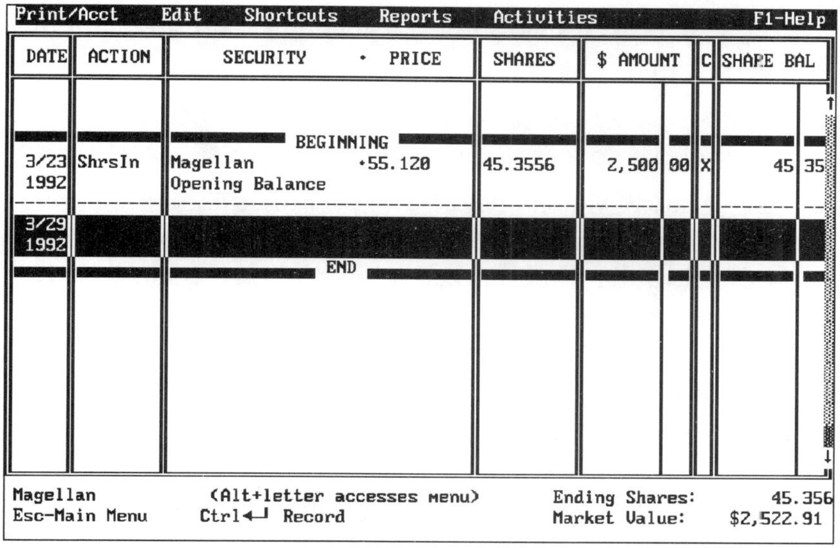

These account differences are reflected in the register screens. But first, look at the components of the register screens that are common to the two account types.

- ▲ The DATE field records the date of each transaction.
- ▲ The ACTION field specifies the nature of the transaction, such as shares sold or purchased, dividends reinvested, and so on. You'll learn more about the various investment account actions later in this chapter.
- ▲ The SECURITY field records the name of the security involved in the transaction. In a mutual fund account, this will always be the single security in the account. In a regular account, this field can contain various security names. Note, however, that each individual transaction is for a single security only.
- ▲ The PRICE field records the per-share price of the security.
- ▲ The SHARE field records the number of shares that the transaction involved.

- The $ AMOUNT field records the total dollar amount of the transaction.
- The C (Cleared) field indicates whether the transaction has been cleared.
- The "Memo:" field (directly below the SECURITY field) can be used to hold a note about the transaction.
- The "Market Value:" field is not part of an individual transaction, but is located in the lower-right corner of the screen. It displays the total market value of the account, based on the most recently entered share prices.

The register screens for the two account types differ in the field located in the right-most column on the screen:

- In the mutual fund account register, this field is called SHARE BAL (share balance). This field displays the total number of shares of the account's single security that are owned after each transaction. The current share balance is also displayed in the lower-right corner of the screen.
- In the regular account register, this field is called CASH BAL (cash balance). This field displays the account's cash balance after each transaction. The current cash balance is also displayed in the lower-right corner of the screen.

Using the Investment Account Register

Many actions you take in the investment account register are the same as you have already learned for the checking account register. You use the same procedures to:

- Move the cursor between fields.
- Enter and edit information in a field.
- Change the date.
- Record a transaction.
- Add a new transaction or delete an existing transaction.
- Scroll through the register.

The Investment Account Register

The major differences between the investment account register and the checking account register are in the ACTION and SECURITY fields.

The ACTION Field

When you enter a transaction in an investment register, the ACTION field describes the nature of the transaction. For example:

- ▲ You are buying or selling shares.
- ▲ You are transferring shares or cash into or out of the account.
- ▲ You have received or reinvested interest, dividends, capital gains, or return of capital from a security.
- ▲ You are paying interest on your margin account.
- ▲ Shares have split.

To maintain accurate account records and create valid reports, it's important that the ACTION field entry be correct for each transaction. This can be a bit confusing, since many of the "action" terms will not be familiar to you if you are new to investing. The statements you receive from your broker or mutual fund will contain detailed information on each transaction, and you can use that information to determine which action to assign your Quicken transactions to. The various actions are divided into a number of categories. Those actions marked with an asterisk are available only with regular investment accounts, not with mutual fund investment accounts.

The "Add/Remove shares" category describes when shares are added to or removed from the account. When you add shares, the shares (or money used to buy them) do not come from a Quicken account. When you remove shares, the shares (or proceeds of the sale) do not go to a Quicken account. The actions in this category are:

ShrsIn Adds shares to the account

ShrsOut Removes shares from the account

The "Buy shares" category describes when you purchase shares using money in a Quicken account. The actions in this category are:

Buy* Buys shares using money in the investment account.

BuyX Buys shares using money transferred from another Quicken account.

The "Capital Gains distr(ibutions)" category describes when a security pays you cash based on capital gains. Note that the capital gains actions listed below distinguish between long-term and short-term capital gains. This is because Federal tax laws used to tax these two types of capital gains at different rates. As of this writing, the tax code no longer treats long- and short-term capital gains differently, but Quicken provides the two categories just in case the law changes again. The actions in this category are:

CGLong* Receives cash from long-term capital gains distribution and keeps it in the investment account.

CGLongX Receives cash from long-term capital gains distribution and transfers it out of the investment account.

CGShort* Receives cash from short-term capital gains distribution and keeps it in the investment account.

CGShortX Receives cash from short-term capital gains distribution and transfers it out of the investment account.

The Dividends category describes cash that you receive from security dividend income. The actions in this category are:

Div* Receives cash from dividends and keeps it in investment account.

DivX Receives cash from dividends and transfers it out of investment account.

The Interest category refers to interest you pay or receive. The actions in this category are:

IntInc* Receives cash from interest paid on the account's cash balance.

MargInt* Pays interest on a margin loan using cash in the account.

The Reinvest category refers to purchasing additional security shares using money from interest, dividends, or capital gains. Note that many investments, particularly mutual funds, are usually set up to automatically reinvest income. The actions in this category are:

ReinvDiv Purchases shares using funds from income or dividend distributions.

ReinvInt Purchases shares using funds from interest distributions.

ReinvLG Purchases shares using long-term capital gains distributions.

ReinvSG Purchases shares using short-term capital gains distributions.

The "Sell shares" category describes when you sell security shares held in the account. The actions in this category are:

Sell* Sells shares and leaves the cash proceeds in the account.

SellX Sells shares and transfers the cash proceeds to another Quicken account.

The "Transfer cash" category describes the moving of cash between an investment account and another Quicken account. The actions in this category are:

XIn* Transfers cash into the investment account from another Quicken account.

XOut* Transfers cash out of the investment account into another Quicken account.

The "Other transactions" category covers several miscellaneous actions:

MiscExp* Miscellaneous expenses paid using cash in the account.

MiscInc* Miscellaneous income, with cash left in the account.

Reminder Reminds you of upcoming events related to the security. This "action" works in conjunction with the Billminder program. Further details are given later in this chapter.

RtrnCap* Receives cash from the return of capital.

StkSplit Changes the number of shares and price of a security due to a stock split.

Entering Actions in the ACTION Field

When you are entering transactions in the investment register, you can simply type the action directly in the ACTION field.

Quicken also offers some special features that make it easier to enter actions:

1. Type the first few letters of the desired action, then press **Enter** or **Tab**. If the letters you typed match only one action, Quicken enters that action in the ACTION field and moves the cursor to the next field. If the letters match more than one action, Quicken displays a list of matching actions. Highlight the correct action, then press **Enter**; Quicken enters it in the ACTION field.
2. Move the cursor to the ACTION field, then press **Ctrl+L**. Quicken displays a list of action categories (Figure 12.3). Select the desired action category and Quicken displays a short list of related actions for you to choose from.

When you are working with a mutual fund investment account, the action list contains only those actions that are applicable to that account type.

The Investment Account Register

▼ Figure 12.3. The Quicken Action List

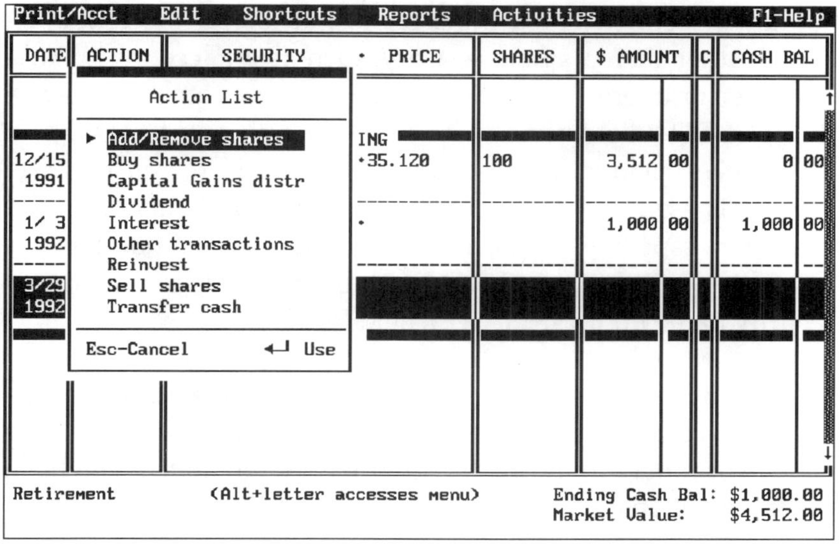

CHECK YOURSELF

Practice using Quicken's action list to enter an action into an investment account transaction.

ANSWER

1. Display the investment account register.
2. Move the cursor to the ACTION field.
3. Press **Ctrl+L** to display the action List.
4. Use the Up and Down arrow keys to highlight the desired action, then press **Enter**.
5. If necessary, select from the short list that is displayed.

The SECURITY Field

The SECURITY field records the name of the individual security that the transaction affects. In a mutual fund investment account, which can contain only a single security, Quicken automatically fills in the SECURITY field with the name of the account's security. For a transaction that affects the entire account rather than a single security, such as an account maintenance fee or interest earned on a cash balance, you should leave the SECURITY field blank.

Quicken maintains a list of all securities in the current file. This list is used to verify security names that you enter (to guard against misspellings) and also to provide some shortcuts for entering security names. You have three methods for entering a security name in the SECURITY field:

1. Type in the full security name, then press **Enter** or **Tab**. If the name matches one in the security list, it is entered and the cursor moves to the next field. If it does not match, you have three options:

   - ▲ Press **Esc**, then edit the security name.
   - ▲ Add the new name to the security list.
   - ▲ Select a name from the security list.

2. Type in the first few letters of the security name (enough to distinguish it from any other name on the list), then press **Enter** or **Tab**. Quicken fills in the entire name.
3. With the cursor in the SECURITY field, press **Ctrl+Y**; or select Shortcuts from the menu, then select Security List from the pull-down menu. Quicken displays the Security List window (Figure 12.4). Use the Up and Down arrow keys to highlight the desired security name, then press **Enter**.

The Security List

As you've seen, you can use the security list to enter a security name in the transaction register. This list provides several columns of information about each security (Figure 12.4).

- ▲ The Security column lists the security name.
- ▲ The Symbol column lists the security's symbol, if you entered one when setting up the security.

The Investment Account Register

▼ *Figure 12.4. The Security List Window*

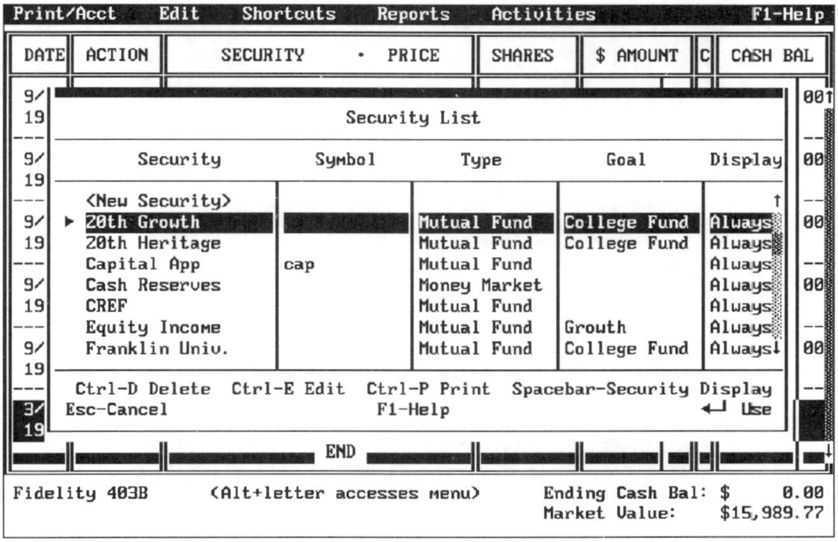

▲ The Type column lists the type of the security—stock, mutual fund, and so on.

▲ The Goal column lists the investment goal associated with the security, if you entered a goal when setting up the security.

▲ The Display column determines whether the security is displayed on the Update Prices and Market Value screen (described later in this chapter). To change a security's display status, highlight the security name, then press **Spacebar** one or more times to switch between the following display options:

Always—the security is always displayed.

Never—the security is never displayed.

Open—the security is displayed only if you own it, or a short position in it, as of the current date.

There are several commands you can issue while in the Security List window:

▲ Press **Ctrl+D** to delete the highlighted security. Quicken asks for confirmation before deleting. You cannot delete a security for which you have any transactions.

- ▲ Press **Ctrl+E** to edit information about the highlighted security. The Edit Security window will be displayed. In this window, you can modify the security name, symbol, type, and goal. If you modify the security name, Quicken automatically makes the change in all transactions involving the security.
- ▲ Press **Ctrl+P** to print a copy of the security list.

Adding a New Security

You must add securities to the security list when first setting up your investment account (as described in Chapter 11). You'll also need to add securities as you modify and expand your investments. You add a security using the Set Up Security window (Figure 12.5). There are two ways to display this window:

1. Display the Security List window, highlight the selection <New Security> at the top of the list, then press **Enter**.
2. Enter the new security name in the SECURITY field of a register transaction, press **Enter**, then select "Add to Security List."

▼ ***Figure 12.5. The Set Up Security Window***

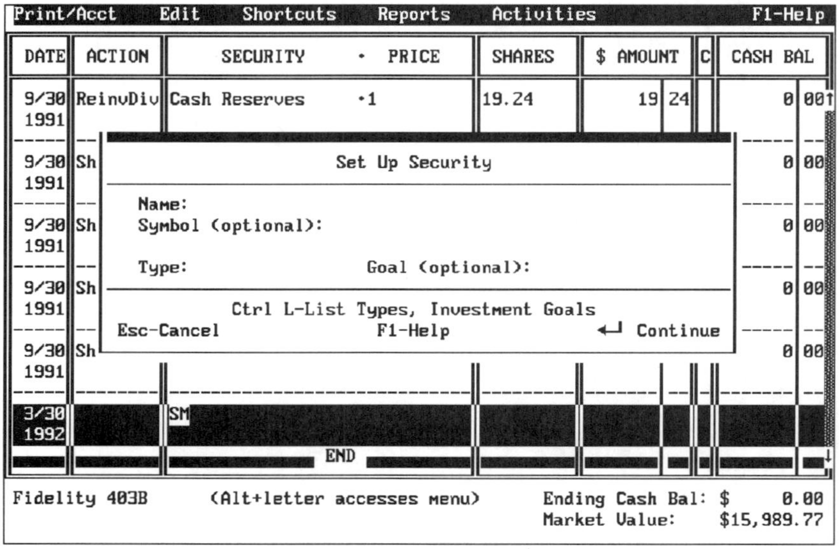

Adding a New Security

To set up the new security, make the following entries in this window:

- ▲ In the "Name:" field, enter the security name.
- ▲ In the "Symbol:" field, you can enter the symbol for the security. This is necessary only if you plan to import security price data from a file, or if you want to track different lots of a security. Otherwise, you can leave this field blank.
- ▲ In the "Type:" field, enter the type of the security (stock, bond, and so on). You can enter the security type directly, or press **Ctrl+L** to display a list of security types from which you select.
- ▲ In the "Goal:" field, you can enter a goal for this investment, if desired. The goal can be a specific purpose, such as "Retirement" or "College Fund," or it can be more general, such as "Growth" or "Income." If you enter goals for your investment accounts, Quicken can group data by goal in your investment reports. Type in a goal, or with the cursor on this field, press **Ctrl+L** to display a list of goals from which you can select.

When you have filled in the desired fields, press **Ctrl+Enter**. The new security will be recorded and added to the security list.

Entering a New Security Type

When you are entering or editing a security and the cursor is in the "Type:" field, you can press **Ctrl+L** to display a list of defined security types. Quicken comes preconfigured for the four most commonly used security types: stock, bond, mutual fund, and CD (certificate of deposit). If you have invested in a security that does not fit into one of these categories, you can set up a new security type.

To set up a new security type:

1. Display the list of security types.
2. Highlight the selection <Set Up New Type> at the top of the list, then press **Enter**. Quicken displays the Set Up Security Type window (Figure 12.6).

▼ *Figure 12.6. The Set Up Security Type Window*

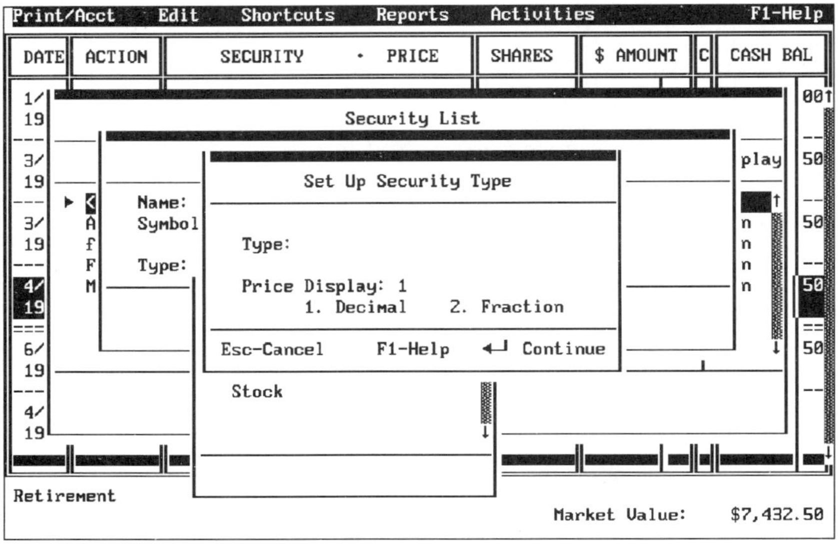

3. In the "Type:" field, enter the name of the new security type. The name can contain up to 15 letters, numbers, or spaces.
4. In the "Price Display:" field, enter **1** for standard decimal price display, **2** for prices to display as multiples of 1/16. For example, "2.50" is decimal display, "2 1/2" is fraction display.
5. Press **Enter** or **F10** to add the new type to the security type List.

CHECK YOURSELF

Add one or more securities to your file's security list. If you plan to start your own Quicken investment account, you can add the securities that you have invested in.

ANSWER

1. Display the investment account register.
2. Press **Ctrl+Y**, or select Shortcuts then select Security List.

3. Highlight <New Security>, then press **Enter**.
4. Fill in the security name and other information, then press **Ctrl+Enter**.

Adding a New Security

Entering Investment Transactions

You now know the most important aspects of the investment account register and are almost ready to start entering transactions. This section covers the remaining details of investment account transactions.

Share Price

The PRICE field records the price per share of the security. Share price is recorded to the nearest $0.0005, and displayed to the nearest $0.001. For stocks and mutual funds, the share price is obvious, but for other securities that may be tracked in an investment account, the share price is not. Here are some guidelines:

- For a stock or mutual fund, enter the actual per-share price.
- For a money market fund or certificate of deposit, enter **$1.00**.
- For a bond, enter 1/10 of the market value of each bond (this matches the way that bond prices are reported).
- For a precious metal, enter the per-ounce price.
- For a collectible (coins, stamps), enter **1**.

You can enter a share price as a decimal number (for instance, **15.625)** or as a number plus a fraction. For the latter, enter the whole dollar amount followed by a space, then the fraction (for instance, **15 5/8**).

Number of Shares

In the SHARE field, you enter the number of shares involved in the transaction up to four decimal places.

- For a stock or mutual fund, enter the actual number of shares involved in the transaction.
- For a certificate of deposit or a money market fund, enter the total dollar amount of the transaction. Since share price is fixed at $1.00 for these types of accounts, the number of shares and the dollar amount are always the same.
- For a bond, enter ten times the number of bonds (to match the way bond prices are quoted). For example, for six bonds with a total value of $6000, enter **60** in the SHARE field.
- For a precious metal, enter the number of ounces.
- For a collectible, enter **1**.

The $ AMOUNT Field

The $ AMOUNT field records the total dollar amount of the transaction. Quicken "knows" that there is a relationship between amount, share price, and number of shares so that:

AMOUNT = (PRICE) x (SHARES)

If you fill in any two of these fields, Quicken uses this formula to calculate the correct value for the third, and automatically enters it in the proper field. The only exception to this is when a transaction involves a commission or fee, as explained in the next section.

Commissions and Fees

When you buy or sell shares of a security, you usually have to pay a commission to your broker. Quicken lets you keep track of commissions in your investment accounts. When you enter a

Entering Investment Transactions

buy or sell action, Quicken adds a field labeled "Comm/Fee:" (Commission/Fee) to the transaction, immediately below the SHARE field (Figure 12.7). This is where the transaction commission amount is recorded.

You have two ways to enter the amount of the commission or fee:

1. Enter the transaction share price, shares, and amount, as you usually would, disregarding the commission. Then, enter the commission amount in the "Comm/Fee:" field. Quicken automatically adds it (for a buy action) or subtracts it (for a sell action) from the $ AMOUNT field.
2. Enter the share price and number of shares for the transaction. In the $ AMOUNT field, enter the actual dollar amount of the transaction, including the commission. Quicken will note that the dollar amount does not equal the share price times the number of shares, and will automatically enter the difference in the "Comm/Fee:" field (Figure 12.8).

Note that when you buy shares, the dollar amount will be equal to the share price times the number of shares, *plus* the

▼ *Figure 12.7. The "Comm/Fee:" Field*

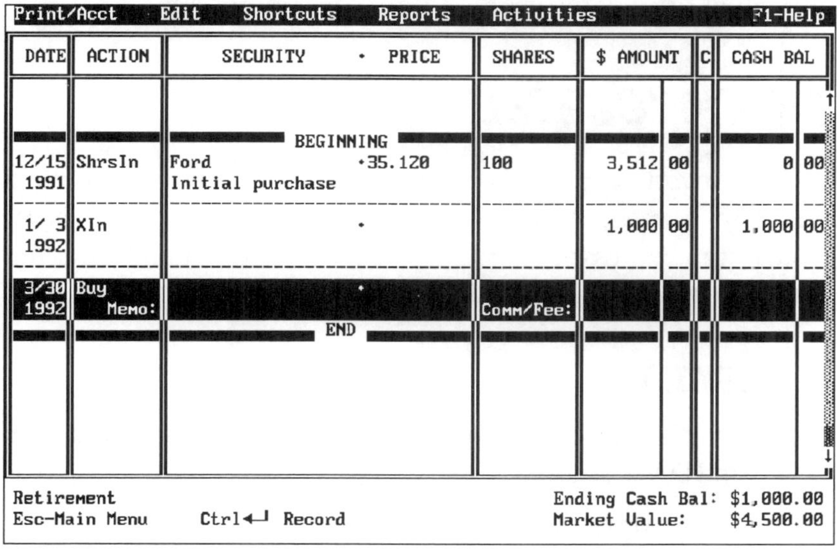

▼ ***Figure 12.8. The Total Dollar Amount of a Buy or Sell Transaction, Including the Commission or Fee***

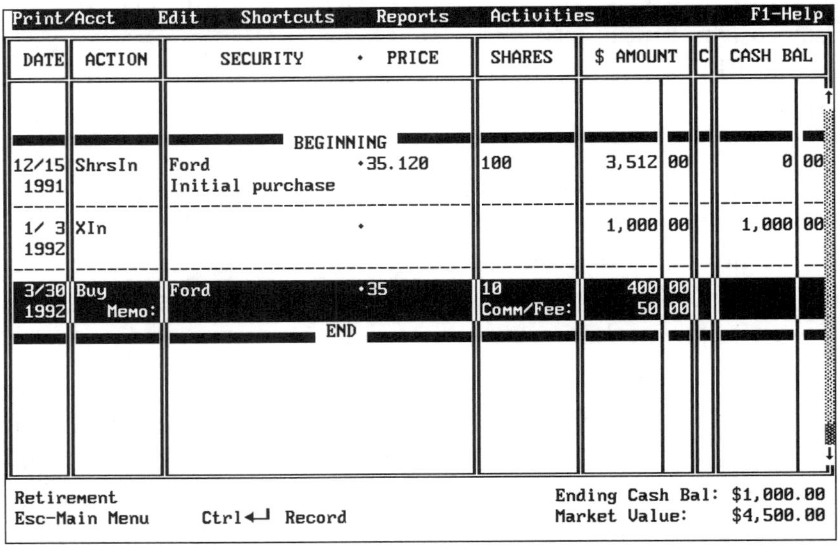

commission. This is because the total amount you pay is the purchase price of the shares plus the commission. In contrast, when you sell shares, the dollar amount will be equal to the share price times the number of shares, *minus* the commission. This is because the total amount of cash you receive is equal to the selling price of the shares, minus the commission.

CHECK YOURSELF

Enter an investment transaction that includes a commission into a regular investment account. For example, you purchased 100 shares of American Express at $19.50 per share, with a $55 commission. You used cash in the account for the purchase.

ANSWER

1. Display the account register, then enter the transaction date in the DATE field.
2. In the ACTION field, enter **Buy**.

3. In the SECURITY field, enter **American Express**, then press **Enter**. If this is a new security for your file, add it to your security list.
4. In the PRICE field, enter **19.50**.
5. In the SHARE field, enter **100**. Quicken automatically enters 1950.00 in the $ AMOUNT field.
6. In the "Comm/Fee:" field, enter **55**. Quicken automatically adjusts the value in the $ AMOUNT field to read 2005.00.
7. Press **Enter** to record the transaction.

Transactions that Involve Transfers

Certain investment account actions involve a transfer of money between the investment account and another Quicken account. When you select one of these actions, Quicken adds the "Account:" field to the transaction (Figure 12.9). In this field, you enter the name of the account that the money is being transferred to or from. In a mutual fund account (but not in a regular

▼ ***Figure 12.9. Account Field Added to the Register***

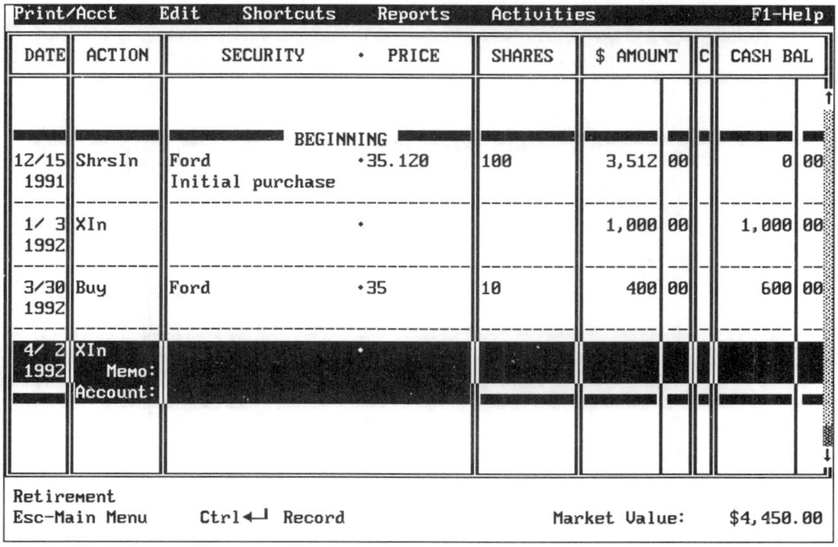

account), another field labeled "Xfer Amt:" (transfer amount) is also added. You enter the transfer amount in this field. (In a regular account, the transfer amount is entered in the $ AMOUNT field.)

To enter a transaction that involves a transfer:

1. Enter the action in the ACTION field.
2. Move the cursor to the "Account:" field.
3. Press **Ctrl+C**, or select Shortcuts, then select Categorize/ Transfer from the pull-down menu.
4. Quicken displays a list of accounts in the current file. Highlight the transfer account name, then press **Enter**.
5. Move the cursor to the $ AMOUNT field, then enter the transfer amount. Enter a positive amount to transfer money into the investment account or a negative amount to transfer money out of the investment account. In a mutual fund account, Quicken transfers the amount to the "Xfer Amt:" field.
6. Fill in the remaining transaction fields, then press **Ctrl+Enter** to record the transaction (Figure 12.10).

▼ ***Figure 12.10. A Regular Account Register with a Transfer Transaction Recorded***

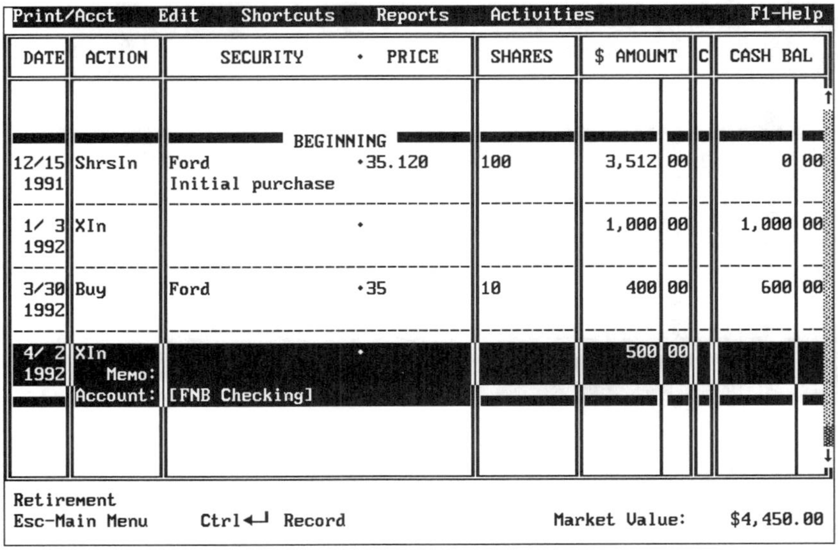

Update Prices and Market Value

Update Prices and Market Value

Quicken's calculation of your investment account's market value is based on the current prices of the securities you own. To Quicken, a security's "current" price is the most recent price you entered, even if it's several months old. Quicken provides an easy way for you to update your security prices so that your account's market value figure is accurate. Prices are updated on the Update Prices and Market Value screen, shown in Figure 12.11.

Remember, the display of securities on the Update Prices and Market Value screen is controlled by the entry in the Display column of the Security List window for each security (as explained earlier in this chapter). Now look at the components of this screen:

- ▲ The Security Name column lists each security name.
- ▲ The Type column lists the security type.
- ▲ The Mkt Price column lists the most recent per-share market price that Quicken knows. An asterisk (*) after the price indicates that the price is estimated based on a price entered

▼ ***Figure 12.11. The Update Prices and Market Value Screen***

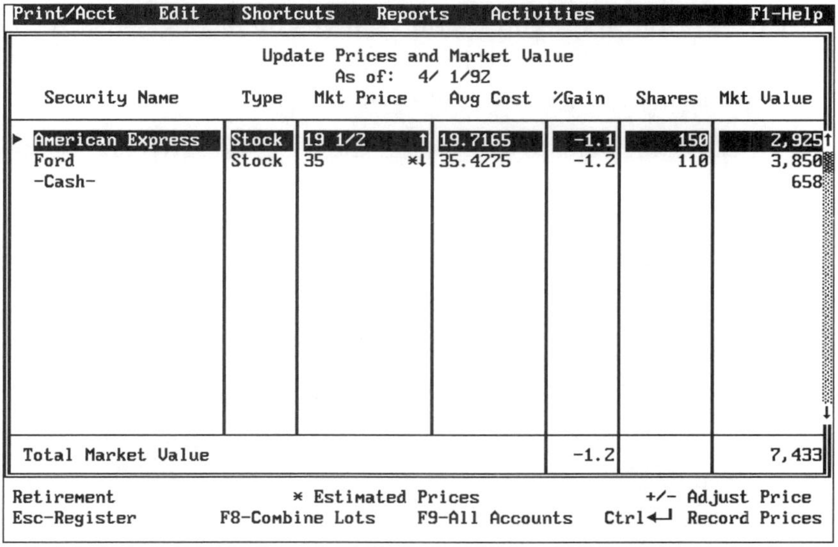

before the current date. An Up arrow or Down arrow after the price indicates that the price is higher or lower than the previous price.

- The Avg Cost column displays the average cost per share. Quicken calculates average cost by dividing the security's cost basis (total cost of shares) by the number of shares.
- The %Gain column displays the security's unrealized gain, expressed as a percentage of the average cost per share. The %Gain equals the difference between the market price and average cost, divided by the average cost and multiplied by 100 percent. A negative number for %Gain indicates an unrealized loss. When average cost is unknown, Quicken displays "NA."
- The Shares column displays the total number of shares of the security you have, rounded off to a whole number.
- The Mkt Value column displays the security's market value, equal to the market price per share times the number of shares. Values over $9,999,999 display as rows of asterisks.

To update your security prices:

1. Obtain a list of current share prices, such as from your newspaper's business section.
2. To display the Update Prices and Market Value screen, press **Ctrl+U** from the Main Menu or Investment Register screen. From the Register screen, you can also select Activities then select Update Prices from the pull-down menu.
3. If necessary, press **F9** to toggle the display between securities in all accounts or securities in the current account. This is applicable only if you have more than one investment account in the current file.
4. Use the Up and Down arrow keys to move between securities, then enter the current market price for each. When entering market prices, you have the following keys available:
   - Type **+** or **-** to increase or decrease the price to the next 1/8 (0.125).

- Type a single or double quote (' or ") to make the price equal to the one immediately above.
- If the estimated price displayed is unchanged, type an asterisk (*) to tell Quicken that the price is correct. The displayed asterisk will disappear.
- If you make an error and want to redisplay the estimated price, type *.

Update Prices and Market Value

5. Press **Ctrl+P** if you want to print a hard copy of the screen. When you are finished updating prices, press **Ctrl+Enter** or **F10** to record the new prices, then press **Esc** to close the screen.

CHECK YOURSELF

Update the market prices for the securities in your investment account.

ANSWER

1. From the Main Menu or Investment Register screen, press **Ctrl+U**.
2. Use the Up and Down arrow keys to move the cursor between securities.
3. Enter the current per-share price for each security.
4. Press **F10** to record the new prices, then press **Esc**.

Using Reminders

A *reminder* is a dated note that you place in an investment register. You use reminders to remind yourself of investment-related events that will occur at some time in the future. For example, you could write a reminder that a certificate of deposit is maturing on June 1.

Reminder memos work only if you have installed the Quicken Billminder program. When you start your computer, Billminder will display a message indicating that you have a reminder memo. The Billminder program will be covered in *Appendix B: The Billminder Program*. This section explains how to enter a reminder memo in your investment account register.

To enter a reminder memo:

1. Display the investment register. In the DATE field, enter the date of the memo (the date you want to be reminded *on*).
2. In the ACTION field enter **Reminder**. If you use the action list, select "Other transactions" then select Reminder.
3. Enter the text of the memo in one or both lines of the SECURITY field.
4. Record the reminder transaction by pressing **Ctrl+Enter**.

A reminder memo is recorded in your investment account register like any other transaction (Figure 12.12). To turn off a reminder memo, you can delete the entire reminder memo transaction.

▼ ***Figure 12.12. A Reminder Memo in the Register***

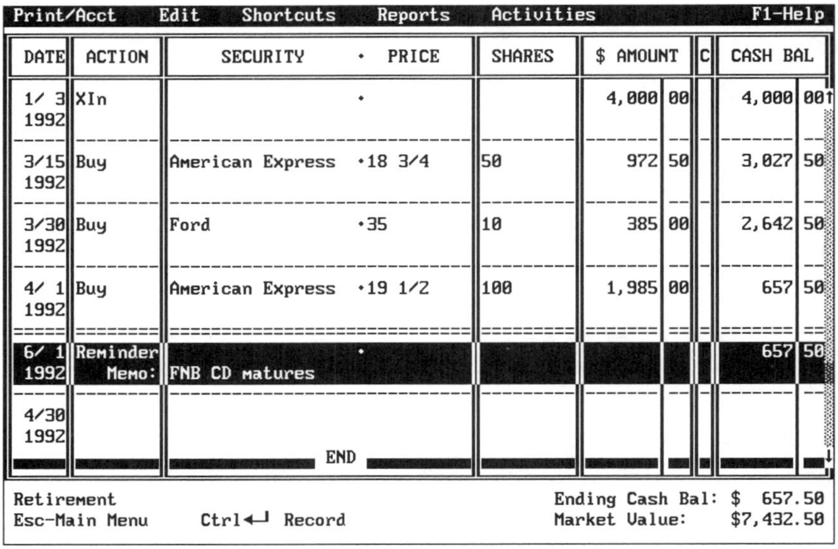

If you want to turn off a reminder memo while retaining a record of it in the register:

1. Display the register, then highlight the reminder memo transaction.
2. Move the cursor to the SECURITY field, then press **Right** arrow to move the cursor to the C field.
3. Enter **X** or *.
4. Press **Ctrl+Enter** or **F10** to record the changed transaction.

QUICK COMMAND SUMMARY

To enter an action in the ACTION field:

1. Move the cursor to the ACTION field.
2. Type in the entire action name.

   or:

   Type the first few letters of the desired action, then press **Enter** or **Tab**.

   or:

   Press **Ctrl+L**, then select the desired action from the list that is displayed.

To enter a security name in the SECURITY field:

1. Move the cursor to the SECURITY field.
2. Type in the full security name, then press **Enter** or **Tab**.

   or:

   Type in the first few letters of the security name (enough to distinguish it from any other name on the list), then, press **Enter** or **Tab**.

   or:

   Press **Ctrl+Y**. Select the desired security name from the list that is displayed, then press **Enter**.

To add a new security to the security list:

1. Display the investment register and, with the cursor in the SECURITY field, press **Ctrl+L**.
2. Highlight the selection <New Security> at the top of the list, then press **Enter**.
3. Enter information about the new security in the window.
4. When all information has been entered, press **Ctrl+Enter**.

To update the market prices for your securities:

1. From the Main Menu or Investment Register screen, press **Ctrl+U**.
2. Press the **Up** and **Down** arrow keys to move the cursor between securities.
3. Enter the current per-share price for each security.
4. Press **F10** to record the new prices, then press **Esc**.

PRACTICE WHAT YOU'VE LEARNED

This chapter covered the details of the investment account register and showed you how to enter investment transactions. Here are some main points to practice to help you retain what you have learned. Use either your own Quicken account or a dummy account that you set up specifically for these exercises.

1. Enter a variety of transaction types in the account. Be sure to include at least the following action types, which you will probably encounter most often with a real account:
   - ▲ Add and remove shares.
   - ▲ Buy and sell shares, including transactions that involve a commission.
   - ▲ Reinvest dividends and capital gains distributions.
   - ▲ Receive interest income.
   - ▲ Transfer cash to and from the account.
2. Update the market prices for the securities in your account.

13

Investment Account Reports

In this chapter, you will learn about Quicken's investment account reports. Once you know how to use investment account reports, you will be able to obtain detailed information about your investments and how they are performing. The topics covered in this chapter include

- ▲ **Different types of investment reports**
- ▲ **Creating an investment report**
- ▲ **Customizing an investment report**

Investment Report Overview

The key to successful investing is information. If you work at all with investments, you'll soon find Quicken's investment reports to be an invaluable tool. Quicken's report generating capabilities can handle your investment transaction information with the same power and flexibility that it does for your personal account information. Quicken makes it easy to obtain accurate data about your past investment activities and the performance of your stocks, bonds, and mutual funds. Investment reports are also a great help at tax time, when your investment income and losses must be reported to Uncle Sam.

Creating Investment Reports

As you work with investment reports, you will see that many of the procedures and options are the same as for the personal reports that you learned about in Chapter 8. Most of what you learned there can be applied to investment reports as well.

In this section, you will learn the basic steps that are common to all of the investment reports. Later in the chapter, you will be shown each of the five report types individually.

To create an investment report:

1. From the Main Menu, select Create Reports; or from the register or the Write Checks screen, select Reports.
2. Quicken displays the Reports menu. From this menu, select Investment Reports.
3. Another menu is displayed listing the five types of investment reports. Select the desired report type.
4. A setup window for the selected report is displayed. For example, Figure 13.1 shows the setup window for the Portfolio Value Report.

▼ *Figure 13.1. The Setup Window for the Portfolio Value Report*

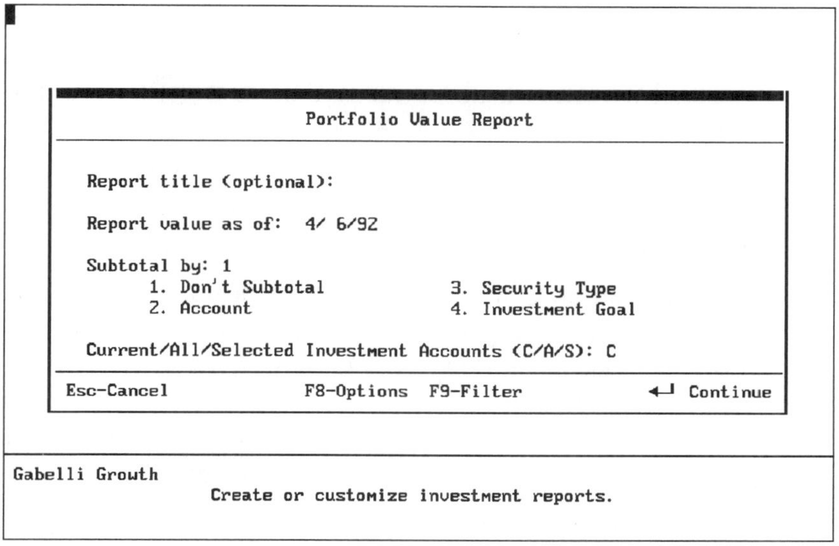

Creating Investment Reports

5. If desired, enter a title in the "Report title:" field. If you do not specify a title, Quicken will use the report name as the title and display it at the top of the report.
6. All investment report types (except the Portfolio Value report) require you to enter a start and a stop date. The report will include information from transactions within the date range. To include all transactions, enter a start date before the earliest transaction and today's date as the stop date. For the Portfolio Value report, you enter only a single date, and the report will summarize the status of your investments as of that date.
7. All investment report types give you the option of subtotaling by various criteria. For example, you can subtotal by period (month, quarter, or year), by security, or by account. If you want subtotals, specify this in the report setup window. Quicken's default is for no subtotaling.
8. The setup window also lets you specify which investment accounts are to be included in the report. Specify All to have the report include information from all investment accounts

in the current file, specify Current to have the report include information from only the current account. To include only selected accounts in the report, specify Selected. When you close the setup window, Quicken will display a list of all investment accounts in the current file. Use the Up and Down arrow keys to highlight account names, and press **Spacebar** to toggle each account between included and excluded (as indicated in the right column). Press **F9** to toggle all accounts between included and excluded.

9. Press **Ctrl+Enter**. Quicken creates the report and displays it on your screen. You can scroll to view different parts of the report by pressing the **Up** and **Down** arrow keys and the **PgUp** and **PgDn** keys. If the report is wider than your screen, you can scroll horizontally by pressing the **Left** and **Right** arrow keys, as well as the **Home** and **End** keys.
10. While the report is displayed on the screen, you can print it by pressing **Ctrl+P** or by selecting File/Print then selecting Print Report.
11. Press **Esc** to close the report and return to the report setup window. From this window, you can modify the setup and redisplay the report, or press **Esc** again to close the setup window.

Once you've entered all the necessary information in the report setup window, Quicken displays the report on the screen.

CHECK YOURSELF

Try your hand at creating an investment report. To do so, you must have entered some transactions in an investment account. To begin, display a Portfolio Value report.

ANSWER

1. From the Main Menu select Create Reports.
2. Select Investment Reports.

3. Select Portfolio Value.
4. Enter today's date in the "Report value as of:" field in the report setup window, then press **Ctrl+Enter**.
5. Quicken creates the report and displays it on the screen.

Creating Investment Reports

Investment Report Types

Quicken offers five different types of investment reports, all of which are based on transactions in investment accounts. The preset investment reports cover the most frequently needed investment information and, as with all Quicken reports, they can be customized to meet special situations.

The Portfolio Value Report

The Portfolio Value report shows the total value of each security in your investment accounts as of the date you specify in the report setup window. For each security, the following information is displayed:

- ▲ The security name.
- ▲ The number of shares of the security owned (to the nearest 0.01).
- ▲ The current per-share price. Estimated prices are marked with an asterisk.
- ▲ The cost basis for the security (see Chapter 11 for a definition of cost basis). If, when setting up the investment account, you did not enter full historical information and you did not enter the cost basis for the security, Quicken displays 0.00.
- ▲ The unrealized gain or loss for the security. This is calculated as current price multiplied by the number of shares, minus the cost basis.

▲ The market value of the security as of the report date. This is calculated as current price multiplied by the number of shares.

You use the Portfolio Value report to obtain a summary view of your investment holdings and their current value. Because of the way that cost basis is calculated, however, you cannot use the gain/loss figure from this report as an indicator of how well your investment is doing.

A Portfolio Value report is shown in Figure 13.2. Note that overall totals for the cost basis, gain/loss, and balance columns are listed at the bottom of the report. If you had requested subtotals when setting up the report, these three columns would be subtotaled by the specified category as well.

The Investment Performance Report

The Investment Performance report calculates and displays the average annual total return on your securities for a specified time period. The average annual total return takes into account dividends, interest payments, and capital gains distributions that

▼ ***Figure 13.2. A Portfolio Value Report with the Current Value and Gain/Loss on All of the Securities***

File/Print Edit Layout Reports Activities F1-Help

PORTFOLIO VALUE REPORT

INVEST-All Investment Accts As of 4/ 7/92
4/ 7/92

* Estimated Prices

Security	Shares	Curr Price	Cost Basis	Gain/Loss	Balance
20th Heritage	129.05	8.570 *	955.68	150.30	1,105.98
20th Ultra	82.47	14.620 *	1,205.80	0.00	1,205.80
Franklin Univ.	152.05	7.915 *	1,175.92	27.59	1,203.51
Gabelli Growth	62.22	18.220 *	1,000.00	133.67	1,133.67
Total Investments			4,337.40	311.56	4,648.96

20th Ultra
Esc-Leave report

Investment Report Types

you have received in cash or reinvested. It also takes into account any increase or decrease in the per-share price.

You use the Investment Performance report to see how well your investments are doing and to compare one investment's performance with another's. The average annual total return calculated by this report is the annual percentage rate you would need to receive on a regular savings account to obtain the same return on your investment. For example, if you invested in a mutual fund a year ago and the Investment Performance Report indicates an average annual total return of 20 percent, you would probably feel quite satisfied with the investment since its return is much better than you would find on a savings account. If, however, the investment's average annual total return was only two percent, you would no doubt conclude that you would have been better off putting your money in a savings account that earns five percent.

Quicken cannot calculate an average annual total return of over 10,000 percent or under -99.9 percent. In addition, certain transaction timings can make it impossible to calculate an accurate figure. In these cases, Quicken displays "N/A" (not available) on the report.

In the setup window for the Investment Performance report, you have the option of displaying cash flow details in the report. If you request cash flow details, the report will include each individual transaction that Quicken is using to calculate the annual return value.

Figure 13.3 shows an Investment Performance report. For this report, subtotal by security was requested in the report setup window.

The Capital Gains Report

The Capital Gains report provides information on realized gains or losses that you have incurred by selling securities. The term *capital gain* refers simply to the profit (or loss) that results when you sell something for more (or less) than you paid for it. Use this report to obtain the capital gains information required for tax preparation.

▼ ***Figure 13.3. An Investment Performance Report Subtotaled by Security***

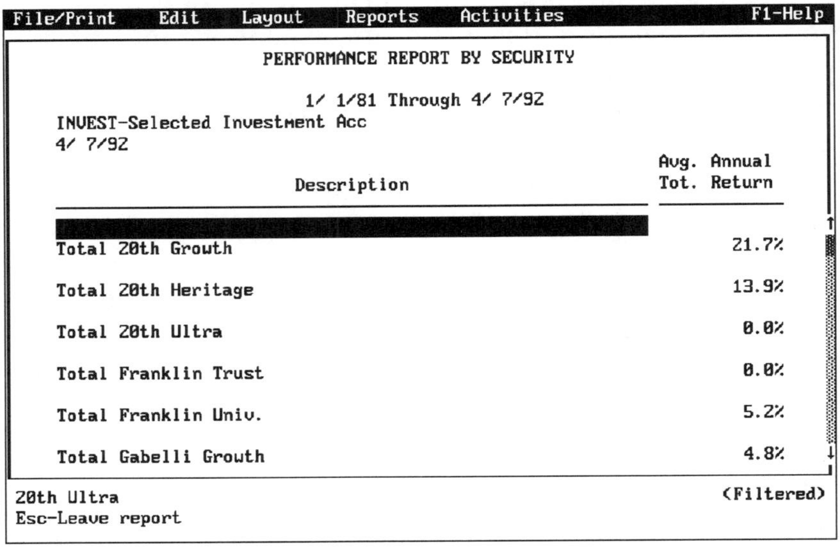

Quicken can distinguish between short-term and long-term capital gains. The difference between these is the length of time you owned a security before selling it. In the past, short- and long-term capital gains were taxed at different rates. As of this writing, they are not treated differently, although the tax law may change again in the future. On the Capital Gains report Setup window, you can enter the maximum holding period for short-term capital gains. The default value is 365 days.

Note that the Capital Gains report does not include capital gains distributions in mutual funds. For information on mutual fund capital gains distributions, use the Investment Income report. If you sell only a portion of the shares of a security, Quicken calculates capital gains based on the assumption that the shares you sold are the ones you've held the longest.

Figure 13.4 shows a portion of a Capital Gains report. (The entire report is too big to fit on the screen.) This report was subtotaled by short- vs. long-term gains.

▼ *Figure 13.4. A Portion of a Capital Gains Report*

File/Print Edit Layout Reports Activities F1-Help

CAPITAL GAINS REPORT

1/ 1/81 Through 4/ 7/92

RETIRE-Fidelity 403B
4/ 7/92

Security	Shares	Bought	Sold	Sales Price	Cost Basis	Gain/Loss
Equity Income	1.8881	7/ 3/91	7/16/91	46.84	45.43	1.41
Equity Income	0.0151	7/ 3/91	7/31/91	0.37	0.36	0.01
Equity Income	0.0818	7/16/91	7/31/91	2.02	2.03	-0.01
	TOTAL SHORT TERM			1,852.78	1,616.03	236.75
	LONG TERM					
Equity Income	0.4702	7/31/86	12/ 2/88	12.00	13.29	-1.29
Magellan	0.605	8/ 1/86	8/28/89	38.36	30.56	7.80
Magellan	0.569	8/27/86	8/28/89	36.08	30.56	5.52

Fidelity 403B
Esc-Leave report

Investment Report Types

The Investment Income Report

The Investment Income report summarizes your investment income and expenses by category. Note that the categories used in this report are not the income and expense categories you use in your Quicken bank accounts (for instance, groceries and utilities), but are the predefined investment-related categories, such as dividend income, capital gains distributions, and so on. Use this report to obtain investment income information needed for tax preparation. Figure 13.5 shows an Investment Income report for a single account, with no subtotals.

The Investment Income report offers a number of options. To set these options, press **F8** from the report setup window. The Report Options window will be displayed, as shown in Figure 13.6.

The following options are available in this window:

▲ In the "Report organization:" field, select "Income and expense" if you want the report to have separate sections for income, expense, and transfer transactions. Select "Cash flow

▼ *Figure 13.5. An Investment Income Report*

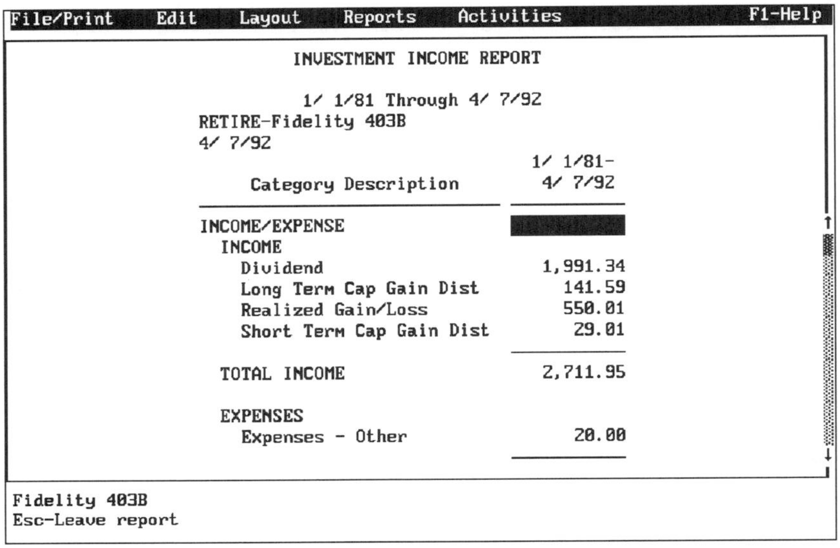

basis" to have one section for all inflows (including income and transfers into the account) and another section for all outflows (including expenses and transfers out of the account). The default setting is "Income and expense."

▼ *Figure 13.6. The Investment Income Report Options Window*

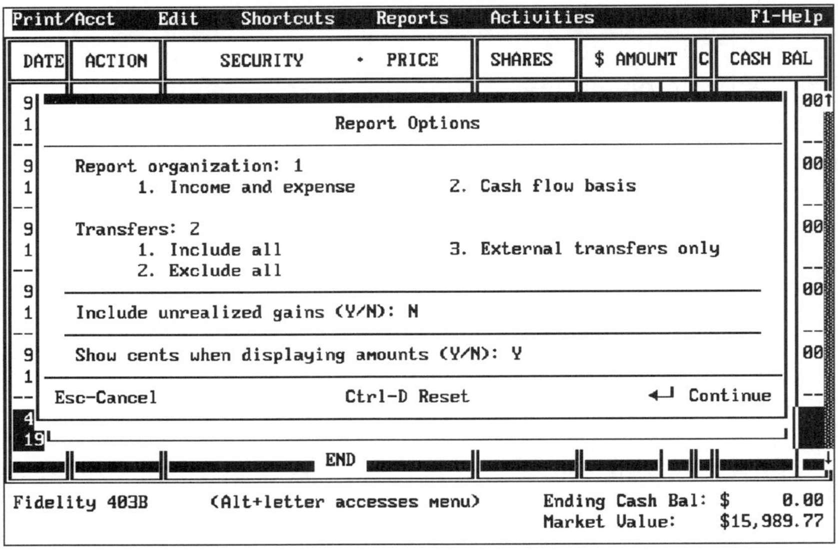

Investment Report Types

- In the "Transfers:" field, select "Include all" if you want the report to include all transfers from and to the accounts included in the report. Select "Exclude all" if you want the report to omit all transfers. Select "External transfers only" if you want the report to include only those transfers between accounts included in the report and accounts not included in the report. This last option excludes transfer transactions that essentially cancel each other out in the report. The default setting is "Include all."
- In the "Include unrealized gains:" field, enter **Y** if you want the report to include unrealized gains and losses reflecting the increases and decreases of the value of your securities as their prices change. Enter **N** to exclude this information. The default setting is N.

After specifying the options you want, press **Ctrl+Enter** to close the Report Options window and return to the report setup window. Any time the Report Options window is open, you can press **Ctrl+D** to reset all options to their default values.

The Investment Transactions Report

The Investment Transaction report displays individual transactions from your investment accounts and shows how each transaction affected the market value or cost basis of the investment and the cash balance in the account. Use this report to obtain detailed information about the history of your investments.

Press **F8** while the Investment Transactions setup window is displayed. Notice that you have the same report options available as described for the Investment Income report (as shown in Figure 13.6). Make selections in this window as described earlier in the *The Investment Income Report* section.

The "Include unrealized gains:" field affects the information displayed by the Investment Transactions report. For example, if unrealized gains are included, the report displays the change in market value caused by each transaction. If unrealized gains are not included, the report shows the change in cost basis caused by each transaction.

▼ Figure 13.7. The Left Part of an Investment Transaction Report

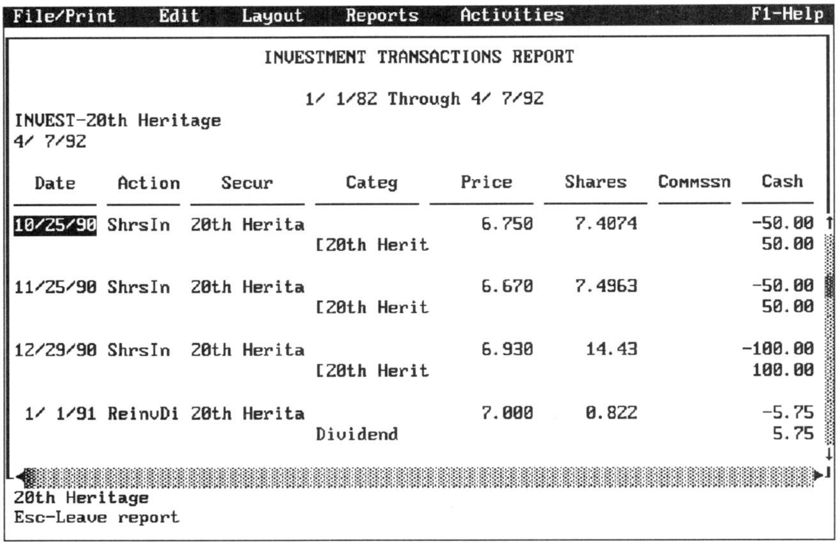

An Investment Transaction report is shown in Figures 13.7 and 13.8. (This type of report is usually too wide to fit on one screen.)

▼ Figure 13.8. The Right Part of an Investment Transaction Report

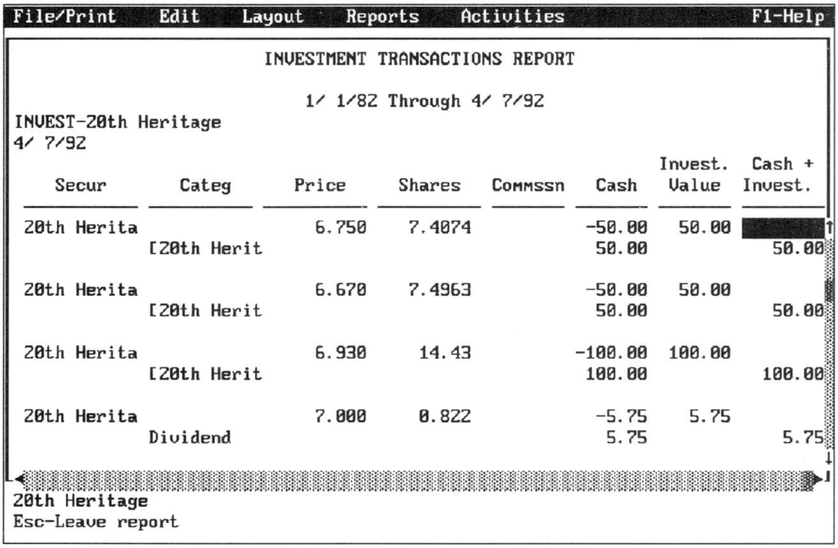

Investment Report Types

The columns in the report contain the following information:

- ▲ The Date column lists the date of the transaction. Transactions are sorted by date. If you specified any subtotals in the report, transactions are sorted by date within subtotal categories.
- ▲ The Action column lists the action of the transaction: Buy, Sell, Reinvest Dividend, and so on.
- ▲ The Secur column lists the security that the transaction involved.
- ▲ The Categ column lists the category (if any) of the transaction.
- ▲ The Price column gives the per-share price of the security.
- ▲ The Shares column gives the number of shares involved in the transaction.
- ▲ The Commssn column lists the commission, if any.
- ▲ The Cash column lists the change in the account's cash balance.
- ▲ The "Invest. Value" column lists the change in either the cost basis (if unrealized gains are excluded) or market value (if unrealized gains are included) of the security.
- ▲ The "Cash + Invest." column gives the sum of the amounts in the Cash and "Invest. Value" columns.

For each subtotal section (if requested) and for the entire report, sums are displayed for the Cash, "Invest. Value," and "Cash + Invest. Value" columns. Note that certain complex investment transactions are listed on two or more lines in the report, with one line for each component of the transaction. For example, a reinvested dividend transaction will be on two lines. The first line will be a "Buy" transaction, the second line an "Income" transaction for the same amount.

CHECK YOURSELF

To familiarize yourself with Quicken's five preset investment reports, display each type on your screen in turn.

ANSWER

1. From the Main Menu, select Create Reports.
2. Select Investment Reports.
3. A menu is displayed listing the five types of investment reports. Select the desired report type.
4. A setup window for the selected report is displayed. Fill in the necessary information, then press **Ctrl+Enter**.
5. Quicken creates the report and displays it on your screen. Scroll to view different parts of the report, if necessary.
6. Press **Esc** twice to close the report and return to the Reports menu. Return to Step 3 to display another report type, or press **Esc** twice more to return to the Main Menu.

Customizing Investment Reports

Quicken's preset investment reports are suitable for many needs, particularly when you're just beginning to keep track of your investments. As with other Quicken reports, investment reports can be customized when necessary.

Changing Report Layout

The Layout menu is used to control the appearance of your report. The commands on this menu do not affect what information the report contains, only how that information is presented. The layout commands for investment reports are the same as you learned for non-investment reports in Chapter 8, and will not be repeated here.

Filtering Investment Reports

Customizing Investment Reports

As you learned in Chapter 8, when you filter a report, you are instructing Quicken to limit the report to transactions that meet certain criteria. For example, you could filter an investment report to include only your stock investments and to exclude mutual funds and bonds. Or, you could create a report limited to transactions where the action was reinvestment of dividends.

When you create a filter for a report, Quicken remembers the filter and will automatically use it the next time you create a report unless you explicitly remove it or recall a memorized report with a different filter setting. You can specify a filter either before or after displaying the report.

To specify a filter for an investment report:

1. Before displaying the report, press **F9** while the report setup window is displayed (such as in Figure 13.1), or while the report is displayed on the Reports screen, select Edit then select Filter Transactions.
2. Quicken displays the Filter Investment Transactions window (Figure 13.9). For some investment report types, only a subset of the filter options shown in Figure 13.9 will be available.

TIP

While the Filter Investment Transactions window is displayed, press *Ctrl+D* to return all filter settings to the defaults (unfiltered).

3. First is the "Security contains:" field. If you make an entry in this field, the report will be filtered to contain only transactions where the SECURITY field contains the text you entered. You can also use the special match characters you learned about in Chapter 3.
4. The next field is the "Memo contains:" field, which is present only for Investment Income and Investment Transaction reports. Make an entry here to filter for transactions based on the contents of the MEMO field.

▼ Figure 13.9. The Filter Investment Transactions Window

```
                 Investment Transactions Report

                  Filter Investment Transactions

      Restrict report to transactions matching these criteria
         Security contains:
         Memo contains    :

      Select actions to include...          (Y/N): N
      Select categories to include...       (Y/N): N
      Select securities to include...       (Y/N): N
      Select security types to include...   (Y/N): N
      Select investment goals to include... (Y/N): N

   Esc-Cancel              Ctrl-D Reset              ↵ Continue

Gabelli Growth      Version 5.0, Copyright 1989-1991 Intuit
                    Create or customize investment reports.
```

5. The next five (or fewer, for some report types) fields accept yes or no (Y/N) entries. Enter a **Y** in each field to filter for the corresponding transaction attribute; you can choose from actions, categories, securities, security types, and investment goals. For example, if you want to filter your report by action and by security type, enter **Y** in the "Select actions to include:" and "Select security types to include:" fields.
6. Once you have made all the desired entries in the Filter Investment Transactions window, press **Ctrl+Enter**. What happens next depends on whether you entered **Y** in any of the Y/N fields in the Filter Investment Transactions window.
7. If you did not enter **Y** in any of the Y/N fields and you started from the report setup window, you are returned there; complete entering information in this window (if necessary) and press **Ctrl+Enter** to view the filtered report. If you did not enter **Y** in any of the Y/N fields and started from the Reports screen, the report is immediately displayed with the filter(s) in effect.
8. If you did enter **Y** in one or more of the Y/N fields in the Filter Investment Transactions window, Quicken next dis-

plays a window in which you specify details of the filter. For example, if you entered **Y** in the "Select actions to include:" field, Quicken will display the Select Actions to Include window (Figure 13.10).

9. Use the Page Up, Page Down, Up arrow, and Down arrow keys to move the highlight between selections in the window. Press **Spacebar** to toggle a single selection between included and not included. Press **F9** to toggle all selections between included and not included. For example, in Figure 13.10 the actions "Buy security" and Dividend are included and other actions are not included.
10. Once all items in the window are marked as included or not included, press **Enter**. If you had entered **Y** in another Y/N field in the Filter Investment Transactions window, the selection window for that criteria is displayed. Return to Step 9 to select items to include in the report.
11. When finished with the final selection window, press **Enter**. You are returned to either the report setup window or the Reports screen.

Customizing Investment Reports

▼ Figure 13.10. The Select Actions to Include Window

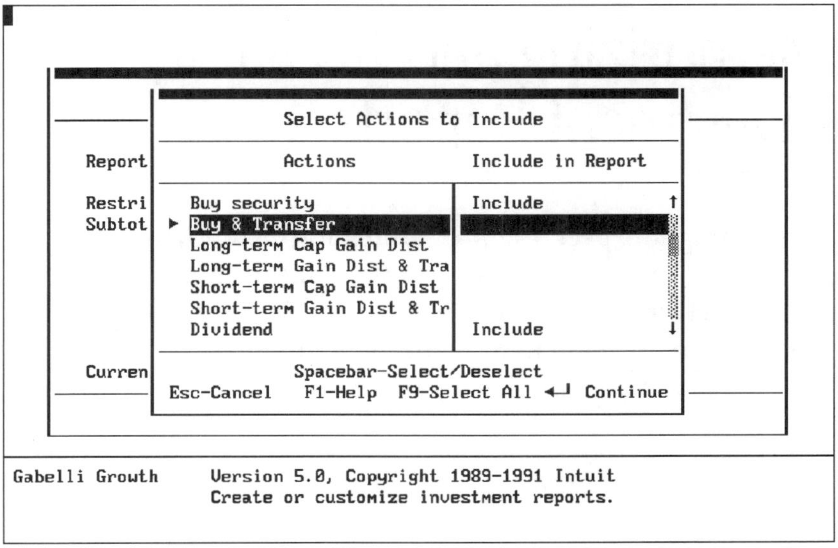

TIP

When a filter is in effect Quicken displays "(Filtered)" in the report setup window and in the lower-right corner of the Reports screen.

CHECK YOURSELF

Report customization is a powerful tool, letting you create exactly the reports you need. Create a report, then customize it.

ANSWER

1. Display one of Quicken's preset investment reports.
2. Select Edit.
3. Select Filter Transactions.
4. Enter the desired filter information, then press **Ctrl+Enter**.
5. Select Layout.
6. Select commands to customize the report layout.

Memorizing and Recalling Investment Reports

As you might expect, the procedures for memorizing and later recalling an investment report are the same as those for personal reports, which you learned in Chapter 8. Please refer to that chapter if you need to refresh your memory.

QUICK COMMAND SUMMARY

To display one of Quicken's preset investment reports:

1. From the Main Menu, select Create Reports; or from the register or the Write Checks screen, select Reports.
2. From the next menu, select Investment Reports.
3. From the next menu, select the desired report type.
4. In the report setup window, fill in the necessary information
5. Press **Ctrl+Enter**. Quicken displays the report on your screen.

To create a filtered investment report:

1. Display the desired unfiltered report.
2. From the Reports screen, select Edit.
3. Select Filter Transactions.
4. In the Filter Investment Transactions window, enter information for the filter you want.
5. Press **Ctrl+Enter**.

PRACTICE WHAT YOU'VE LEARNED

Spend some time becoming familiar with Quicken's investment reports and the various report customizations available. For practice, you can do the following:

1. Display all five of the preset investment reports.
2. Try filtering the reports in various ways.
3. Customize the report layout to best suit your needs.
4. Memorize some of the custom reports you create.
5. Recall your memorized reports.

14

Asset and Liability Accounts

This chapter teaches you how to use Quicken asset and liability accounts. You will learn

- ▲ When to use an asset account or a liability account
- ▲ How to set up asset and liability accounts
- ▲ How to use the asset and liability registers
- ▲ How to keep track of loans
- ▲ How to update the value of your assets and liabilities

What Are Assets and Liabilities?

An *asset* is anything you own or anything that is owed to you. A *liability* is something that you owe. You can use Quicken asset and liability accounts to keep track of your assets and liabilities. Asset and liability accounts are relatively advanced Quicken features, and many users do just fine without using them. For a complete picture of your financial situation, however, you may find them useful.

The money you're tracking in your Quicken checking account is an asset and the balance owed in your Quicken credit card account is a liability. This is why Quicken's asset and liability accounts are called "Other asset" and "Other liability" accounts. This is not to imply that *only* these account types can be used for assets and liabilities. There are, however, certain types of assets and liabilities that are best handled by this type of account.

Asset and liability accounts are in many ways like other Quicken accounts. Transactions in them can be assigned to categories and classes, and you can create summaries or detailed reports on account activities as needed. You can also make transfers between asset and liability accounts and other types of accounts.

Using Asset and Liability Accounts

Generally, you will use an asset or liability account to keep track of assets and liabilities that you are not tracking in another type of Quicken account. Once you become familiar with them, you will probably find it easy to decide when to use these accounts and when to use another account type. Typically, asset and liability accounts are used to keep track of:

- Balances owed on your mortgage and other loans.
- The market value of your home.

Using Asset and Liability Accounts

- Investments that do not fluctuate in value, such as Treasury bills and certificates of deposit.
- Collectibles, such as coins, stamps, or artwork.
- Money owed to you—for instance, accounts receivable for a small business.
- The cost of home improvements, so that you have a record for tax purposes.

Note that Quicken cannot calculate investment performance on an asset account. For assets on which you want to know the rate of return, you should use an investment account rather than an asset account.

Setting Up an Asset or Liability Account

An asset account can be used to track a single asset or a group of two or more assets. The same is true of liability accounts. The choice is yours. If each account contains only a single asset or liability, it is easier to update the value. Combining multiple items in a single account can, however, make reports more concise.

To set up an asset or liability account:

1. From the Main Menu, choose Select Account.
2. Use the Up and Down arrow keys to highlight the <New account> selection at the top of the list, then press **Enter**.
3. The Set Up New Account window is displayed (Figure 14.1). In the "Account Type:" field, enter **4** to set up an asset account or enter **5** to set up a liability account.
4. In the "Name for this account:" field, enter the account name. Use a descriptive name such as "Home Mortgage," "Coin Collection," or "CD."

▼ ***Figure 14.1. The Set Up New Account Window***

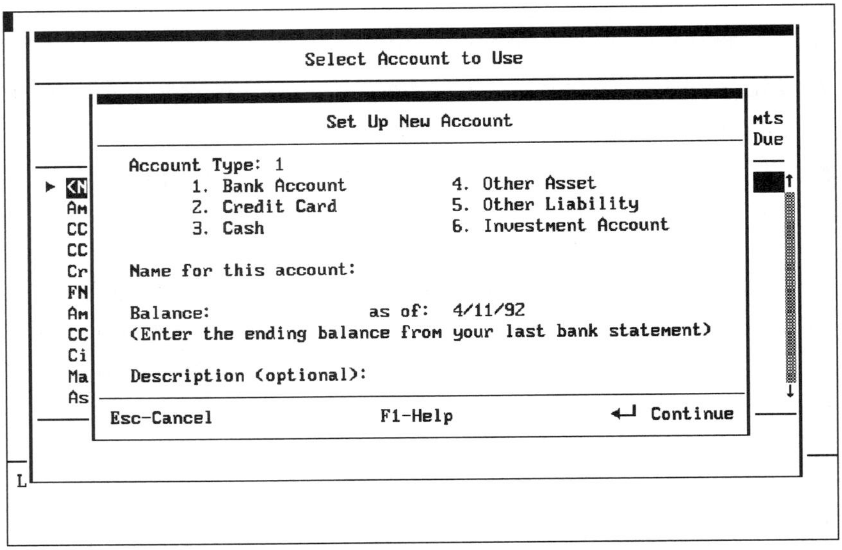

5. If the account will contain a single asset or liability, enter the current value of the asset or the current amount owed on the liability in the "Balance:" field. Do not enter a negative number for a liability—amounts in a liability account are automatically assumed to be owed. If the account will contain more than one asset or liability, enter **0** in the "Balance:" field. Later in this chapter, you'll enter individual transactions in the account for each asset or liability's opening balance.
6. Enter an account description, if desired, then press **Enter**. The account is created and added to the account list.

CHECK YOURSELF

Set up an account for a single asset or liability. For an asset account, you might use the value of your home or your car; for a liability account, your mortgage or car payment. Don't worry if you are not sure of the exact values of the asset or liability—you can always go back and make corrections later if necessary.

ANSWER

Setting Up an Asset or Liability Account

1. From the Main Menu, choose Select Account, highlight <New Account>, then press **Enter**.
2. In the "Account Type:" field, enter **4** to set up an asset account, or enter **5** to set up a liability account.
3. Enter a name for the account.
4. In the "Balance:" field, enter the current value of the asset or the current amount owed on the liability.
5. Enter an account description, if desired, then press **Enter**.

Entering Transactions

For asset and liability accounts, entering transactions in the register is very similar to entering transactions in other accounts. The registers for these two account types are almost identical, as shown in Figures 14.2 and 14.3

Look closely and you'll see that the only difference between these two registers is that the position of the INCREASE and DECREASE fields is reversed. In both account types, an increase is any transaction that increases the total account balance—how much you *owe* if it's a liability account, and how much you *have* if it's an asset account.

The balance in an asset or liability account can be adjusted in two ways: by entering a transaction or by using the Update Account Balance command. The following are some general guidelines on when to use each technique:

- ▲ Enter a transaction when adding a new item to an asset or liability account. For example, you are using an asset account to track your CD's and you purchase another CD.

▼ *Figure 14.2. The Other Asset Account Register Screen*

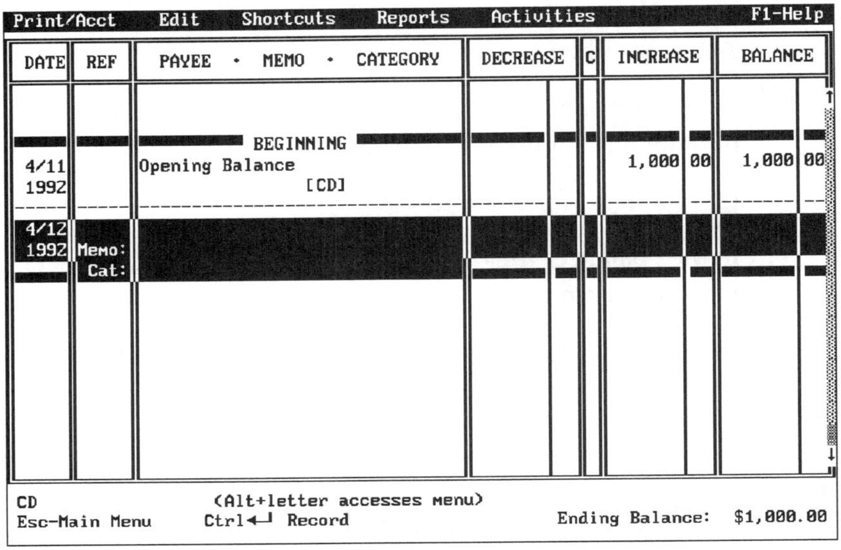

▲ Enter a transaction when money is being transferred to or from another Quicken account. For example, you are using a liability account to track your auto loan and you write a check to pay off your balance.

▼ *Figure 14.3. The Other Liability Account Register Screen*

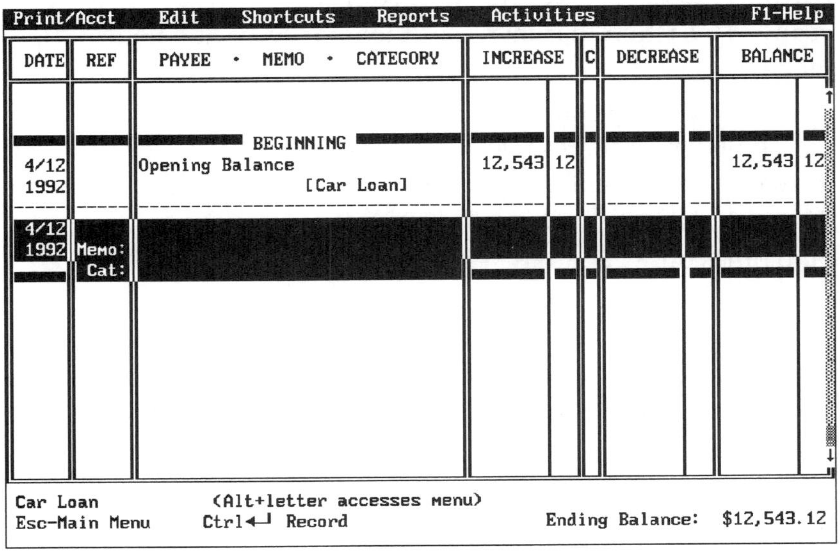

Entering Transactions

- Use the Update Account Balance command only with accounts that track a single asset or liability.
- Use the Update Account Balance command when the value of the account changes without anything actually being added to or taken out of the account. For example, you are using an asset account to track the value of your coin collection and the market value of your coins increases.

The Update Account Balance command is discussed in more detail later in this chapter.

To make entries in an asset or liability account register:

1. Display the account register. If necessary, press the **PgDn** key to move the highlight to the first blank transaction.
2. Enter the transaction date in the DATE field. Try using Quicken's special date keys that you learned about earlier in this book.
3. The REF field is generally left blank, but you can make an entry here for your own reference, if desired.
4. In the PAYEE field, enter information about the transaction. This is usually not a "payee" in the literal sense, but merely a description of the transaction. For example, when setting up a new CD in an asset account, the initial transaction might have "5% CD at First Federal" in the PAYEE field. Likewise, if your grandfather gives you his prized $20 gold piece for your coin collection, the PAYEE field might read "Granddad's $20 gold."
5. Enter the transaction amount in the appropriate field. Remember, make an entry in the INCREASE field for any transaction that increases the account balance, and an entry in the DECREASE field for any transaction that decreases the account balance.
6. Enter a memo in the MEMO field, if desired.
7. In the CATEGORY field, enter the category to which you want the transaction assigned. Use of categories in asset and liability accounts is discussed in more detail below.

8. Check your entry for errors. If you need to make corrections, press **Tab** and **Shift+Tab** to move between fields, and edit the information as needed. Once everything is correct, press **Ctrl+Enter** to record the transaction.

Transactions in asset and liability accounts can be assigned to categories just like any other transactions. They can also be left uncategorized by leaving the CATEGORY field blank, but this is not recommended. Because of the nature of asset and liability accounts, it's sometimes not clear what category to assign transactions to. For example, imagine that you're using an asset account to track the value of your home. Real estate values in your neighborhood increase, and you estimate that your home's value has increased by $20,000. When you add $20,000 to your asset account, what category do you use? You should set up special categories for transactions such as these, so that the transaction amounts are treated properly when you generate reports. For this example, "Real estate appreciation" would be an appropriate category.

Entering Initial Balances

You learned earlier in this chapter that when you are setting up an asset or liability account to track a collection of assets or liabilities, you do not enter the account's initial balance during the setup procedure. Rather, you enter **0** during setup, then later enter each individual asset or liability's initial balance as a separate transaction in the account register.

Entering the initial balance for an asset is no different than entering any other transaction. When you do so, however, be sure to enter the proper category for the transaction. The category should be the name of the asset or liability account. This is called a *self-transfer.* A self-transfer is used to prevent the initial balance amounts from showing up as uncategorized income or expenses in reports. Then, assign each transaction to a class to differentiate them from one another.

The following is an example: You have three certificates of deposit (CD's) from different banks and want to set up an asset

Entering Transactions

▼ ***Figure 14.4. A Transaction with the Initial Balances Entered and the Account Name Used as the Category***

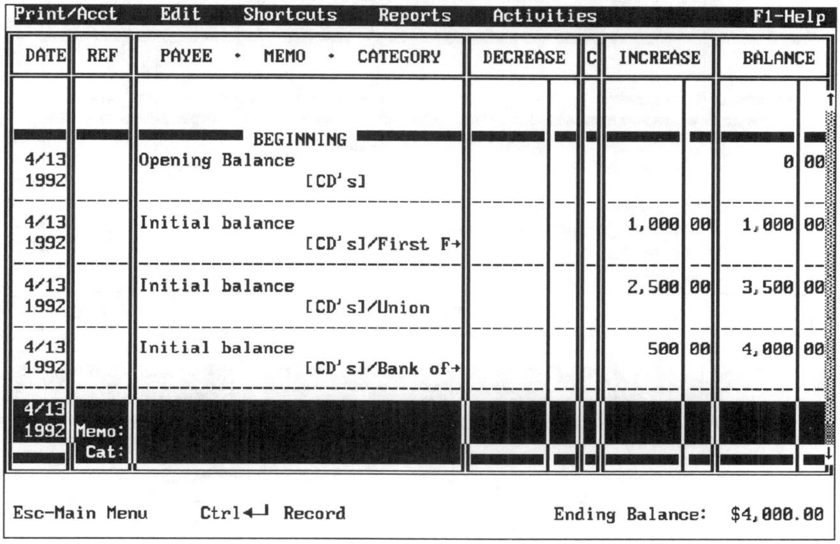

account (which you will call **CD's**) to keep track of them. When you first set up the account, you enter **0** as the initial balance. Then, enter a separate transaction for the initial balance of each CD in the account register. For each transaction, enter **CD's** (the account name) as the category and some distinguishing information, such as the bank name, as the class. When you're finished, your register should look similar to Figure 14.4.

Updating Account Balances

Quicken lets you update the balance in an asset or liability account without entering a transaction. Quicken will automatically create the required transaction for you, and assign it to the category you specify.

To update an account balance in an asset or liability account:

1. Display the register for the account.

▼ Figure 14.5. The Update Account Balance Window

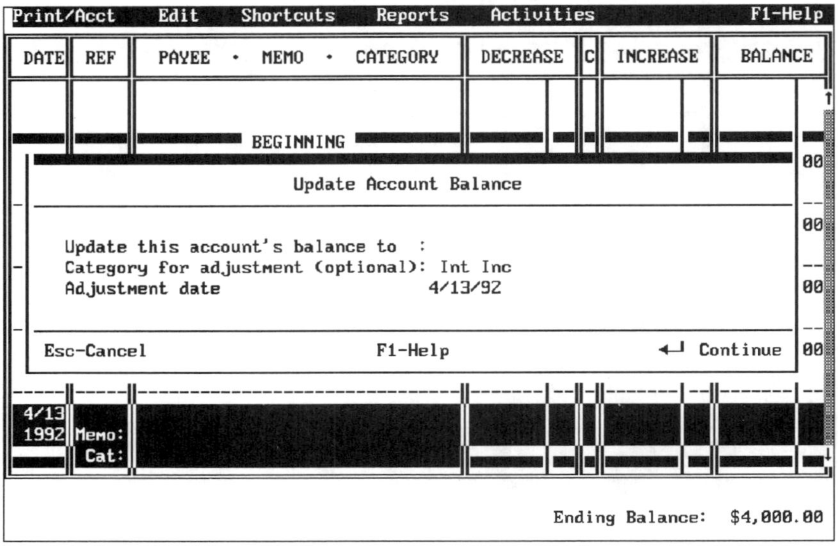

2. Select Activities, then select Update Account Balance.
3. The Update Account Balance window is displayed (Figure 14.5). In the window, enter the new account balance and optionally, the category for the adjustment to be assigned to.
4. Change the adjustment date if you don't want today's date used.
5. Press **Ctrl+Enter**. Quicken adds a balance adjustment transaction to the register (Figure 14.6).

CHECK YOURSELF

Update the account balance in one of your asset or liability accounts.

ANSWER

1. From the account's Register screen, select Activities, then select Update Account Balance.
2. Enter the new account balance.
3. Enter the category for the adjustment to be assigned to.

Updating Account Balances

▼ ***Figure 14.6. A Balance Adjustment Transaction Added to the Account Register***

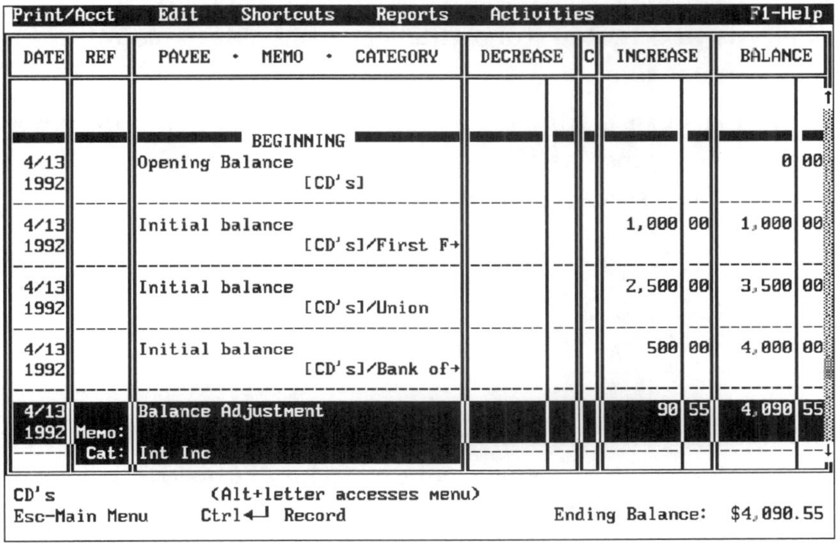

4. Enter a date for the adjustment transaction.
5. Press **Ctrl+Enter**.

Transfers

You can use Quicken's transfer feature to transfer money between asset/liability accounts and other Quicken accounts. You can even transfer money between an asset account and a liability account. Remember, you can enter a transfer in either the source account (where the money's coming from) or the destination account (where the money's going to). In either case, you enter the name of the other account in the transaction CATEGORY field, and Quicken automatically enters the matching transaction in the other account. Here are some example situations where a transfer involving an asset or liability account could be used:

- You write a check to pay off a loan balance (transfer from checking account to liability account).
- You sell some coins from your collection and invest the proceeds in a mutual fund (transfer from asset account to investment account).
- You cash in a CD and use the money for home improvements that increase the market value of your house (transfer from one asset account to another asset account).

Tracking Loans

One of the more common uses for liability accounts is to keep track of loans. By keeping accurate track of your loan balances, you will always know the amount you still owe. You'll also be able to use Quicken's Net Worth report to obtain an exact net worth figure.

To keep track of a loan, first set up a liability account for the loan. Enter the total loan amount as the initial account balance. You should use a separate liability account for each loan you are tracking. Then, whenever you write a check for a loan payment, make a transfer to the loan account for that portion of the payment that is being applied to the loan principal. With each such transfer, Quicken will automatically enter a transaction decreasing your loan liability by the proper amount.

This technique is applicable to the standard type of fixed loan, where you borrow a certain sum and then have fixed monthly payments over a set time period. Most mortgages and car loans fall into this category. Remember that each monthly payment you send in goes for both interest and principal. Only the portion that goes toward the loan principal reduces the amount you owe on the loan. Therefore, when you enter a loan payment check you must split the transaction and assign the proper amounts to interest and principal. Only the principal amount should be transferred to the loan's liability account. The amount of each payment that goes toward interest and toward principal can be found in a *loan amortization table*. If your bank

Tracking Loans

▼ ***Figure 14.7. A Loan Payment Split between Interest and Principal***

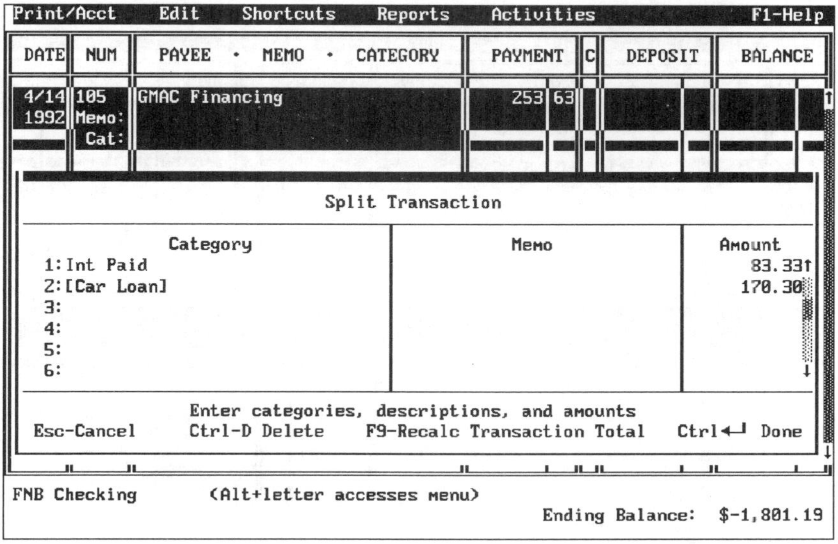

does not provide such a table for your loan, you can use Quicken's loan calculator to generate one. The loan calculator is described in the next section.

For example, say you have set up a liability account to keep track of your car loan. The total loan is for $10,000, and the first payment of $253.63 is comprised of $83.33 in interest and $170.30 toward principal. When you enter the check for this payment, you would split the transaction as shown in Figure 14.7.

Once you've recorded this transaction in your Quicken checking account, a parallel transaction is automatically created for the transfer in the Car Loan liability account, as shown in Figure 14.8.

The Loan Calculator

Quicken's loan calculator calculates the periodic payment on a loan based upon the loan amount, term, and interest rate. It can also display an amortization table for a given loan. Use the calculator to perform comparisons between different loans and to

▼ *Figure 14.8. The Principal Portion of the Loan Payment Is Transferred to the Loan's Liability Account*

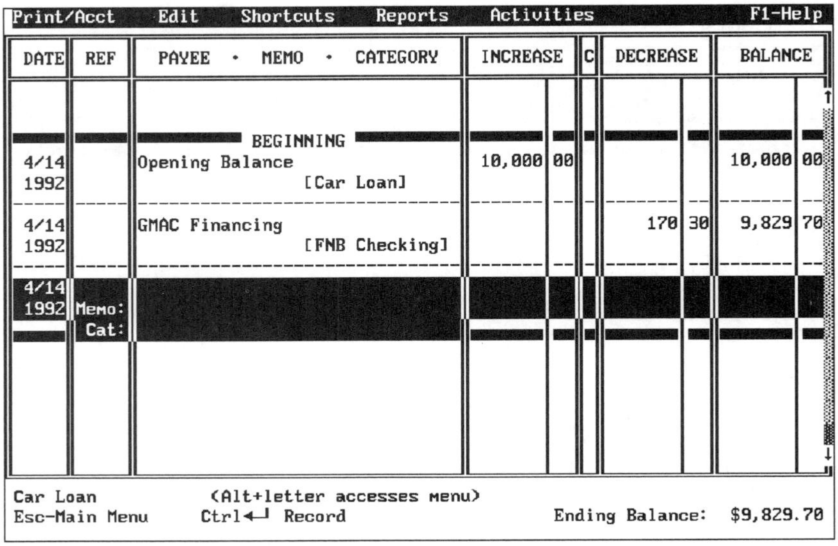

determine what proportion of your payments are going for interest and for principal.

To use the loan calculator:

1. From the Register screen, select Activities.
2. From the pull-down menu, select Loan Calculator. The calculator is displayed. (Figure 14.9).
3. In the "Principal:" field, enter the total loan amount.
4. In the "Annual interest rate:" field, enter the percentage rate of the loan.
5. In the "Total years:" field, enter the duration of the loan payment schedule in years.
6. In the "Periods per year:" field, enter the number of loan payments you must make each year.
7. Quicken calculates and displays the periodic loan payment. If you go back and change the information in any of the input fields, Quicken immediately updates the payment amount.

The Loan Calculator

▼ *Figure 14.9. Quicken's Loan Calculator*

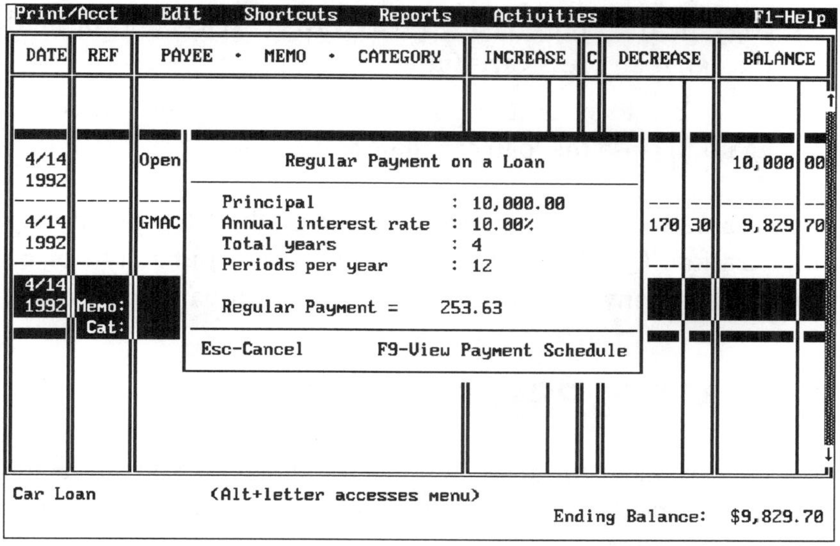

8. To view the amortization chart, or payment schedule, for the loan, press **F9**. This chart shows the interest amount and the principal amount for each loan payment, and also shows the remaining loan balance (Figure 14.10).

▼ *Figure 14.10. A Loan Payment Schedule, or Amortization Chart*

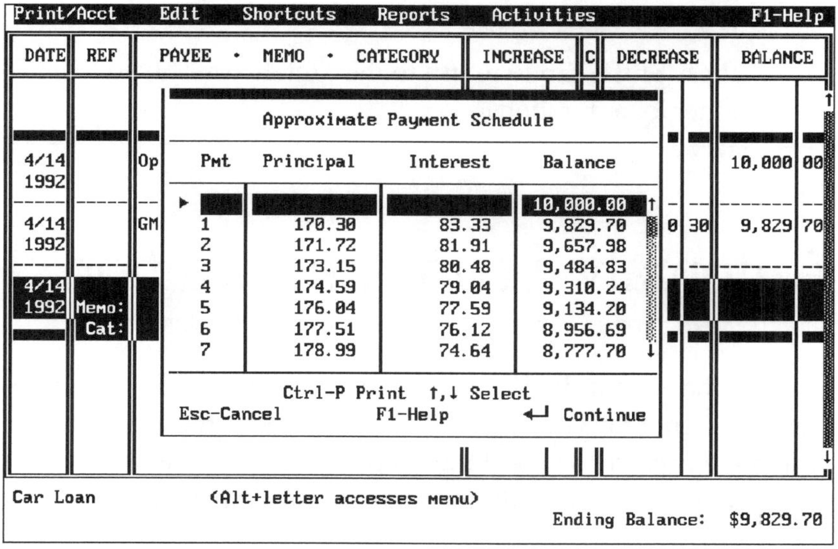

9. Use the Up arrow, Down arrow, Page Up, Page Down, Home, and End keys to scroll through the chart. To print a copy of the entire chart, press **Ctrl+P**, select the desired printer, then press **Ctrl+Enter**.
10. Press **Esc** to close the payment schedule, then press **Esc** again to close the loan calculator.

Note: Some banks may use a different method for calculating amortization. Quicken's figures will be close, but may not be exact to the penny. You should check with your bank if unsure.

CHECK YOURSELF

Use the loan calculator to see how the duration of a loan affects the monthly payments. You could try a loan of $9,000 at 10% for three, four, and five years.

ANSWER

1. From the register or the Write Checks screen, select Activities, then select Loan Calculator.
2. Enter the loan amount and interest rate.
3. Enter **3** in the "Total years:" field, then press **Enter**. The payment amount is calculated and displayed.
4. Press **Shift+Tab** to return to the "Total years:" field to enter other loan durations.

Automatic Loan Amortization

Quicken has a handy feature that will automatically amortize loan payments for you. You tell Quicken about the loan, then as you make each subsequent payment, Quicken automatically assigns the correct amounts to interest and principal. Quicken's

Automatic Loan Amortization

loan amortization feature is usually used in conjunction with a loan liability account.

To set up an amortized loan payment:

1. Set up the liability account for the loan. Enter the amount you currently owe on the loan as the initial balance.
2. Switch to the checking account that you will be using to make payments on the loan.
3. In the register or the Write Checks screen, enter the Payee and Amount information for the loan payment.
4. Press **Ctrl+M** to memorize the transaction.
5. Press **Ctrl+T** to display the list of memorized transactions.
6. Use the arrow keys to highlight the just-memorized transaction, then press **F9**. The Set Amortization Information window is displayed (Figure 14.11).
7. Under Loan Information, the "Regular payment:" field is already filled in with the payment amount from the memorized transaction. Enter the other details of the loan in the

▼ *Figure 14.11. The Set Amortization Information Window*

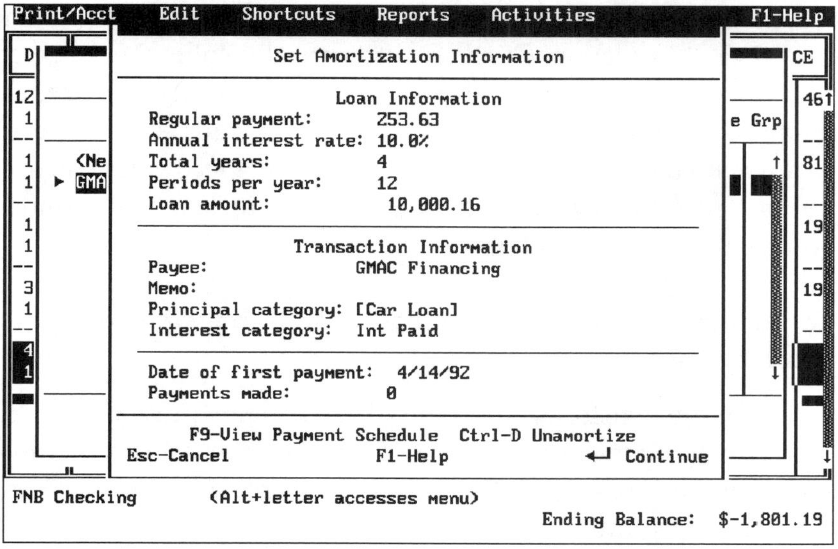

appropriate fields—"Annual interest rate," "Total years," and "Periods per year." Quicken calculates the total loan amount from this information. The value that Quicken calculates may be slightly different from the actual loan amount because of different calculation methods.

8. Under Transaction Information, the "Payee:" field is already filled in with the name of the payee from the memorized transaction. Enter a memo to be saved with each transaction. In the "Principal category:" field, enter the name of the category to which you want the principal portion of each payment assigned. If you're using a liability account to track the loan, this will be the liability account name. In the "Interest category:" field, enter the name of the category to which you want the interest portion of each payment assigned. This will usually be Int Paid.
9. Enter the date of first payment. In the "Payments made:" field, enter the number of loan payments that have already been made. If it's a new loan, enter **0**. For an existing loan, enter the actual number of payments you have already sent in.
10. Press **Enter**. Quicken records the amortization information and associates it with the memorized loan payment transaction.

To use an amortized payment transaction, you simply recall the transaction in the usual way, enter the payment date, then record the transaction. Quicken automatically splits the transaction and, based on the payment number, assigns the proper amounts for interest and principal to the categories you specified when you set up the amortized payment. Once you've made the last scheduled payment on the loan, Quicken will remind you that the loan is paid off.

To remove amortization information from a memorized payment transaction:

1. From the register or the Write Checks screen, press **Ctrl+T** to display the memorized transaction list. Transactions that include amortization information are displayed with an A in the Split column.

Automatic Loan Amortization

2. Use the arrow keys to highlight the transaction, then press **F9**.
3. The payment's amortization information is displayed. Press **Ctrl+D**, then **Enter** to delete it.

CHECK YOURSELF

Set up an amortized loan payment in your checking account.

ANSWER

1. Display the register or the Write Checks screen for the checking account
2. Enter the payee and amount information for the loan payment transaction.
3. Press **Ctrl+M** to memorize the transaction.
4. Press **Ctrl+T** to display the list of memorized transactions.
5. Highlight the new transaction, then press **F9**
6. Under Loan Information, enter the details of the loan.
7. In the "Principal category:" and "Interest category:" fields, enter the categories in which you want the principal and interest portions of each payment assigned.
8. Enter the date of the first payment. In the "Payments made:" field, enter the number of loan payments that have already been made.
9. Press **Enter**.

Closing Items

Asset and liability accounts do not need to be reconciled. You can, however, use the C (cleared) field to mark items in the account that are closed. An item is considered "closed" when it is no longer active as an asset or liability. For example, you pay off a loan or sell part of your coin collection. You would not want these items included in most reports, but for record keeping purposes you might not want to delete them from your accounts. If you mark them as "closed," you can then exclude them from reports by applying a filter.

To mark an item as closed, enter an asterisk (*) in the C field in the account register. If an item has more than one transaction associated with it, be sure to mark them all as closed.

QUICK COMMAND SUMMARY

To set up an asset or liability account:

1. From the Main Menu, choose Select Account, then highlight <New Account> and press **Enter**.
2. In the "Account Type:" field, enter **4** for an asset account, or enter **5** for a liability account.
3. Enter the account name.
4. Enter the account's current value in the "Balance:" field.
5. Enter an account description, if desired, then press **Enter**.

To update the balance in an asset or liability account:

1. From the Register screen, select Activities.
2. Select Update Account Balance.
3. Enter the new account balance.
4. Enter the category for the adjustment to be assigned to.
5. Enter a date for the adjustment transaction.
6. Press **Ctrl+Enter**.

To set up an amortized loan payment:

1. Display the register or the Write Checks screen.
2. Enter the transaction payee and amount information.
3. Press **Ctrl+M** to memorize the transaction.

4. Press **Ctrl+T** to display the list of memorized transactions.
5. Highlight the new transaction, then press **F9**.
6. Under Loan Information, enter the details of the loan.
7. In the "Principal category:" and "Interest category:" fields, enter the desired categories.
8. Enter the date of the first loan payment.
9. In the "Payments made:" field, enter the number of loan payments that have already been made, if any.
10. Press **Enter**.

PRACTICE WHAT YOU'VE LEARNED

Depending on the details of your financial situation, you may find asset and liability accounts very useful. The following practice activities will help you become comfortable with using these types of accounts. You can use your own real accounts, or create "dummy" accounts to work with.

1. Set up several asset and liability accounts, some containing only a single asset or liability and some with multiple items.
2. Enter some transactions that change the value of your accounts.
3. Use the update account balance feature to change account balance.
4. Call up the loan calculator and determine the payments on some loans you might need. Display and print the payment schedule table for one of these loans.
5. Use the automatic amortization feature to set up a memorized payment transaction for a loan.

15

Electronic Bill Paying with CheckFree

This chapter shows you how to use Quicken to pay bills with the CheckFree electronic payment service. You will learn how to

- ▲ **Use CheckFree**
- ▲ **Set up Quicken to use CheckFree**
- ▲ **Use the electronic payee list**
- ▲ **Write electronic checks**
- ▲ **Transmit your transactions**

What Is CheckFree?

CheckFree is an electronic bill payment service developed and operated by the CheckFree Corporation of Columbus, Ohio. CheckFree is not associated with Intuit (the company that created Quicken), but for a modest monthly fee, Quicken users can use the service to make payments electronically.

Using CheckFree

To use CheckFree, you must have a Hayes-compatible modem connected to your computer. Almost all modems are Hayes-compatible. If you are not sure, check your modem documentation or contact the dealer from which you purchased the modem. You can also purchase a modem from CheckFree.

You must also set up an account with CheckFree. Your Quicken package includes a form and instructions for setting one up. When you send in the CheckFree Service Form, you authorize CheckFree to make electronic payments from your bank account. After your application is processed, you will receive a package of information including your CheckFree account number, modem access telephone number, and other information.

How CheckFree Works

CheckFree lets you send electronic payments to essentially any organization or individual in the United States (The only exceptions are certain government agencies). Here's how it works:

- You enter information about each payment into Quicken. This process is identical to entering a regular check transaction, except that it is designated as an electronic payment.
- Quicken uses your modem to dial CheckFree and transmit the payment information. CheckFree transmits a confirmation number for each transaction back to Quicken; this number is

What Is CheckFree?

stored in the check register. A password security system ensures that no one but you can access your CheckFree account.

- CheckFree sends payment to the payee. If the payee is set up to receive electronic payments, the transfer is done electronically. Otherwise, CheckFree prints a check and sends it to the payee. In either case, your bank account is debited for the payments, and the payments show up on your regular bank statement.

Is CheckFree for You?

Using the CheckFree service certainly saves the time and trouble of handwriting or printing checks, and stuffing and addressing envelopes. It also saves postage expenses. You must decide if the expense of the CheckFree service (plus the purchase cost of a modem, if you do not already own one) is worth the convenience.

When you sign up with CheckFree, the first month of service is free. After that, you are charged a monthly fee ($9.95 at this time). The monthly fee covers up to 20 payments per month. If you go above 20, there is a small additional per-payment fee.

If you will use CheckFree for 15-20 payments a month, the amount you will save on postage, envelopes, and checks will balance most of the cost of CheckFree. For fewer payments, the "real" cost of using CheckFree will be greater. If you sign up with CheckFree and then change your mind, you can always cancel your CheckFree account and go back to sending checks by mail.

Setting Up Quicken to Use CheckFree

Once you have received your account materials from CheckFree, you can set up Quicken for electronic payments. There are several steps involved, which are covered in the following sections.

Electronic Payment Settings

The electronic payment settings enable Quicken to work with your modem to transmit information to the CheckFree service. To establish electronic payment settings, you need to know:

- The communications port your modem is attached to. On most systems, this will be COM1 or COM2; less frequently COM3 or COM4 will be used. If you are unsure, ask your computer dealer or try COM1. If that doesn't work try different settings until your modem works.
- The *baud rate* to use. Baud rate is a measure of how fast information is transmitted by a modem. The information you receive from CheckFree will specify one or more baud rates that you can use. Select a baud rate that is supported by CheckFree and by your modem. If in doubt, try a baud rate setting of 1200.
- Whether your phone system uses tone or pulse dialing.
- The CheckFree telephone number (provided in the information you received from CheckFree).

To enter electronic payment settings into Quicken:

1. From the Main Menu, select Set Preferences.
2. Select Electronic Payment Settings.
3. Select Modem Settings. The Electronic Payment Settings window is displayed (Figure 15.1).
4. In the "Serial port used by modem:" field, specify the communications port. If you are not sure, enter **1** for COM1.
5. In the "Modem speed:" field, specify the baud rate. If you are not sure, enter **2** for 1200 baud.
6. In the "Tone or Pulse Dialing:" field, enter **T** if your phones use tone dialing, **P** if they use pulse dialing.
7. Enter the CheckFree phone number included with your CheckFree confirmation package. Do not enter hyphens or parentheses. If it's a long distance number, be sure to enter

▼ *Figure 15.1. The Electronic Payment Settings Window*

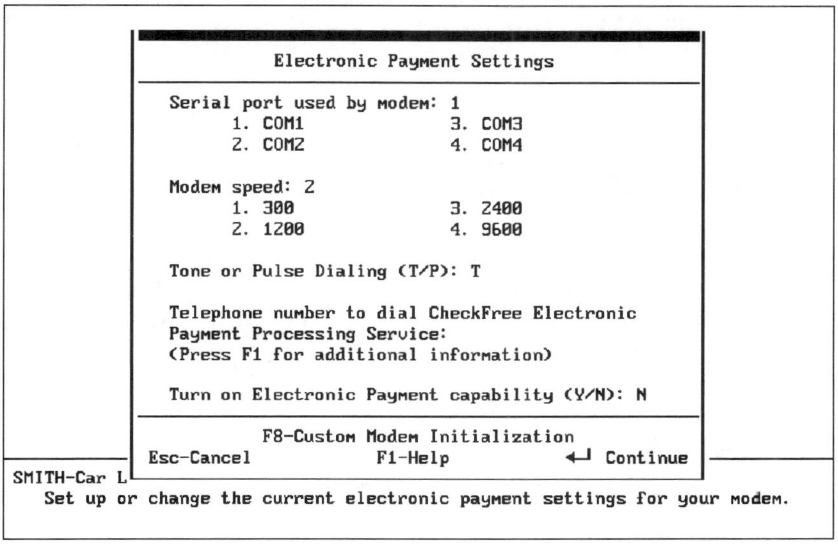

Setting Up Quicken to Use CheckFree

the long distance access code **1** and the area code, for example, **1 800 555 1234**. See below for special phone number considerations.

8. In the "Turn on Electronic Payment capability:" field, enter **Y** to activate electronic payments, then press **Enter**.

Quicken is now set to communicate with CheckFree. Before you can make any electronic payments, you must also set up your Quicken bank account to work with CheckFree and establish an electronic payee list.

In some situations, you will need to enter special codes in the CheckFree phone number. For example, if you are using an office phone and must dial 9 to get an outside line, the "9" must be included in the phone number you enter in the Electronic Payment Settings window. If you have a call waiting service on your phone line, you must disable it when calling CheckFree or it may interfere with data transmission. This is done by dialing a special code before the CheckFree number (usually *70). Check with your phone company if you are not sure how to disable it. Finally, you can enter one or more commas in the phone number to tell Quicken to pause during dialing. Here are some examples:

9, 1 800 555 1234	Dial an outside line, pause to wait for a dial tone, then dial CheckFree.
*70, 1 800 555 1234	Turn off call waiting, pause, then dial CheckFree.

CHECK YOURSELF

Go through the steps to set up Quicken to work with CheckFree. If you have enrolled in CheckFree and received your confirmation package, and have a modem installed, you'll have all the information you need to actually go ahead and set up. If not, you can practice a "dry run."

ANSWER

1. From the Main Menu, select Set Preferences.
2. Select Electronic Payment Settings.
3. Select Modem Settings.
4. Specify your modem's communications port and baud rate.
5. Enter **T** if your phones use tone dialing, **P** if they use pulse dialing.
6. Enter the CheckFree phone number.
7. Enter **Y** in the "Turn on Electronic Payment capability:" field, then press **Enter**.

Bank Account Settings

Before you can make payments with CheckFree, you must set up a Quicken bank account for electronic payments. This can be an existing account or a new account. It must, of course, be the same account you specified on the CheckFree Service Form. Before setting up your bank account, you must enter the modem settings as described above. If you plan to set up a new account for use with CheckFree, you must first set up the Quicken bank account using the procedures you learned earlier in the book.

Setting Up Quicken to Use CheckFree

To set up an existing Quicken bank account for electronic payments:

1. From the Main Menu, select Set Preferences.
2. Select Electronic Payment Settings.
3. Select Account Settings.
4. The Set Up Account for Electronic Payment window is displayed. This window contains a list of bank accounts in the current file. Use the Up and Down arrow keys to highlight the name of the account you want to set up, then press **Enter**.
5. In the next window, enter **Y**, then press **Enter**.
6. The Electronic Payment Account Settings window is displayed (Figure 15.2).
7. Enter your name, address, and phone number in the fields in the window. The phone number is required, and should be entered with the area code first.
8. In the "Social Security Number:" field, enter your CheckFree System Identification Number (provided in your CheckFree confirmation package). In most cases, CheckFree uses your Social Security number for this purpose.

▼ ***Figure 15.2. The Electronic Payment Account Settings Window***

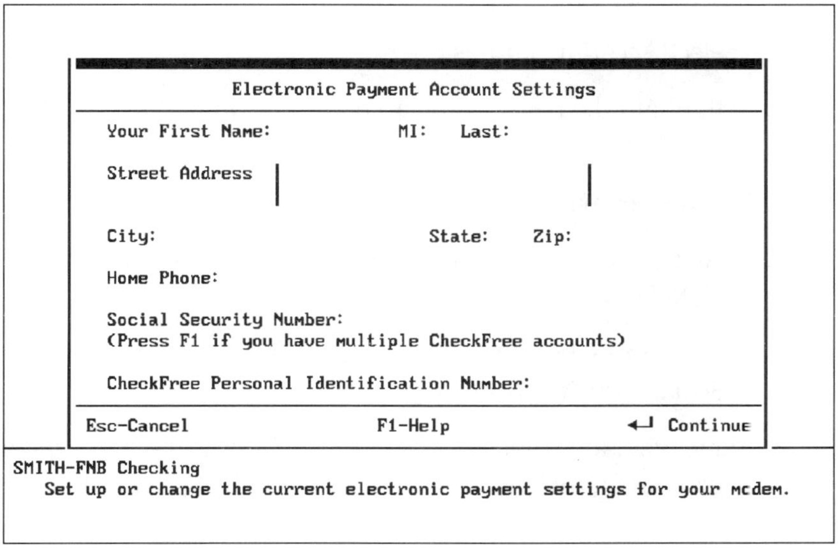

9. In the "CheckFree Personal Identification Number:" field, enter the four-digit Personal Security Code provided by CheckFree.
10. Press **Enter**. Quicken displays the Set Up Account for Electronic Payment window again. The word "Enabled" is now displayed next to the account name in the "Electronic Pmts" field.
11. Press **Esc** until the Main Menu is displayed.

Your account is now ready to make electronic payments. Whenever you display the list of accounts, you will see a small triangle displayed next to the account name in the "Type:" field, indicating that this account is set up for electronic payments.

CHECK YOURSELF

Set up your Quicken checking account to make electronic payments. If you have enrolled with CheckFree, be sure to use the account that you specified on your enrollment forms.

ANSWER

1. From the Main Menu, select Set Preferences.
2. Select Electronic Payment Settings.
3. Select Account Settings.
4. Highlight the name of the account you want to set up, then press **Enter**.
5. In the next window enter **Y**, then press **Enter**.
6. Enter your name, address, and phone number in the appropriate fields.
7. Enter your CheckFree System Identification Number in the "Social Security Number:" field.
8. Enter your four-digit Personal Security Code in the "CheckFree Personal Identification Number:" field, then press **Enter**.

9. Press **Esc** until the Main Menu is displayed.

Setting Up Quicken to Use CheckFree

Electronic Payee List

The next step in getting ready to make electronic payments is adding payees to the Electronic Payee list. Each payee needs be added to the list only once. The information you enter is required by CheckFree to insure that your payment is sent and credited correctly. To enter a payee, you need:

- The payee's name.
- The payee's address (where checks should be sent).
- The payee's phone number. Use the number you would call for billing questions. It is important to enter an accurate phone number since CheckFree uses this number for cross-reference purposes and in case of billing questions. An incorrect phone number could cause payment processing errors.
- Your account number—that is, the number that the payee uses to identify you. Be sure that you enter the proper account number or else the payee may not be able to credit your account with the payments sent by CheckFree. If there is no account number, enter your last name.

To enter payees in your electronic payee list:

1. Display the register or the Write Checks screen for your electronic payment account.
2. Press **Ctrl+Y**, or select Shortcuts, then select Electronic Payee List. Quicken displays a list of electronic payees.
3. Highlight <Set up a new payee>, then press **Enter**. Quicken displays the Set Up Electronic Payee window (Figure 15.3).
4. Enter payee information in the appropriate fields in the window. After entering the account number, press **Enter**.
5. Return to Step 3 to enter additional payees, or press **Esc** until you return to the Main Menu.

▼ *Figure 15.3. The Set Up Electronic Payee Window*

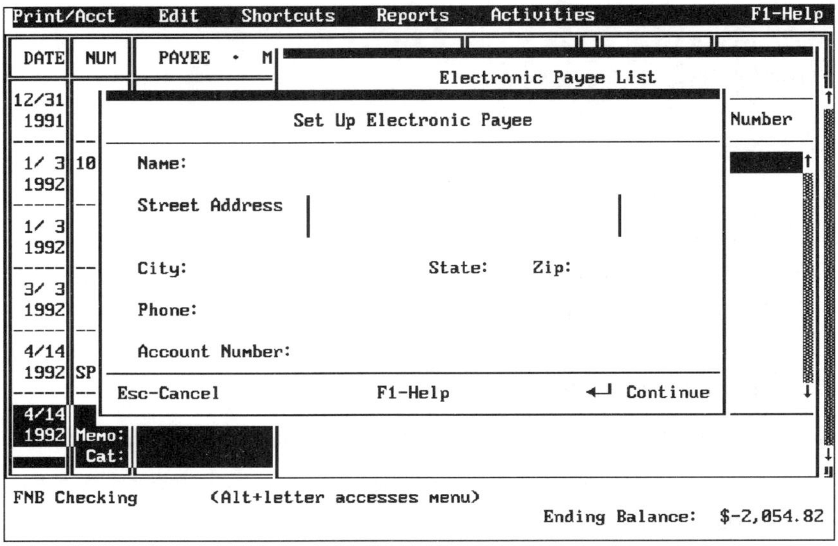

If you have completed all of the preparations outlined above, you are ready to write your first electronic checks. But first you need to be aware of some guidelines for avoiding late payments.

CHECK YOURSELF

If you know some payees that you will be sending electronic payments to, enter them in the electronic payee list. Remember, it's very important to enter accurate address, phone number, and account number information in this list.

ANSWER

1. From the register or the Write Checks screen, press **Ctrl+Y**, or select Shortcuts, then select Electronic Payee List.
2. Highlight <Set up a new payee>, then press **Enter**.
3. Enter payee information in the appropriate fields in the window. After entering the account number, press **Enter**.

4. Return to Step 2 to enter additional payees; press **Esc** when finished.

Setting Up Quicken to Use CheckFree

Avoiding Late Payments

You may need to allow a little extra time for CheckFree payments. If your payee is set up to accept electronic payments directly, then your payment is sent and received almost instantly (on the date you specify), and there should be no problems with lateness.

Many payees, however, cannot accept electronic payments directly, so CheckFree must print a check and mail it from Ohio to them. In addition, the check that your payee will receive from CheckFree is accompanied by a payment stub that's in a different format than the merchant is accustomed to receiving. This forces some merchants to process CheckFree payments as "exception items" that require special handling (and more time).

When you date your payments, you specify the date that CheckFree will print and mail a check. Be sure to allow sufficient lead time so that your payment can be received and processed before the payment due date.

CheckFree guarantees that your payments will be sent as you request. They cannot, however, be responsible for mail delays, or delays in processing your payment once it is received. CheckFree suggests the following guidelines to minimize the likelihood of late payments:

- The payment date (the date CheckFree sends payment to the payee) should be at least five business days prior to the payment due date.
- The transmission date (the date you transmit payment information to CheckFree) should be 10 business days prior to the due date.

In addition, it's crucial that the name, address, and account number information for each payee is correct.

Writing Electronic Checks

The procedure for writing an electronic check is very similar to the procedures for writing a paper check. You can write an electronic check from the Write Checks screen or the register.

Writing Electronic Checks from the Write Checks Screen

To write an electronic check from the Write Checks screen:

1. Make the electronic payment account current.
2. From the Main Menu, select Write/Print Checks to display the Write Checks screen.
3. Press **F9**, if necessary, to display the screen in electronic payment format (as shown in Figure 15.4).

▼ ***Figure 15.4. The Write Checks Screen in Electronic Payment Format***

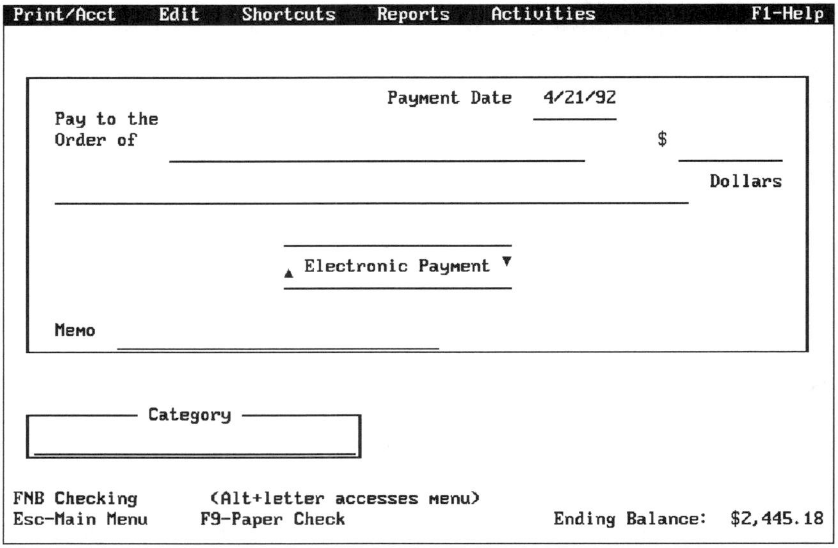

Writing Electronic Checks

4. Quicken automatically postdates the "Payment Date" field by five business days from the current date. You can enter a different date, but it must be postdated by at least five days.
5. In the "Pay to the Order of" field, enter the name of the payee. You can also enter the first few letters of the payee's name then press **Enter**. One of three things happens:
   - ▲ If what you entered matches a single entry in the electronic payee list, Quicken completes the entry if necessary and moves the cursor to the "$" (amount) field.
   - ▲ If what you entered matches more than one entry in the electronic payee list, Quicken displays the list so you can select one payee from it.
   - ▲ If what you entered does not match any entry on the electronic payee list, Quicken displays screens so you can either select from the list or add a new entry to the list.
6. Enter the appropriate information in the "$," "Memo," and "Category" fields. Note that the Memo information is not sent to the payee along with the payment, so you cannot use this field for messages to the payee. Entering categories, splitting transactions, and using transfers is no different than for non-electronic payments.
7. Press **Ctrl+Enter** to record the payment. Quicken records it, and displays another blank check. Quicken does not transmit payment information to CheckFree at this time, but only stores it for later transmission.

Note: Quicken will not accept an electronic payment that appears to duplicate an earlier payment (has the same information in the "Date," "Pay to the Order of," and "$" fields).

Electronic payments that you enter in the Write Checks screen are added to the account register. They appear just like other check transactions except that the NUM field contains "E-PMT" (electronic payment) for electronic checks that have been entered and transmitted, and ">>>>>" for electronic checks that have been entered but *not* transmitted. For example, the highlighted transaction in the register in Figure 15.5 is for an

▼ ***Figure 15.5. Untransmitted Electronic Checks Appear in the Register with ">>>>>" in the NUM Field***

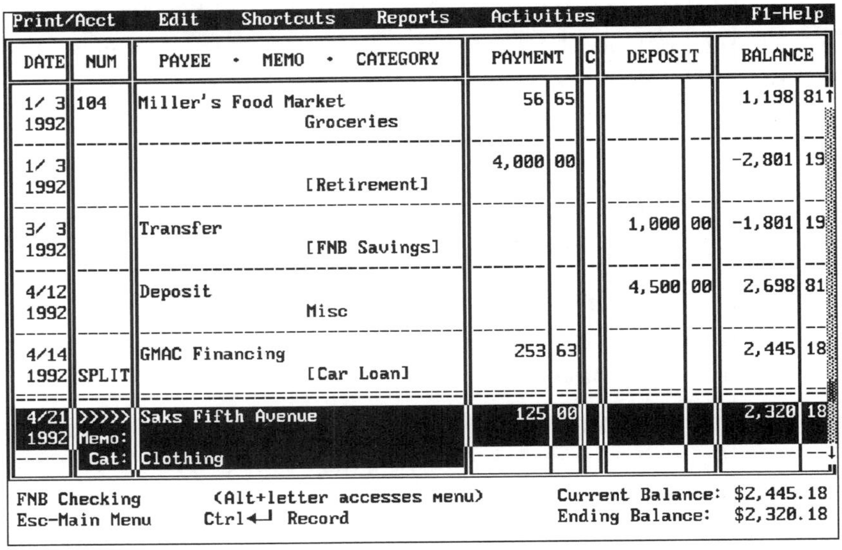

untransmitted electronic check. Also note in this figure, that in the register, postdated transactions are preceded by a double-dashed line.

Writing Electronic Checks from the Register Screen

To enter an electronic check in the register:

1. Display the register, then highlight the first blank transaction.
2. The DATE field displays today's date. Change it if desired.
3. In the NUM field, enter a single greater-than symbol (>). Quicken automatically fills the remainder of the NUM field with five > symbols. Quicken also changes the transaction date, if necessary, to postdate the payment by at least five working days.
4. Enter the payee in the PAYEE field. As described above for the Write Checks screen, Quicken compares your entry with

Writing Electronic Checks

the electronic payee list and lets you select a payee or add a new payee, if necessary.

5. Complete the remainder of the fields in the usual fashion, and press **Ctrl+Enter** to record the transaction.

Note: If you enter a single > in the NUM field and it does not immediately expand to fill the field, then electronic payments have not been enabled for this account.

CHECK YOURSELF

Enter some electronic payments. Try doing so from both the Write Checks screen and from the register.

ANSWER

From the Write Checks screen:

1. Press **F9**, if necessary to display the screen in electronic payment format.
3. Enter a date that is postdated by more than five business days, if desired.
4. Enter a payee, or select one from the electronic payee list.
5. Enter the payment amount, memo, and category.
6. Press **Ctrl+Enter** to record the transaction.

From the register:

1. Highlight the first blank transaction.
2. Enter > in the NUM field.
3. Check the DATE field, and change it if necessary.
4. Enter a payee, or select one from the electronic payee list.
5. Enter the payment amount, memo, and category.
6. Press **Ctrl+Enter** to record the transaction.

Transmitting Transactions to CheckFree

Entering your electronic transactions into Quicken is only the first part of the procedure. You must transmit these transactions to CheckFree so that they can process them and make the payments you have requested. Transmissions can also include additions or changes to your electronic payee list, stop payment orders, and inquiries to CheckFree. (These last two items are discussed later.)

To transmit to CheckFree:

1. Display the Write Checks screen or the register for the electronic payment account.
2. Press **Ctrl+I**, or select Print/Acct, then select Transmit Payments.
3. Quicken displays a window telling you how many payments you have to be transmitted. Press **F9** to preview the information to be transmitted.
4. Quicken displays a list of transactions and other information that is about to be transmitted. Review the list for accuracy. If you see an error, press **Esc** twice to return to the register or to the Write Checks screen. Make any needed changes, then return to Step 2.
5. Be sure that your modem is turned on, if it's an external model, and that the phone line is free. Press **Enter** to start transmitting.
6. Quicken dials the CheckFree number and transmits the information. As it works, it displays messages informing you of its progress. If you receive an error message, press **Esc** to terminate the transmission procedure and repeat the entire procedure. If errors persist, press **F1** for help, or refer to the *CheckFree Troubleshooting* section in your Quicken manual.

CHECK YOURSELF

Transmit your electronic payments to CheckFree. This is impossible to practice, as any transmission to CheckFree is a real one. If unsure, you might want to start with a small number of less important transactions. You could even have CheckFree send a check to a friend, to be sure everything is working.

ANSWER

1. From the Write Checks screen or the register, press **Ctrl+I**, or select Print/Acct, then select Transmit Payments.
2. Press **F9** to preview the information to be transmitted. Review the list for accuracy.
3. Be sure that your modem is turned on, if it's an external model, and that the phone line is free. Press **Enter** to start transmitting. Quicken displays messages informing you of its progress, and informs you when transmission is complete.
4. If you receive an error message, press **Esc** to terminate the transmission procedure, then repeat the entire procedure.

Your Confirmation Number

After CheckFree successfully receives your transmission, it sends a confirmation number back to Quicken. Quicken automatically stores each confirmation number, and uses it if you later send an inquiry or stop payment message to CheckFree.

If you want to see the confirmation number:

1. Display the register, and highlight an electronic payment transaction that has already been transmitted (that is, displays E-PMT in the NUM field).
2. Select Edit.

3. Select Electronic Payment Inquiry. Quicken displays a window containing information about that transaction, including the confirmation number.

Stopping Electronic Payments

If you enter an electronic payment in error, you can correct or cancel it at any time before you transmit it. Simply display the register, highlight the transaction, then make corrections or press **Ctrl+D** to delete it.

You may discover that the payment is in error after transmitting it to CheckFree. You can stop the payment if you do not wait too long. It can take CheckFree as long as five days from the time it receives your transmission to the time it actually sends payment.

To stop a payment:

1. Display the register, then highlight the transaction you want to stop.
2. Select Edit.
3. Select Transmit Stop Payment Request.
4. Based on the date that the transaction was transmitted, Quicken tells you if it is possible to stop it. If it is possible, enter **Y**.
5. Quicken immediately dials the CheckFree number and transmits the stop payment request. If the payment is successfully stopped, Quicken receives and records a stop payment confirmation number, and marks the transaction as VOID in the register.

If Quicken tells you the payment cannot be stopped, you may still be able to stop the payment by calling CheckFree directly and speaking with a representative. See the CheckFree literature for information. There is no fee for stopping payment using Quicken, but there is a fee if you call directly.

Memorizing and Recalling Electronic Payments

Memorizing and Recalling Electronic Payments

You can memorize and recall electronic payments using the same techniques you use for non-electronic transactions.

To memorize an electronic payment:

1. Enter the payment information you want memorized in the Write Checks screen (in electronic payment format) or in the register. If using the register, be sure the electronic payment symbol (>>>>>) is entered in the NUM field.
2. Press **Ctrl+M** to memorize the transaction.
3. Complete the transaction if you wish, or delete it by pressing **Ctrl+D**.

To recall a memorized electronic payment:

1. Display the Write Checks screen (in electronic payment format) or a blank transaction on the register screen.
2. Press **Ctrl+T** to display a list of memorized transactions. In this list, electronic transactions display as "Epm" in the "Type:" field.
3. Highlight the desired transaction, then press **Enter**.
4. Fill in the remaining transaction information.

QUICK COMMAND SUMMARY

To set up Quicken to work with CheckFree:

1. From the Main Menu, select Set Preferences.
2. Select Electronic Payment Settings.
3. Select Modem Settings.
4. Specify your modem's communications port and baud rate.
5. Enter **T** if your phones use tone dialing, **P** if they use pulse dialing.

6. Enter the CheckFree phone number.
7. Enter **Y** in the "Turn on Electronic Payment capability" field, then press **Enter**.

To set up your Quicken checking account to make electronic payments:

1. From the Main Menu, select Set Preferences.
2. Select Electronic Payment Settings.
3. Select Account Settings.
4. Highlight the name of the account you want to set up, then press **Enter**.
5. In the next window, enter **Y**, then press **Enter**.
6. Enter your name, address, and phone number in the appropriate fields.
7. Enter your CheckFree System Identification Number in the "Social Security Number:" field.
8. Enter your four-digit Personal Security Code in the CheckFree Personal Identification Number:" field, then press **Enter**.

To make entries in the electronic payee list:

1. From the register or Write Checks screen, press **Ctrl+Y**, or select Shortcuts, then select Electronic Payee List.
2. Highlight <Set up a new payee>, then press **Enter**.
3. Enter payee information in the fields in the window, making sure the information is accurate. After entering the account number, press **Enter**.
4. Return to Step 2 to enter additional payees; press **Esc** when finished.

To transmit your electronic payments to CheckFree:

1. From the Write Checks screen or the register, press **Ctrl+I**, or select Print/Acct, then select Transmit Payments.

2. Press **F9** to preview the information to be transmitted. Review the list for accuracy.
3. Be sure that your modem is turned on, if it's an external model, and that the phone line is free. Press **Enter** to start transmitting. Quicken displays messages informing you of its progress, and informs you when transmission is complete.
4. If you receive an error message, press **Esc** to terminate the transmission procedure and repeat the entire procedure.

PRACTICE WHAT YOU'VE LEARNED

It's difficult to practice electronic payments, since any transmission you send to CheckFree is "real" and will result in actual payments being made. One method you can use to ensure everything is working and that you are entering information properly is to send small "payments" to a couple of your friends. If they receive the payments, you can feel confident that it's okay to use Quicken and CheckFree for real payments.

1. Set up Quicken to contact CheckFree, and set up a checking account to make electronic payments.
2. Make some entries in your electronic payee list.
3. Enter some electronic payments into your account.
4. Transmit the payments to CheckFree.
5. Use the stop payment feature to stop payment on one or more of your "practice" payments.

16

Quicken Settings

Quicken has a number of settings that control certain aspects of the program's operation. You can change these settings to customize Quicken to suit your own preferences. In this chapter, you'll learn how to

- ▲ **Change Quicken's screen display**
- ▲ **Set up Quicken to use your printer**
- ▲ **Protect your data with passwords**
- ▲ **Change transaction, check, and report settings**

Screen Settings

Quicken gives you control over certain aspects of your screen display, such as color. To a certain extent, the screen options available to you depend on the type of video display hardware your system has.

To change Quicken's screen settings:

1. From the Main Menu, select Set Preferences.
2. From the next menu, select Screen Settings. Quicken displays the Screen Settings menu (Figure 16.1).
3. Select the screen setting you want to change, then on the next menu select or enter the desired choice. The available screen options are explained in the next sections.

Screen Colors

Quicken offers eight different screen color schemes. Some of the schemes are usable only if you have a color monitor. Others can

▼ *Figure 16.1. The Screen Settings Menu*

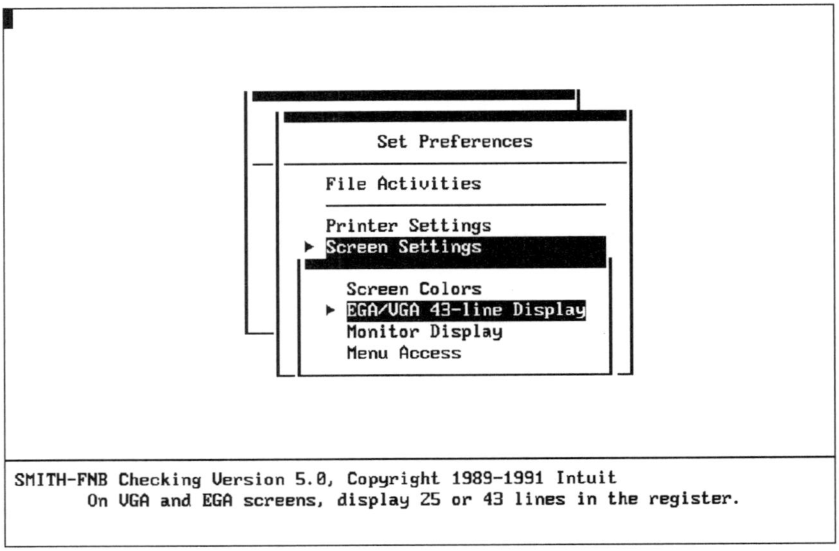

be used on either color or monochrome monitors. The available color schemes are:

Monochrome	For black-and-white monitors that cannot display shades of gray.
Reverse monochrome	Monochrome with black and white reversed.
Navy/Azure	Quicken's default color scheme for color monitors.
White/Navy	Optional color scheme.
Red/Gray	Optional color scheme that may improve visibility for certain color blind individuals.
Shades of gray	For black-and-white monitors that can display shades of gray (for instance, VGA monochrome).
Purple/White	Optional color scheme.
Green/Yellow	Optional color scheme.

When you make a selection from the Change Color Scheme menu, the change takes effect immediately. You can try different settings and see which one you prefer.

EGA/VGA 43-Line Display

If your system is equipped with an EGA or VGA video display, you have the option of displaying 43 lines of text on the screen instead of the default 25 lines. Letters and numbers are smaller, but this option allows you to view more information at one time.

To change the number of lines displayed, select EGA/VGA 43-line Display from the Screen Settings menu, then select either 25 lines or 43 lines. If your video system does not support a 43-line display, Quicken tells you that the option is not available.

Monitor Display

Quicken can send information to your video monitor at two speeds: fast and slow. On some older video systems, use of the default fast display mode will cause "snow" to appear on the screen. To get rid of the snow, select Monitor Display from the Screen Settings menu, then select Slow.

Menu Access

Quicken offers you two methods of menu access: Alt key and function key. With the Alt key method, you select a menu command by pressing **Alt** and then typing the letter that is highlighted in the menu display. With the function key method, you select a command by typing the number displayed next to the item. The Alt key method conforms to a new industry standard called Systems Applications Architecture (SAA). You're likely to see more and more programs using the SAA standard in the future. The function key method is used by earlier Quicken versions and some other popular PC programs. Both methods work equally well—you can use the one you prefer.

To set the menu access method:

1. Select Menu Access from the Screen Settings menu.
2. Enter **1** for function key access, **2** for Alt key access.
3. Press **Enter**. The new menu access method will take effect the next time you start Quicken.

CHECK YOURSELF

Spend some time experimenting with Quicken's different screen settings. If you have a color monitor, you might want to try different screen color settings to find the one you prefer.

ANSWER

1. From the Main Menu, select Set Preferences.

Screen Settings

2. Select Screen Settings.
3. Select the screen setting you want to change: Screen Colors, EGA/VGA 43-line Display, Monitor Display, or Menu Access.
4. Select the desired option setting.
5. Return to Step 2 to make additional screen setting changes, or press **Esc**.

Printer Settings

Quicken lets you set up three different printer definitions. These could actually be three different printers attached to your system, or (more likely) they could be three different settings for the same printer, allowing it to print in three different ways. The three printer definitions are called the Check Printer, the Report Printer, and the Alternate Report Printer. The procedure for setting up each of these printer definitions is the same. You may need only one definition, in which case you need not set up the other two.

For each printer definition, you must provide Quicken with:

- The brand name and model of the printer.
- The printing style to use. *Style* refers to the number of characters printed per inch and the orientation of lines on the page. There are two orientations: *portrait* is the normal orientation, with lines of print parallel to the short edge of the paper; *Landscape* orientation prints lines parallel to the long edge of the paper. Landscape orientation is not available on all printers. Each printer has a certain number of styles available.
- The printer settings. The settings include things such as how the printer is connected to your computer, the number of lines to print per page, and the left indentation.

To set up or modify a printer definition:

1. From the Main Menu, select Set Preferences, then select Report Printer Settings. Or, from the register or Write Checks screen, select Print/Acct then, select Change Printer Styles.
2. Quicken displays a list of the three available printer definitions (check, report, and alternate report). Select the definition you want to change.
3. Quicken displays several overlapping windows on the screen (Figure 16.2). The top window lists the styles that are available for the currently selected printer (the name of the current printer is displayed at the top of the Styles window and is also highlighted in one of the other windows). The currently active style is highlighted in the Styles window. For example, Figure 16.2 shows the new selections to be the LaserJet II/IId printer, and 12 cpi (characters per inch) Portrait style.
4. To select a different style, use the Up arrow and Down arrow keys to highlight the style, then press **Enter**. Then, proceed with Step 7.

▼ ***Figure 16.2. The Styles Window with the Available Printing Styles for the Selected Printer Displayed***

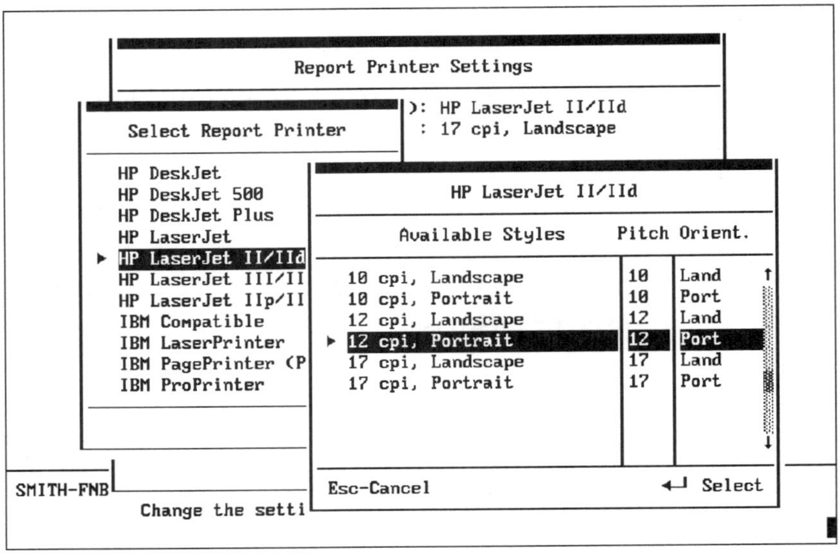

Printer Settings

5. To select a different brand and model of printer, press **Esc** to hide the Styles window; the Select Report Printer window will now be active. Use the Up arrow, Down arrow, Page Up, Page Down, Home, and End keys to highlight the correct printer, then press **Enter**.
6. The Styles window is displayed again, listing styles available for the newly selected printer. Highlight the desired style, then press **Enter**.
7. When you select a style, Quicken displays the Printer Settings window (Figure 16.3). Make entries in this window as described below, then press **Ctrl+Enter**. Your printer is now set up. Return to Step 1 if you want to set up additional printer definitions.

The Printer Settings window contains a variety of fields with information about the printer setup. Quicken fills these fields with information based on the printer and printing style you selected. Most of the time, you will not need to make any changes in this window, except perhaps to the "Print to:" field. However,

▼ *Figure 16.3. The Printer Settings Window*

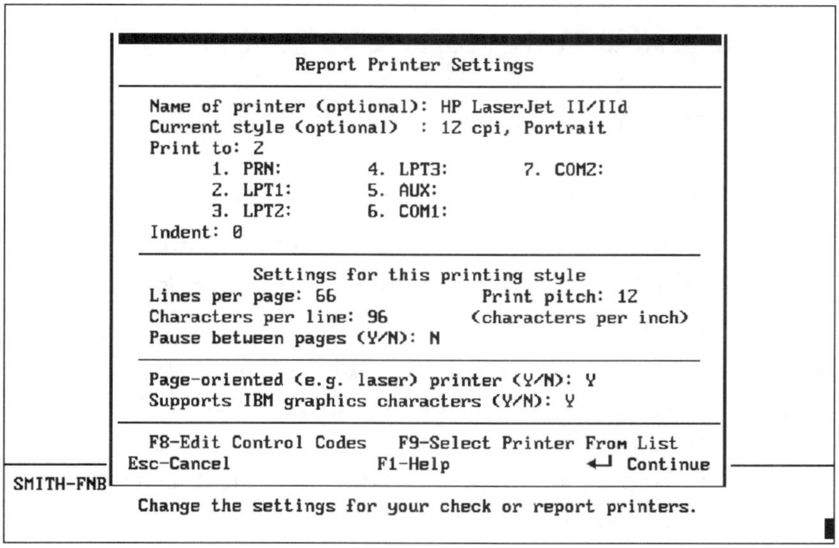

it's a good idea for you to be familiar with the meaning of the information displayed in this window.

- The "Name of printer:" field displays the name of the selected printer.
- The "Current style:" field displays the name of the current style.
- The "Print to:" field specifies the printer port that the printer is connected to. PRN:, LPT1:, LPT2:, and LPT3: are parallel ports. AUX:, COM1:, and COM2: are serial ports. On most systems the printer is attached to the LPT1: port. If your system is different, enter the number corresponding to your printer port in this field. If you select one of the serial ports, another window is displayed when you close the Report Printer Settings window. In this window, you specify the serial port settings. See your printer manual for the settings to use.
- The "Indent:" field specifies how many extra spaces the left margin should be indented. For most printers, this setting is 0.
- The "Lines per page:" field specifies how many lines Quicken prints on a single page.
- The "Print pitch:" field specifies how many characters per inch the printer uses when printing checks.
- The "Characters per line:" field specifies how many characters the printer can place on a single line when printing reports.
- In the "Pause between pages:" field, enter **Y** if you will be hand-feeding single sheets of paper (or checks) to the printer. Enter **N** in this field if your printer uses continuous paper or a paper tray.
- In the "Page-oriented printer:" field, enter **Y** for laser printers (or other sheet-fed printers), and to **N** for dot matrix and other printers that use continuous paper. This setting affects check printing only.
- If your printer can print IBM graphics characters, enter **N** in the "Supports IBM graphics characters:" field. Otherwise, enter **N** in this field. Quicken uses these special characters to generate report headings. If your printer doesn't support them, Quicken uses hyphens and equal signs instead. If

Printer Settings

you're not sure whether your printer supports IBM graphics characters, enter **Y** in this field and print a report. If it prints correctly, then your printer supports graphics characters. If the report heading contains incorrect symbols (Ds and Ms), then your printer does not support graphics characters and you should enter **N** in this field.

After you've made any necessary entries in the Report Printer Settings window, press **Ctrl+Enter**. Your printer definitions are now set up.

If Your Printer Is Not Listed

The Quicken printer list includes almost every popular printer in use today, plus a few of the less popular ones. The great majority of users will find their printer. But what do you do if you cannot find your make and model of printer on Quicken's printer list?

The first step is to look in your printer documentation to see if the printer can emulate another brand of printer that is on Quicken's list. For example, most laser printers can emulate the Hewlett Packard LaserJet, and most dot matrix printers can emulate one of the Epson printers. If you find a supported emulation, select the emulated printer from Quicken's list and your printing should proceed without problems.

If your printer does not have an emulation that Quicken supports, you will have to tell Quicken what printer *control codes* your printer requires. Control codes are instructions that a program sends to a printer to control the way it prints. Entering control codes is an advanced topic that few readers will need. It is beyond the scope of this book. For further information, refer to the Quicken User's Manual.

CHECK YOURSELF

If you have not already done so, set up Quicken to work with your printer. Then, add a new printer definition or modify an existing one to see how it affects your printed output.

ANSWER

1. From the Main Menu, select Set Preferences.
2. Select Report Printer Settings.
3. Select the definition you want to change (check printer, report printer, or alternate report printer).
4. If the selected printer model is correct, use the Up arrow and Down arrow keys to highlight the desired style and press **Enter**. Then, go to Step 6.
5. If the selected printer model is not correct, press **Esc**. Highlight the correct printer model and press **Enter**. Then, return to Step 4.
6. To select a different style, proceed with Step 7.
7. Make entries in the Report Printer Settings window, if necessary.
8. Press **Ctrl+Enter**.

Password Protection

Quicken lets you protect entire files and selected transactions with a password.

File Password

Quicken data files often contain sensitive financial information. If other people have access to your computer, you might want to prevent them from having access to your Quicken files. You can do so by assigning a password to your files. Once a password is assigned, the file cannot be accessed unless the user enters the password correctly.

Password Protection

To password-protect the current file:

1. From the Set Preferences menu, select Password Settings.
2. Select File Password.
3. Type in your password, then press **Enter**. The password can be up to 16 characters long, and can include spaces. Upper- and lowercase letters are treated the same.
4. Type in the password again for confirmation, then press **Enter**.

The next time you try to access this file (after exiting and restarting Quicken or after accessing another file), Quicken will prompt you for the password. You must enter the password exactly to obtain access so be sure to use a password you can remember. You should keep a written record of the password in a safe place.

To change or remove a file password, you must first gain access to the file by entering the original password. Then follow the above procedures, entering the new password, or a blank to remove password protection from the file.

Transaction Password

A transaction password lets you protect certain transactions in a file from unauthorized modification. When you set up a transaction password, you specify a cutoff date. In the future, the password will be required to make modifications to any transaction dated on or before this date. All transactions can be viewed, and transactions after the date can be modified freely. A transaction password can be used along with, or instead of, a file password.

To set up a transaction password:

1. From the Set Preferences menu, select Password Settings.
2. Select Transaction Password.
3. Type the desired password (up to 16 characters, including spaces), then press **Enter**.

4. Enter the cutoff date, then press **Enter**.
5. Type in the password again to confirm it. The transaction password is in effect immediately.

A transaction password is often used to "close" an accounting period. For example, in January, once you are sure that all transactions for the previous year have been entered correctly, you could set up a transaction password with a cutoff date of 12/31. This will prevent you from inadvertently making changes to transactions.

TIP

To make an entire file read-only, set up a transaction password with a cutoff date in the future (for instance, 12/31/99).

CHECK YOURSELF

Assign a password to protect the current file.

ANSWER

1. From the Main Menu, select Set Preferences.
2. Select Password Settings.
3. Select File Password.
4. Type in your password, then press **Enter**.
5. Type in the password again for confirmation, then press **Enter**.

Transaction Settings

Transaction settings affect certain aspects of data entry and the way information is displayed in the register. To view or change your transaction settings, select Transaction Settings from the

▼ *Figure 16.4. The Transaction Settings Window*

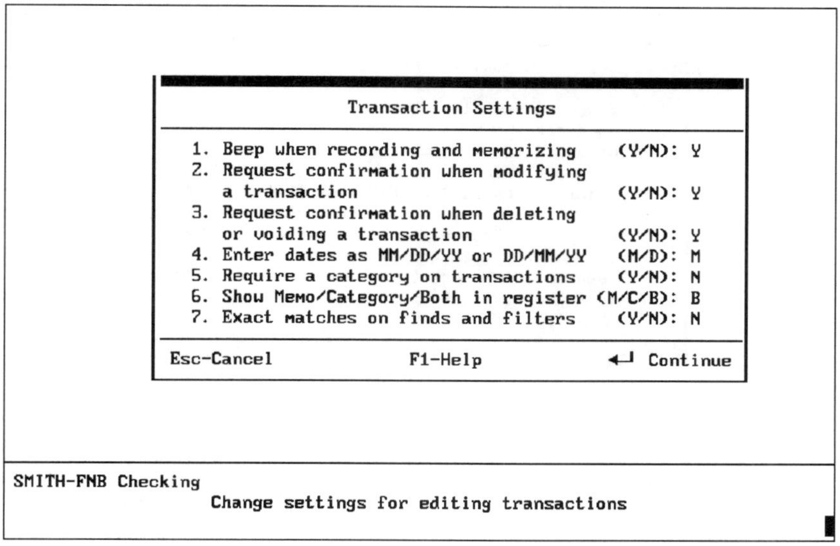

Transaction Settings

Set Preferences menu. The Transaction Settings window is displayed (Figure 16.4).

The option settings in this window are self-explanatory. To change an option, press **Tab** and **Shift+Tab** to move to the field, then enter the letter corresponding to the desired setting. You can also point at a field with the mouse and click to toggle the setting between the valid options. When all options are set as desired, press **Ctrl+Enter** to record them and close the window.

Checks and Reports Settings

Settings for checks and reports affect the way checks and reports appear. To view or modify these settings, select Checks and Report Settings from the Set Preferences menu. The Checks and Reports Settings window is displayed (Figure 16.5).

The settings in this window have the following effects:

▲ *Extra message line on check*—Allows an extra message line to be printed on checks. This extra line is not recorded in the register.

▼ *Figure 16.5. The Checks and Reports Settings Window*

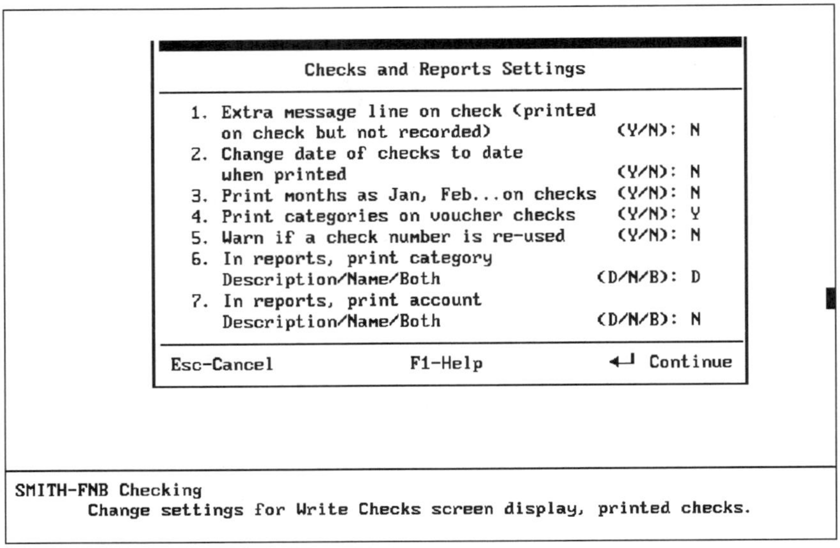

- ▲ *Change date of checks to date when printed*—When you print checks, the date on the check (and in the register) will be changed, if necessary, to today's date.
- ▲ *Print months as Jan, Feb...on checks*—On checks, print the three-letter abbreviations for the month rather than the month number. For example, 12 Mar '92.
- ▲ *Print categories on voucher checks*—When using voucher checks, the transaction category is printed on the check voucher.
- ▲ *Warn if a check number is re-used*—When you enter a check number, Quicken warns you if there is another check with the same number in that account.
- ▲ *In reports, print category Description/Name/Both*—For categories and classes in reports, determines whether the category name, category description, or both is printed.
- ▲ *In reports, print account Description/Name/Both*—For accounts in reports, determines whether the account name, account description, or both is printed.

QUICK COMMAND SUMMARY

To modify Quicken's screen settings:

1. From the Main Menu, select Set Preferences.
2. Select Screen Settings.
3. Select the screen setting you want to change: Screen Colors, EGA/VGA 43-line Display, Monitor Display, or Menu Access.
4. Select the desired option setting.

To set or modify Quicken's printer settings:

1. From the Main Menu, select Set Preferences.
2. Select Report Printer Settings.
3. Select the printer definition you want to change (check printer, report printer, or alternate report printer).
4. If the selected printer model is correct, use the Up arrow and Down arrow keys to highlight the desired style, then press **Enter**. Otherwise, press **Esc**, highlight the correct printer model, then press **Enter**.
5. Make entries in the Report Printer Settings window, if necessary.
6. Press **Ctrl+Enter**.

To assign a password to protect the current file:

1. From the Main Menu, select Set Preferences.
2. Select Password Settings.
3. Select File Password.
4. Type in your password, then press **Enter**.
5. Type in the password again for confirmation, then press **Enter**.

PRACTICE WHAT YOU'VE LEARNED

By modifying Quicken's settings, you can customize many aspects of the program to suit the way you work. You can experiment freely with settings, since they never affect your data. If you assign a password, however, be sure to keep a record of it.

Here are some things to practice:

1. See how the Quicken screen looks with different color settings. Select the one that you find most attractive and easy to read.
2. Experiment with the printer settings. Particularly for reports, printer settings can have a significant impact on the clarity and legibility of your printouts. If you print many wide reports, try a landscape mode setting (if your printer supports it). You'll be able to fit more information across a single page.
3. Experiment with various transaction settings and with checks and reports settings. See how different options affect the way Quicken works.

17

File Activities

Quicken keeps your financial data in disk files. For the most part this process is transparent to you, but there are a few file-related activities that you need to know about. In this chapter, you'll learn about

- **Changing the default data location**
- **Backing up your Quicken data**
- **Year end activities**

Changing the Default Data Location

Quicken can keep its data files anywhere you specify, on a hard disk or a diskette. Quicken's default data location is the drive and directory where it looks for data files, and where it sets up new files. When you first install Quicken on your system, it is set up to look for data files in the same directory where the program files are located (usually this is C:\QUICKEN5).

To change Quicken's default data location:

1. From the Main Menu, select Set Preferences.
2. Select File Activities.
3. Select Set File Location. A window is displayed with the current file location (Figure 17.1).
4. Type in the new drive and/or directory. For example, to store your Quicken files on the diskette in drive B, enter **B:**.

▼ ***Figure 17.1. The Set File Location Window***

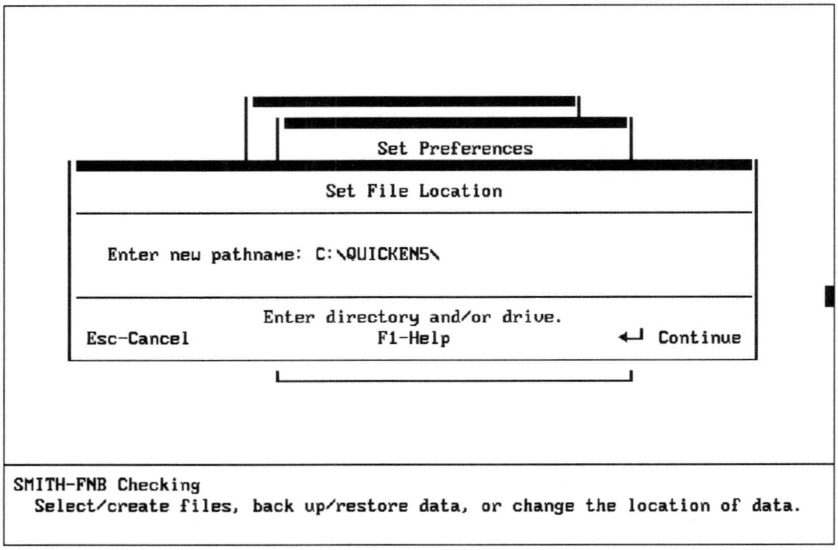

5. Press **Enter**. The new default data location goes into effect immediately.

Changing the Default Data Location

If you change the file location, Quicken will not be able to locate data files that you set up in the old location. To access these files, you will have to change the default file location back to the original disk/directory or copy the Quicken data files to the new location. See your DOS documentation for information on copying files.

Quicken File Names

In Quicken, a "file" is a group of accounts that are stored together. When a Quicken file is stored on disk, it is actually stored as four separate files that contain different parts of the accounts' information. Most users will not have to worry about the names of these disk files, since Quicken handles them for you automatically. However, if you want to use DOS commands to copy your Quicken files from one location to another, you must know their DOS names.

As you may know, each disk file has a two-part identification: the *name*, which can be one to eight characters long, and an *extension* of one to three characters. The four disk files that hold the data for a Quicken "file" all have the same name, which is the name you assigned to the file (QDATA by default). Each of the four files has a different extension. Thus, the Quicken "file" QDATA is stored in four disk files with the identifications:

- ▲ QDATA.QDT
- ▲ QDATA.QNX
- ▲ QDATA.QDI
- ▲ QDATA.QMT

Likewise, if you set up another Quicken "file" with the name RETIRE, it will be stored on disk as the four files:

- ▲ RETIRE.QDT
- ▲ RETIRE.QNX

- RETIRE.QDI
- RETIRE.QMT

If you want to transfer Quicken data from one location to another, you must be sure to copy all four files.

CHECK YOURSELF

Change Quicken's default data location to a different drive and/or directory. Be sure to change it back or you won't be able to access your files.

ANSWER

1. From the Main Menu, select Set Preferences.
2. Select File Activities.
3. Select Set File Location.
4. Type in the new drive and/or directory.
5. Press **Enter**.

Backing Up a Quicken File

It is important for you to *back up* your Quicken data on a regular basis. Backing up means to make an extra copy of your data. If the original is lost or damaged, you can use the backup copy of your data rather than reentering all your transactions. While computer disks are quite reliable, there is always the possibility of a hard disk crash or damage to a diskette. If you make backups and lose your original data, you will need to reenter only those transactions that occurred since your last backup.

To back up your Quicken data:

1. Insert a formatted, blank diskette in a drive (usually A or B).

Backing Up a Quicken File

2. Make sure the file you want to back up is current.
3. From the register or the Write Checks screen, select Print/Acct.
4. Select Back Up File. The Select Backup Drive window is displayed (Figure 17.2).
5. Enter the letter of the drive you are using, then press **Enter**.
6. Quicken copies the data files to the diskette.

The first time you make a backup, you should make two backup copies. Label the diskettes "Quicken data 1" and "Quicken data 2," or something similar. Each time you backup in the future, alternate between the two backup diskettes. By having two backup copies of your data, you guard against the possibility of damaging one of your backup diskettes.

Back up your Quicken data on a weekly or monthly schedule. It may sound like a lot of bother, but it is important to make it a regular habit. Just think of the trouble it would be to reenter hundreds of transactions As the next section will show you, Quicken can even remind you when a backup is due.

▼ Figure 17.2. The Select Backup Drive Window

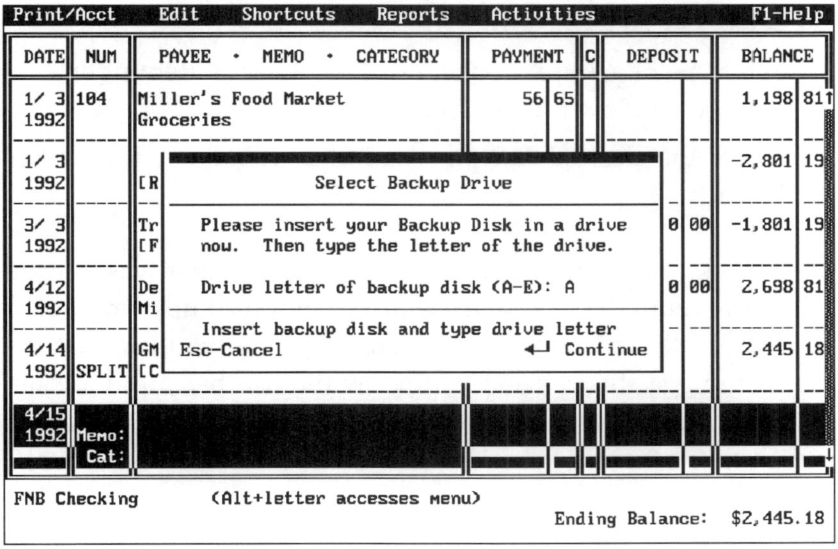

CHECK YOURSELF

Make a backup copy of your Quicken data file. Get in the habit of doing this regularly.

ANSWER

1. Insert a blank formatted diskette in drive A or B.
2. From the register or the Write Checks screen, select Print/Acct.
3. Select Back Up File.
4. Enter the letter of the drive you are using, then press **Enter**.

Automatic Backup Reminders

As do most people, you will sometimes forget when you are due to back up your Quicken data. Fortunately the program can remind you.

To activate automatic backup reminders:

1. From the Main Menu, select Set Preferences.
2. Select File Activities.
3. Select Set Backup Frequency. The Backup Reminder Frequency window is displayed (Figure 17.3).
4. Select the desired backup reminder frequency, then press **Enter**.

A backup reminder applies only to the file that was current when the reminder was activated. When a backup reminder is active, Quicken remembers the date each time you back up the file. If the specified period expires without a backup, Quicken displays a reminder the next time you try to exit Quicken or switch to another file.

▼ *Figure 17.3. The Backup Reminder Frequency Window*

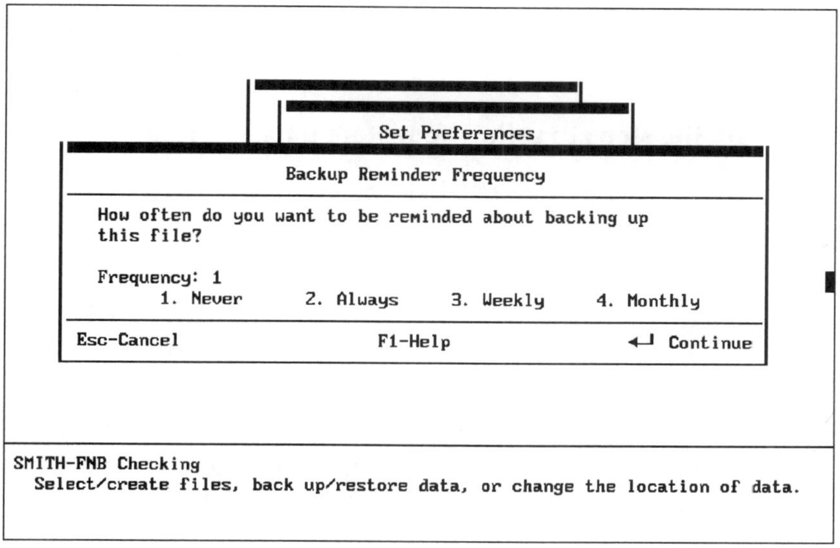

Backing Up a Quicken File

CHECK YOURSELF

Set up Quicken to remind you to make a backup on a weekly basis.

ANSWER

1. From the Main Menu, select Set Preferences.
2. Select File Activities.
3. Select Set Backup Frequency.
4. Enter **3** for weekly, then press **Enter**.

Restoring a Quicken File

If your original Quicken data files are lost or damaged, you will need to use your backup data. If you normally keep your Quicken data on a diskette, you won't need to take any special action.

Simply use your backup diskette in place of your regular data diskette (remember to make a replacement backup). If you normally keep your Quicken data on your hard disk, you will have to restore your data from the backup diskette.

These are the steps to follow to restore data:

1. Insert the backup diskette in a drive.
2. From the Main Menu, select Set Preferences.
3. Select File Activities.
4. Select Restore File.
5. Enter the letter of the drive you are using, then press **Enter**.
6. Select the file to restore, then press **Enter**. Quicken copies the data files from the backup diskette to the default data location. If files of the same name already exist there, you are asked whether you want to replace them.

Year-end Activities

Year-end activities refers generally to procedures that you follow at the end of each year. Quicken does not require you to close-out your accounts or anything else at the end of a year. There are, however, some procedures you may wish to follow.

Quicken permits you to have as many as 65,535 transactions in a file (total for all accounts in the file). Any single account is limited to approximately 30,000 transactions. The typical home user of Quicken will enter between 200 and 1000 transactions per year, so you could keep many years of information in a single Quicken file. This approach enables you to have all your transactions available for reports. If you decide to follow this approach, then there are no "year-end procedures" for you to follow.

Others users are more comfortable with archiving or closing a file. Both of these procedures save certain transactions from your Quicken file into an archive file. They differ in terms of what information is left in the active file. Note that these procedures are called "year-end" because that's when they are usually performed. You can, however, do them whenever you wish.

Year-end Activities

Archiving

When you archive a Quicken file, you create a second file (the archive file) that contains all transactions in the current file that are dated earlier than a specified date. The current file remains your working file and is not changed; after the archiving procedure it still contains all your past transactions.

Let's say you started using Quicken in June 1991. The archive file you create in January 1992 will contain all of 1991's transactions. The archive file you create in January 1993 will contain all of 1991's and 1992's transactions. Your working file will continue to contain all transactions. Use archive files to keep an extra backup, perhaps in your safe deposit box, or to provide information to your accountant.

To create an archive file:

1. From the Main Menu, select Set Preferences.
2. Select File Activities.
3. Select Year End. The Year End window is displayed (Figure 17.4).
4. Enter **1** to select Archive. The Archive File window is displayed (Figure 17.5).
5. The fields in this window are filled in by Quicken with default values. Change them if you wish:

   ▲ The "Archive old Quicken data to:" field specifies the name for the archive file. The default is the current file name with the last two digits of last year appended (for example, SMITH91).

   ▲ The "Location of archive file:" field specifies the drive and/or directory where the archive file is to be stored. The default is Quicken's default data directory.

▼ *Figure 17.4. The Year End Window*

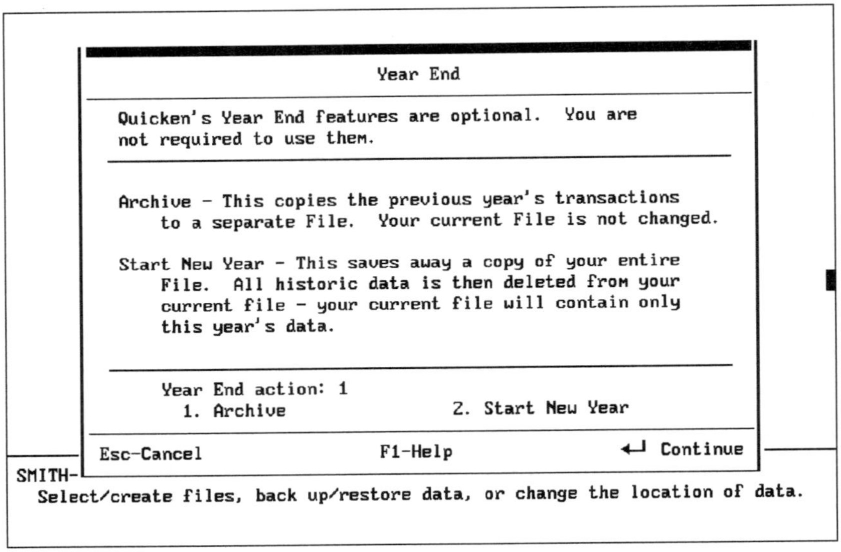

▲ The "Archive transactions prior to and including:" field specifies the last date for which transactions will be archived. The default is December 31 of last year.

▼ *Figure 17.5. The Archive File Window*

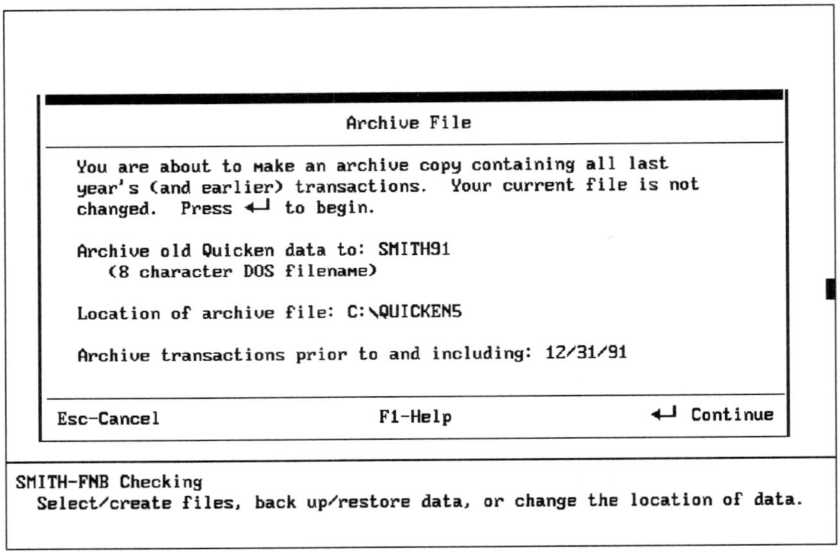

Year-end Activities

6. Press **Enter**. The archive file is created, and all transactions earlier than the specified date are copied to it.

Closing a File

Quicken's "Starting a New Year" procedure, sometimes called closing a file, is similar to archiving in that an archive file is created containing old transactions. It differs in that all transactions prior to the current year are then deleted from the current file. The only exceptions are investment transactions and uncleared transactions, which are kept in the current file no matter what their date.

To start a new file for this year:

1. From the Main Menu, select Set Preferences.
2. Select File Activities.
3. Select Year End. The Year End window is displayed.
4. Enter **2** to select Start New Year. The Start New Year window is displayed (Figure 17.6).

▼ ***Figure 17.6. The Start New Year Window***

```
                          Start New Year

  You are about to save a copy of your current file and
  then delete all historic transactions from your current
  file.  Your current file will contain only this year's
  data plus all investment transactions and any uncleared
  transactions.  Press ↵ to begin.

  Copy all transactions to file:
     (8 character DOS filename)

  Delete transactions from current file older than:  1/ 1/92

Esc-Cancel                   F1-Help                  ↵ Continue

SMITH-FNB Checking
  Select/create files, back up/restore data, or change the location of data.
```

5. Enter a name for the archive file. The name should be one to eight characters, without an extension.
6. Enter a cutoff date for transactions to be deleted. The default date is January 1 of the current year.
7. Press **Enter**. The archive file is created, and all transactions in the current file are copied to it. Next, all transactions (except investment and uncleared transactions) earlier than the specified date are deleted from the current file.

If you need to create archives of your Quicken data, you probably will want to use the Archive procedure rather than the Start New Year procedure. Unless your main Quicken data file has become so large that it is cumbersome to load and backup, there is no real reason for deleting older transactions from it. And you never know when you might need to look at them.

QUICK COMMAND SUMMARY

To change Quicken's default data location:

1. From the Main Menu, select Set Preferences.
2. Select File Activities.
3. Select Set File Location.
4. Type in the new drive and/or directory, then press **Enter**.

To make a backup copy of your Quicken data file:

1. Insert a blank formatted diskette in drive A or B.
2. From the register or the Write Checks screen, select Print/Acct.
3. Select Back Up File.
4. Enter the letter of the drive you are using, then press **Enter**.

To set up Quicken to remind you to backup on a regular basis:

1. From the Main Menu, select Set Preferences.
2. Select File Activities.

3. Select Set Backup Frequency.
4. Specify the reminder frequency, then press **Enter**.

PRACTICE WHAT YOU'VE LEARNED

Except for backing up your data, the procedures covered in this chapter are ones you will be performing infrequently. It never hurts to practice, however—and you really *should* start making backups.

1. Format two new diskettes and label them as your Quicken backups. Back up your Quicken data to both diskettes and store them in a safe place.
2. If you are familiar with DOS commands, you may wish to exit Quicken and set up a new subdirectory for your Quicken data files, such as C:\QUICKEN5\DATA. Copy the data files to the new subdirectory and make it the new default data location.
3. Set up Quicken to remind you about backups.

A

Installing Quicken

This appendix guides you through Quicken installation. This procedure is the same for new users and those who have an earlier version of Quicken installed on their system. To run Quicken you will need

- **An IBM PC/XT/AT or compatible computer**
- **At least 512 kilobytes of memory**
- **A hard disk and one diskette drive, or two diskette drives, one of which must be a high density drive (1.2 megabytes for 5-1/4 inch drives, 1.44 megabytes for 3-1/2 inch drives)**

Installation Procedures

Before you begin installation, you should use the DOS DISKCOPY command to make copies of the master Quicken disks that you received in your Quicken package. Label the duplicates to match the originals, then use the duplicates for installation. Store the originals in a safe place.

Hard Disk Installation

1. Start your computer as usual and wait for the DOS prompt (usually C:\>).
2. Insert the Quicken diskette labeled Install Disk 1 (if installing from 5-1/2-inch diskettes) or Install Disk (if installing from 3-1/2-inch diskettes) into drive A (or B) on your computer.
3. Make the drive that contains the install diskette current by typing **A:** (or **B:**) and pressing **Enter**. Your screen prompt will now read A: (or B:).
4. Type **INSTALL**, then press **Enter**. The diskette will spin for a few seconds, then the install program opening screen will be displayed. Read the information on the screen, then press **Enter**.
5. The next screen asks if you have a color monitor. Enter **1** for Yes, **2** for No, then press **Enter**.
6. On the next screen, type in your name, then press **Enter**.
7. The next screen asks what type of disk you are installing Quicken on. Type **1** for hard disk, then press **Enter**.
8. On the next screen, you must specify the drive letter and directory name where Quicken is to be installed. The default is C:\QUICKEN5. You can accept this, which is recommended, or enter a different drive letter and/or directory.

   Note: If you are upgrading from an earlier version of Quicken, you should specify the drive and directory where the old version is located.

Installation Procedures

9. On the next screen, you are asked to specify the printer you will use with Quicken. Scroll through the list using the Up arrow, Down arrow, Page Up, and Page Down keys until the printer name is highlighted, then press **Enter**.
10. Next, you are asked whether you want to use Billminder. This is a program that works with Quicken to remind you of upcoming payments and other events. See Appendix B for more information on Billminder. Enter **1** to use Billminder, **2** if you don't want to use it.
11. The next screen displays a summary of the installation information you have specified. Check it over for accuracy. If you want to change anything, press **Esc** one or more times to go back to the proper screen and enter the correct information. If the information is correct, press **Enter** to continue.
12. The installation program starts copying Quicken files to the destination directory. If you're installing from 5-1/2-inch diskettes you will be prompted to insert Install Disk 2 into the drive. A message displays when installation is complete. Press **Enter** to end the installation procedure. You are now ready to start Quicken.

Diskette Installation

You will need one blank, formatted high-density diskette. Label this diskette "Quicken Program Disk."

1. Start your computer as usual and wait for the DOS prompt (usually A:\>).
2. Remove all diskettes from the computer drives.
3. Insert the blank formatted diskette in your high-density drive (the drive you will use to run Quicken).
4. Insert the Quicken diskette labeled Install Disk 1 (if installing from 5-1/2-inch diskettes) or Install Disk (if installing from 3-1/2-inch diskettes) into the other drive.
5. Make the drive containing the install diskette current. If the diskette is in drive A, type **A:** and press **Enter**. If the diskette is in drive B, type **B:** and press **Enter**.

6. Type **Install**, then press **Enter**. The diskette will spin for a few seconds, then the install program opening screen will be displayed. Read the information on the screen, then press **Enter**.
7. Follow the instructions in Steps 5 through 12 under *Hard Disk Installation*, except at Step 7 enter **2** to specify floppy disk installation.

Note to Upgraders

When you start Quicken 5 for the first time, it will detect that your data files were created with an earlier version of the program. Quicken can translate your old format data files into Quicken 5 files. You will be offered the option of backing up the files before they are translated. Unless you are sure that you have an up-to-date backup of your data, you should tell Quicken to make backups before translating.

B

The Quicken Billminder Program

Billminder is a program that is provided as part of your Quicken package. It is separate from the Quicken program, but works in conjunction with your Quicken data files to remind you of tasks you need to perform. Billminder will remind you to

- **Print checks**
- **Transmit electronic payments**
- **Take investment actions (see Chapter 13)**

How Does Billminder Work?

If you have Billminder installed, it is activated every time you start your computer. Billminder scans your Quicken data files looking for overdue or upcoming (postdated) items. If it finds any, a reminder message is displayed on the screen. It is then up to you to start Quicken and take care of the pending tasks.

Installing Billminder

When you first installed Quicken, you were given the option of also installing Billminder. If you answered YES, the program was installed for you, and you don't need to take any further action—Billminder is already at work (although you may not have seen any messages if you had no overdue items or had not activated Billminder).

If you did not install Billminder when you installed Quicken, you can do so now. You have two options. You can go through the entire Quicken installation procedure again, this time asking that Billminder be installed. Quicken will be reinstalled in the same directory, but your data and settings will not be affected. Or, if you are familiar with DOS commands and file editing, you can edit your AUTOEXEC.BAT file to install Billminder.

This latter procedure should not be attempted unless you are familiar with your AUTOEXEC.BAT file and know how to edit it. You need to add a line at the end of your AUTOEXEC.BAT file. This line will start Billminder and tell the program where your Quicken program files are located. Normally, the Billminder program is located in the same directory as your Quicken program files. Assuming this is C:\QUICKEN5, the line you add to the end of AUTOEXEC.BAT is:

```
C:\QUICKEN5\BILLMIND C:\QUICKEN5
```

Installing Billminder

If you installed Quicken into a directory named C:\Q5, the line would read

```
C:\Q5\BILLMIND C:\Q5
```

You have the option to ask Billminder to pause after it displays its reminder message until you press **Enter**. To turn on the pause option, include the /P switch on the AUTOEXEC.BAT line:

```
C:\Q5\BILLMIND C:\Q5 /P
```

Once the correct command line is added to AUTOEXEC.BAT, Billminder will run every time you start your computer. If Billminder has been activated from within Quicken and it finds overdue items in your files, it will display a message. Otherwise, it does nothing.

Activating Billminder

Even if it is installed, Billminder does nothing until you activate it from within Quicken. When you activate Billminder, you also specify how far in advance you want to be reminded of pending events.

To activate Billminder:

1. From the Main Menu, select Set Preferences.
2. Select Automatic Reminder Settings. The Automatic Reminder Settings window is displayed.
3. In the first field, enter the number of days of advance warning you want Billminder to provide.
4. In the next field, enter **Y** to activate Billminder, then press **Enter**.

The next time you start your computer, Billminder will scan all the data files in your Quicken directory and report on any pending items. To deactivate Billminder, follow the above procedures, but enter **N** in the window's last field.

Index

C

P

Q

R

U

V

W

X

Y